STYLE AND THE FUTURE
OF COMPOSITION STUDIES

STYLE AND THE FUTURE OF COMPOSITION STUDIES

EDITED BY
PAUL BUTLER, BRIAN RAY, AND
STAR MEDZERIAN VANGURI

UTAH STATE UNIVERSITY PRESS
Logan

© 2020 by University Press of Colorado

Published by Utah State University Press
An imprint of University Press of Colorado
245 Century Circle, Suite 202
Louisville, Colorado 80027

All rights reserved

The University Press of Colorado is a proud member of the Association of University Presses.

The University Press of Colorado is a cooperative publishing enterprise supported, in part, by Adams State University, Colorado State University, Fort Lewis College, Metropolitan State University of Denver, Regis University, University of Colorado, University of Northern Colorado, University of Wyoming, Utah State University, and Western Colorado University.

ISBN: 978-1-64642-010-0 (paperback)
ISBN: 978-1-64642-011-7 (ebook)
https://doi.org/10.7330/9781646420117

Library of Congress Cataloging-in-Publication Data

Names: Butler, Paul, date, editor. | Ray, Brian, date, editor. | Vanguri, Star Medzerian, date, editor.
Title: Style and the future of composition studies / edited by Paul Butler, Brian Ray, Star Vanguri.
Description: Logan : Utah State University Press, an imprint of University Press of Colorado, [2020] | Includes bibliographical references and index.
Identifiers: LCCN 2020014457 (print) | LCCN 2020014458 (ebook) | ISBN 9781646420100 (paperback) | ISBN 9781646420117 (ebook)
Subjects: LCSH: Literary style—Study and teaching. | English language—Style—Study and teaching.
Classification: LCC PN203 .S788 2020 (print) | LCC PN203 (ebook) | DDC 428.0071—dc23
LC record available at https://lccn.loc.gov/2020014457
LC ebook record available at https://lccn.loc.gov/2020014458

The University Press of Colorado gratefully acknowledges the generous support of the University of Houston toward the publication of this book.

Cover image © Netfalls Remy Musser / Shutterstock

CONTENTS

Foreword
　Frank Farmer　vii

Acknowledgments　xv

Introduction: Moving Forward with Style
　Paul Butler, Brian Ray, and Star Medzerian Vanguri　3

SECTION 1: STYLE MEDIATES RELATIONSHIPS

1. Cans of Worms: Tracing an Undergraduate Thesis-Writer's Style Knowledge over Time
　Andrea R. Olinger　23

2. "Here's What I Would Like for You to Know": Epistolary Style as an Invitation to Read and Write Metonymically
　Melissa A. Goldthwaite　37

3. "Clarity" Really Means Rhythm: Toward a Psychoanalytic Poetics of Prose
　T. R. Johnson　53

4. Erasmus in the Professional Writing Classroom: Workplace Genre, Designing and Writing for the Web, and the Future of Style
　Tom Pace　66

SECTION 2: STYLE CONVEYS IDENTITY

5. The Stylized Portrayal of the Writing Life in Spike Jonze's *Her*
　Cydney Alexis and Eric Leake　85

6. Stance as Style: Toward a Framework for Analyzing Academic Language
　Laura L. Aull and Zak Lancaster　98

7. Looking Forward to a Nice, Stupid, Future Style. R U?
　Jimmy Butts　114

8. Metaphorical Translingualisms: The Hip-Hop Cipher as Stylistic Concept
   Eric A. House   133

SECTION 3: STYLE FORMS STRATEGY

9. Expectations of Exaltation: Formal Sublimity as a Prolegomenon to Style's Unbounded Future
   Jarron Slater   147

10. Civil Style: Reexamining Discourse and Rhetorical Listening in Composition
    Laura L. Aull   160

11. Applied Legal Storytelling: Toward a Stylistics of Embodiment
    Almas Khan   173

12. What Style Can Add to Genre: Suggestions for Applying Stylistics to Disciplinary Writing
    Anthony Box   185

SECTION 4: STYLE CREATES AND TRANSCENDS BOUNDARIES

13. Point of Departures: Composition and Creative Writing Studies' Shared Stylistic Values
    Jon Udelson   199

14. The Danger of Using Style to Determine Authorship: The Case of Luke and Acts
    Mike Duncan   213

15. Words, Words, Words, or Leveraging Lexis for a Pedagogy of Style
    William T. FitzGerald   227

About the Authors   245
Index   247

FOREWORD

Frank Farmer

When histories of our discipline first began to be written, scholars were often hard-pressed to explain the emergence of modern composition studies. How did this momentous change occur? What, exactly, were the historical conditions that brought it about? Or, put a bit differently, what were the antecedents—intellectual, material, institutional, pedagogical—from which we could acquire a better understanding of this new discipline, now widely known as rhetoric and composition? Some historians, such as Edward P. J. Corbett and Frank D'Angelo, pointed to a revived interest in classical rhetoric, and others noted the more recent advances in rhetorical theory, as signaled in the work of Chaïm Perelman and Lucie Olbrects-Tyteca, and, of course, Kenneth Burke.

At the same time, however, others saw the 1960s as a watershed moment, not merely because of a revived interest in rhetoric but also because of a newfound freedom that began to appear in the writing classrooms of the day. Taken together, these pedagogies later came to be known under the broad rubric of expressivism and were largely understood to be a remedy to the "skill and drill" writing instruction of preceding decades. Experimentalism, verbal or otherwise, was often the prized value in such classes and was not only encouraged but sometimes required. As an undergraduate in the last years of that decade, I recall a group project that involved one member reading Lawrence Ferlinghetti's "The World Is a Beautiful Place," while Pink Floyd's *Atom Heart Mother* played in the background and remaining group members performed an interpretive dance with brightly colored streamers. It was indeed (*pace* Geoffrey Sirc) nothing less than a happening. It was also the English course I remember best from my undergraduate days.

Still, while a restored interest in rhetoric, accompanied by a new emphasis on personal expression, emerged in the 1960s, and while both of these developments added to the formation of a new discipline, a more favored explanation was provided by the philosopher of science Thomas Kuhn (1970), who introduced the concept of a *paradigm* to explain how scientific knowledge changes. Historians of composition borrowed this concept to draw a stark contrast between the old paradigm for writing instruction, current-traditional rhetoric, and the new paradigm—namely, process approaches to the teaching of writing. By the early 1970s it was obvious that a paradigm shift had occurred, and that the most important consequence of this shift was the consolidation of a new field, the discipline that most readers of this volume, I assume, profess.

In order to make the contrasts between these two paradigms clear, and in order for current-traditional rhetoric to be construed as a useful foil,[1] it had to be defined as something beyond the simplistic "teaching rhetoric" of the first half of the twentieth century (Fogarty 1959, 11). To this end, a number of composition scholars—James Berlin, Richard Young, Maxine Hairston, Sharon Crowley, to name just a few—explicated a variety of understandings, but perhaps the one most frequently cited was Richard Young's. As he characterized current-traditional rhetoric, its salient features included:

> The emphasis on the composed product rather than the composing process; the analysis of discourse into words, sentences and paragraphs; the classification of discourse into description, narration, exposition, and argument; the strong concern with usage (syntax, spelling punctuation) and with style (economy, clarity, emphasis); the preoccupation with the informal essay and the research paper, and so on. (1978, 31)

A few observations about this definition. First, as may be inferred here, its function was to draw a distinction between product and process approaches to the teaching of writing. Second, it could not have been written without an awareness that current-traditional rhetoric was still very much with us (then, as it is now). And third, it tended to endorse the view that our paradigm shift was also a canonical shift, that is, a shift from the rhetorical canon of style to the rhetorical canon of invention. Such a shift was likely necessary, especially if a process paradigm was to prevail. After all, the very idea of process is a rather vacated one if invention is not vigorously embraced, understood, and taught. Indeed, much composition scholarship during the 1970s and early 1980s was centrally concerned with the problem of understanding invention and how it might be taught in our writing classrooms.

There is, no doubt, much to lament about my capsule description of composition's early history, not least of which is its brevity. But my purpose in offering this thumbnail sketch is to remind how, from its origins as a discipline, rhetoric and composition has disparaged style as a legitimate concern. If the canon of style is to be forever yoked to a current-traditional paradigm, and if that paradigm was thought to be replaced by a process paradigm, with its emphasis on invention, then it is hard to imagine why any scholar or teacher in this new field would take up style as a worthy intellectual pursuit. Never mind that Young's mention of style reveals a narrow understanding of what it is or might be. And never mind that explaining a paradigm shift in terms of rhetorical canons might be reductive. Style, nonetheless, became something of an easy target for those who sought to elevate rhetorical invention by diminishing the importance of style. I am perhaps overstating this contrast for effect, but there can be little doubt that narratives that aimed to explain the origins of rhetoric and composition did so, in part, by minimizing style's importance to this new discipline.[2]

And yet.

I grew up in the profession as a graduate student in the mid- to late 1980s, and I can vouch for the fact that there was no dearth of available scholarship on style during these years. Paul Butler, one of the editors of this volume, has named the period from the 1960s through the mid-1980s as the "Golden Age" of style. Butler (2008) points to the volume of published scholarship on style that emerged during this period, and the important developments that occurred as well, for example, sentence combining pedagogies, generative rhetorics, a renewed interest in imitation, and so on. And while it is somewhat disconcerting to realize that one has lived through *any* golden age, I think Butler is right: style enjoyed a prominence then that it has not enjoyed since.

But how can this be? If it is true that there was a general discrediting of style during this period, how could there be so much published literature in composition about style? I admit I was aware of this tension in my own early work. When I revealed that I planned to do a thesis on imitation, more than one faculty mentor was (to put it delicately) less than enthusiastic. Their concerns, however, were well-founded and doubtless were told to me with my interests in mind. They worried that because of my chosen topic, I might not find a suitable entry-level position that would launch me into a successful career. Then, as now, taking up stylistic inquiries might be considered, for some in our field, an occupational hazard.

In what follows, I want to offer a way to explain the waxing and waning of style's fortunes, both within and outside of our discipline. The fact that style can be simultaneously discredited and embraced ought not to surprise us, and I want to enlist the help of yet another, more distant mentor to show why.

· · · · ·

In the opening pages of his very long essay "Discourse in the Novel," Mikhail Bakhtin makes a distinction between two large, sociohistorical forces in language, forces that he names *centripetal* and *centrifugal.* Bakhtin suggests that there exists an uninterrupted struggle between these "two tendencies" in language . . . [the first] "a centralizing (unifying) tendency, the other, a decentralizing tendency (that is, one that stratifies languages)" (1984 [1981], 267). Forces that aspire to a seamless verbal unity, to a consolidated "verbal-ideological world," to a "monologic" universe that permits no language diversity—these are centripetal forces (270), and it is clear Bakhtin does not look favorably upon them, even while he acknowledges their constancy. Opposed to these are centrifugal forces (272) in language, scattering forces that aim to decentralize and disunify, forces that result in *heteroglossia,* that is, the layering of multiple languages that Bakhtin so desires and that he sees as a condition of possibility for authentic dialogue (292).

Though he does not elaborate this distinction at length, he does add some characteristics that are useful to consider. First, he claims that while centrifugal forces—dispersive, multiple, heteroglossic—may be understood as a *given,* centripetal forces must always be *posited* (1984 [1981], 270), and thus they constitute forces that must, in some measure, be imposed and maintained. Second, while Bakhtin introduces this distinction by framing it in terms of broad, historical tendencies, he points out that the "struggle" between these "two tendencies" is so pervasive that it is possible to discern both in the individual utterance itself, no matter how ordinary that utterance may be. As Bakhtin says, "Every concrete utterance of a speaking subject serves as a point where centrifugal as well as centripetal forces are brought to bear" (272). Finally, Bakhtin does not imagine this struggle to be one that is ultimately resolved. There are no victors here, no dialectical "finishing off" that results in a scenario where one tendency might be proclaimed a final winner. Yes, there may be periods when one tendency prevails, but the struggle itself is always present (272). The two tendencies exist alongside one another, in perpetuity, as it were. If what Bakhtin says about language tendencies is likewise true of style (how could it not be?), then maybe this explains, in part, why I received my professional training in a time when style was both impugned and celebrated in our scholarship.

In its own relatively brief history, composition studies has been more than a little complicit in the unifying, centripetal forces discussed here—that is, the forces of standardization, centralization, and homogeneity. But it would be utterly misleading to overlook the fact that composition has also opposed these same forces. From the CCCC's 1974 resolution, *Students' Right to Their Own Language*, to recent inquiries into translanguaging; from our disavowal of Standard American English (and the prescriptive grammars that go with it) to our recent understanding of the racist underpinnings of assessment practices; from our challenge to the conventional idea that a written text *must* be an alphabetic text to our realization that the writing process is incomplete without an understanding of how texts circulate—in all of these aspects, and more, composition has shown its willingness to dispute the centripetal forces of uniformity and consolidation and, instead, embrace the decentralizing tendency of centrifugal forces. But may the same be said of style? How might Bakhtin's distinction translate to our typical stylistic concerns?

It seems to me that unifying centripetal forces are present whenever stylistic fixity is a sought-after norm. Our near obsessive (and, I would offer, misguided) wish to define style "once and for all," so to speak, is symptomatic of this desire. I will spare the reader a review of all the definitions of style that have been handed down through the ages and, instead, remain content to point out that a definition, no matter how useful, is always an imposed limit on whatever it is we seek to define. It is an essentializing move, a hoped-for last word that preempts the need for any future definitions.

Centripetal forces are also present in the familiar tendency to conflate stylistic concerns with grammatical ones. One unhappy feature of this kinship is that just as we have prescriptive grammars, we have prescriptive style advice too, and lots of it. Strunk and White (2000), in the opinion of many, is still the most revered in this genre, and, of course, there are far too many others to mention here. What they share in common, though, is a desire to nail down, to codify that which makes a good style available to every writer, everywhere, in every moment. Some decades ago, Richard Lanham (1974), famously and brilliantly, challenged stylistic orthodoxies by bringing to bear upon them the importance of rhetorical context to any enlightened understanding of style. Not surprisingly, the usual advice of style books did not fare especially well in Lanham's critique. Once context, rhetorical or otherwise, gains entry into discussions of style, the presumed infallibility of much stylistic advice falters, becomes disputable, or, to use Bakhtin's term, dialogized.

Finally, a centripetal motive may be witnessed in our desire to name individual styles. We need only remind ourselves of Cicero's Plain, Grand, and Middle styles—or perhaps more recently, Walker Gibson's Tough, Sweet, and Stuffy—to document this tendency in the history of style. To be sure, the desire to name specific styles is not entirely without value. Indeed, for readers and writers alike, it is certainly helpful to notice the internal commonalities in particular styles. But if what Bakhtin says is true—namely, that both centripetal and centrifugal forces can be discovered in the individual utterance—ought we not to, at least, entertain the possibility that a named style is not quite as unified or consistent as it might pretend to be? In other words, might we be well advised to look for, listen for, traces of other styles that surpass the name given to any particular one?

• • • • •

I think of the chapters gathered here as an answer to the centralizing forces so often aligned with the history of style in composition studies. Taken as a whole, these chapters gesture to a freedom and openness that resists the enclosures of our received understandings of style and resists, too, the imposition of stylistic orthodoxies upon any future intimations of what style may yet be.

Yes, to be sure, much that is familiar about style can be found in the pages to follow. Rethinkings of classical concepts are included here, as are pedagogical ideas for the writing classroom, as are empirical studies on style. All of these approaches, no doubt, reprise certain traditions of stylistic inquiry in composition. But at the same time, this collection pushes against settled definitions, pushes against unified understandings, prescriptive advice, and well-traveled commonplaces. Put a bit differently, this volume encompasses, at once, both continuities and provocations. Heard as a complete utterance, all of the chapters here oppose the dominance of centripetal forces that seek a fixity or unity upon what style could mean and how it might be studied. Such is why *Style and the Future of Composition Studies* anticipates a hopeful future for style and for style's importance to the discipline of composition studies.

Thus, in its commitment to thematic and conceptual diversity, *Style and the Future of Composition Studies* celebrates various and multiple understandings of style, and this is certainly one of its outstanding and most readily noticed virtues. But as Bakhtin reminds, the mere fact of multiple languages does not guarantee that heteroglossia becomes dialogue. For that to happen, any particular language must first become conscious that other languages exist and that one's own language must now be understood in light of all others, and is, in fact, conditioned by this knowledge. Such is a precondition for dialogue between languages and, as I maintain here, a precondition for dialogue between different understandings of style as well.

More so than any other collection in recent memory, the chapters gathered here engage in such a dialogue. They talk to one another—sometimes directly, sometimes obliquely, sometimes implicitly, always revealing any particular author's awareness of what the other contributors in this volume are saying in their respective utterances on style. In this sense, *Style and the Future of Composition Studies* is a true colloquy, a dialogue on style, but a dialogue that is not always explicit and that, in fact, occasionally requires careful listening to be heard (or overheard) at all. I assure you the effort, dear reader, is well worth the effort.

I close with a musical analogy. Imagine a composition structured along the familiar lines of tension and release, and imagine this piece of music nearing its completion as the tension rises and the listener anticipates a pleasant ending to the piece in question. But just as this music nears the brink of being happily resolved, it suddenly, and without notice, modulates and changes key, thereby embarking upon a new musical journey, a journey much like the one that brought the listener to this threshold point to begin with.

I think of the history of style in composition this way, and I invite readers to regard this collection as an important moment in that history—a key change, if you like, a timely and much needed one at that. I believe you will find it to be a pleasurable one too.

NOTES

1. I use the term *foil* here, but Robert Connors, in his *Composition-Rhetoric* (1997), referred more sharply to current-traditional rhetoric as "a convenient whipping boy" for any practice in the field that certain scholars considered benighted or passé.
2. I quote Richard Young's famous passage here, but James Berlin also had little good to say about the style canon. See, especially, his *Rhetoric and Reality: Writing Instruction in American Colleges, 1900–1985* (1987).

REFERENCES

Bakhtin, M. M. 1984 (1981). "Discourse in the Novel." In *The Dialogic Imagination: Four Essays*, edited by Michael Holquist, translated by Holquist and Caryl Emerson, 259–422. University of Texas Press Slavic Series 1. Austin: University of Texas Press.

Berlin, James. 1987. *Rhetoric and Reality: Writing Instruction in American Colleges, 1900–1985*. Carbondale: Southern Illinois University Press.

Butler, Paul. 2008. "The Breadth of Stylistic Interest in Style's 'Golden Age.'" In *Out of Style: Reanimating Stylistic Study in Composition and Rhetoric*, 7–23. Logan: Utah State University Press.

Conference on College Composition and Communication. 1974. *Students' Rights to Their Own Language*, Special Issue *CCC* 25 (3): 1–32.

Connors, Robert J. 1997. *Composition-Rhetoric: Backgrounds, Theory, and Pedagogy.* Pittsburgh: University of Pittsburgh Press.

Fogarty, Daniel. 1959. *Roots for a New Rhetoric.* New York: Russell and Russell.

Kuhn, Thomas S. 1970. *The Structure of Scientific Revolutions*, 2nd ed. Chicago: University of Chicago Press.

Lanham, Richard. 1974. *Style: An Anti-Textbook.* New Haven, CT: Yale University Press.

Strunk, William, and E. B. White. 2000. *The Elements of Style*, 4th ed. New York: Longman.

Young, Richard. 1978. "Paradigms and Problems: Needed Research in Rhetorical Invention." In *Research on Composing: Points of Departure*, edited by Charles Cooper and Lee Odell, 29–47. Urbana, IL: National Council of Teachers of English.

ACKNOWLEDGMENTS

The editors of *Style and the Future of Composition Studies* would like to acknowledge the University of Houston for the generous publication support provided by the Small Grants Program (SGP), sponsored by the Division of Research (DOR), under the leadership of Dr. Amr Elnashai, Vice Chancellor/Vice President for Research and Technology Transfer. We also thank the Research and Scholarship Committee of the University of Houston Faculty Senate for its role in DOR's proposal review process, which resulted in the SGP award for subvention, indexing, proofreading, and copyediting. We are grateful as well to the UH College of Liberal Arts and Social Sciences (CLASS) for its Book Completion Grant and to former CLASS Associate Dean for Faculty and Research, and current Interim Dean, Dr. Daniel P. O'Connor.

Paul is indebted to the Provost's Travel Fund at the University of Houston for supporting professional conference presentations related to the book and to the Department of English's Martha Gano Houstoun Endowment for assisting with participation in the Digital Humanities Summer Institute at the University of Victoria and the Digital Media and Composition Institute at The Ohio State University. Star is recognizant of the travel funding provided by Nova Southeastern University, which allowed her to share her scholarship about this work.

We would like to express our appreciation as well for the professionalism of the editorial team at Utah State University Press and the University Press of Colorado: Rachael Levay, acquisitions editor; Beth Svinarich, sales and marketing manager; Dan Pratt, production manager; Laura Furney, assistant director and managing editor; and Darrin Pratt, director.

We also want to recognize Frank Farmer for writing the foreword to the collection and the volume's authors, without whom this project would not have been possible.

STYLE AND THE FUTURE
OF COMPOSITION STUDIES

Introduction
MOVING FORWARD WITH STYLE

Paul Butler, Brian Ray, and Star Medzerian Vanguri

New uses of language often emerge at critical moments in history. While it is possible to examine many such moments (e.g., recessions, migrant caravans, mass shootings), the phenomenon seems especially powerful during natural disasters, when language change accompanies physical change, uniting the material and discursive. For example, in a blog about Hurricane Katrina, which forever changed the city of New Orleans, Dave Zirin (2007) writes, "To the people I spoke with, Katrina is a noun, an adjective and even a verb." Kat Bergeron (2006) lists such new terms as "Katrina patina" ("the visible coating the storm left on people and things") and "shud" ("the mucky substance deposited by Katrina, a cross between mud and sh–") in her article "SLABBED! And Other Katrinaed Words; Katrina Patina." In its aftermath, writes Zirin, the cyclone became "something ephemeral, a sadness seeped into the humidity. It gets into your clothes, your eyes, your hair."

Zirin's post and Bergeron's article suggest that the most dynamic aspect of language is its ability not only to respond to but also to adumbrate and, indeed, catalyze, *change*. In *Style and the Future of Composition Studies*, we contend the principal way that language and social change emerges is through *style*. While Zirin and Bergeron show how style transformed "Katrina" from a noun to an adjective and verb, coined new phrases, and personified the storm in unusual ways, our claim is that style is further capable of anticipating and enabling innovative ideas, voices, identities, and rhetorics. This is our position as editors, and, more broadly, it is a recurring theme in this volume, in which authors reimagine or invent such concepts as eavesdropping (Goldthwaite), trespass (Udelson), inscrutability and a "translingual style" (House), unconscious rhythm (Johnson), "possible selves" (Alexis and Leake), sublime transdisciplinarity (Slater), and "diplomatic evidentiality" (Aull), among others, to demonstrate *how* style effects change.

As a canon of rhetoric, style has always possessed an adaptive or protean quality that allows writers to shape their messages for particular purposes, audiences, and occasions. Indeed, style serves as a rich palette of choices, enabling writers to mix, match, blend, and combine language and other semiotic forms in ways that allow surprising meanings and possibilities to emerge. The view of style as inventive, as opposed to static or fixed, lies at the heart of work by scholars like M.A.K. Halliday, Mary Bucholtz, Elinor Ochs, Conrad Biber, Zak Lancaster, Laura Aull, and Andrea Olinger (this volume). As John Vance (2014, 140), drawing on Halliday, writes, "Languages are dynamic, open systems whose forms (to the extent that they are 'formal' at all) are contingent on a vast array of local, emergent, 'bottom-up,' functional language practices." The same position undergirds the translingual approach to writing (see Horner et al. 2011; Canagarajah 2013; House, this volume). This dynamic, experimental quality of style reverberates throughout our collection, challenging all of us, as readers and writers, to rethink the ways style *reads and writes us* as a force of disciplinary action and change, and situating style as a crucible in the future of the discipline—its conversations, engagements, and areas of inquiry.

A great deal has changed in the last decade since Susan Peck MacDonald published "The Erasure of Language" (2007), in which she describes the dissociation of sociolinguistics from composition and subsequent decline of attention to sentence-level issues in writing. Like Robert Connors (2000), MacDonald poignantly articulates the impact of language and style's erasure from the discipline—especially on students. In fact, the past several years have seen the very resurgence of style that scholars such as Tom Pace and Paul Butler have anticipated. Articles on style and language have begun appearing in journals again. Books such as *The Centrality of Style* (Duncan and Vanguri 2013), *Style: An Introduction* (Ray 2014), and *Performing Prose* (Holcomb and Killingsworth 2010) have helped to restore the idea of style as a facilitator of agency and creativity.

These recent works have built on foundational texts by Butler, Johnson and Pace, and Lanham. They have also gone well beyond simply lamenting the absence of style from disciplinary conversations and have articulated what style has to offer composition, as well as how new orientations to writing and rhetoric prompt a reconception of style itself. In other words, we have made a central pivot from defending style's place in research and teaching toward exploring it from more diverse perspectives and identifying its latent presence in contemporary scholarship—including discourse analysis, sociolinguistics, language difference, and digital rhetorics. Researchers on style have just begun to articulate the points of connection between our work and these current trends in the field. These new fusions hold a great deal of promise for the study of style, but also for the discipline in general, as they enable unexpected approaches to writing instruction that value and embrace discursive contingency and dexterity. We are now in the process of repurposing style so that it can contribute to the writing instruction designed for the twenty-first century, an era characterized by media convergence, rapid genre evolution, and accelerated globalization. Our shared goals run deep, in that we need to prepare students to be able to compose in a range of settings and circumstances and to adapt to evolving discursive environments.

How does the book reflect the many ways an *inventive style* forces us to recalibrate how we write, read, and, indeed, think about language and meaning in the twenty-first century? The following sections lay out some of the capabilities of style by identifying key actions it performs. These categories could easily be combined or rearranged to reveal even more possibilities, as they merge, blend, overlap, move, and situate themselves in the interest of stylistic virtuosity and transformation.

STYLE MEDIATES RELATIONSHIPS

The future of style in composition studies anticipates style as a vehicle for different and diverse voices to emerge—rhetorically, from exigence, audience, occasion, context. One major focus in research on style involves shifting relationships between rhetors and audiences. Until recently, work on style has prioritized writers and the development of their voices—without a full consideration of the role readers play or how style is co-constructed. In her *Rhetoric Review* piece, "A Sociocultural Approach to Style," Andrea Olinger offers a dynamic definition and theory of style to frame future studies, one that moves beyond a relationship in which "writers engineer style, and the readers, universally, understand the writers' intent" (2016, 124). Olinger draws on research in sociocultural linguistics in order to present a model of style recognizing it as always emerging rather than static and fixed. Her full definition describes style as the "dynamic co-construction of typified indexical meanings (types of people, practices, situations, texts) perceived in a single sign or a cluster of signs and influenced by participants' language ideologies" (125). This definition demonstrates style's function as mediator, in that style refers not just to the writers' choices but the readers' as well, and the meanings they create together. For Olinger, and other authors in this collection, style is always in flux as it negotiates the multiple value systems at play between language users.

The works in this collection share a vision of style as dynamic, shared, co-constructed, emergent, and performed. This model holds a great deal of explanatory power. We can use style not just to inform how we teach students to write well but also as an analytical tool to investigate the language, discourse, and semiotic practices of writers and speakers in a range of contexts, with an emphasis on their relationships with audiences. Specifically, several contributions to this collection offer conceptions of how style mediates relationships between writers and audiences.

Andrea Olinger's chapter in this volume, "Cans of Worms," brings style into dialogue with research on transfer as a way of furthering her project of defining style as co-constructed and dynamic. This piece follows a college student named Corinne, whose understanding of her writing style and that of her advisers adapts as she negotiates their expectations—as well as their performances of style in their own publications. As Olinger shows, "styles may be composed of signs with conflicting or heterogenous indexical meanings," for example, in a short sentence seen by different readers as both "to the point" but also "flowery" if it employs a metaphor (chapter 1). This ethnographic study demonstrates how writers do in fact change their perceptions and practice of styles over time in response to interactions with audiences and also transfer styles across their writing situations and contexts. Readers might see the same stylistic traits differently, use different language to describe those traits, and even contradict themselves and each other when expressing their own perceptions and expectations about style.

Like Olinger, Ellen Carillo (2010, 2014) extends style beyond writers' choices; for Carillo, though, style serves as a way to reinvigorate the importance of reading in composition studies and its connection to writing. For both Carillo and Olinger, style serves as a way to reintegrate reading and writing after a period of their separation, most likely caught in the divide between literary and composition studies. We argue that style unites the process of reading and writing by making the two interactive, a kind of antiphonal effect in which the reader recalibrates the writer and the writer stands in the shoes of, or in the place of, the reader, in an act of rhetorical collaboration.

In "Here's What I Would Like for You to Know" (chapter 2), Melissa Goldthwaite continues the same idea in this volume, stating the important role of eavesdropping in epistolary writing, with the reader occupying the role of eavesdropper: "Readers are always, often unconsciously, negotiating their identifications and disidentifications—the ways they are or are not the intended audience for a piece of writing. Epistolary writing, however, makes that negotiation more explicit, encouraging readers either to identify with the audience being invoked or to consciously inhabit the role of eavesdropper." Goldthwaite sees this negotiable process at work in Ta-Nehisi Coates's *Between the World and Me*. She writes:

> Because the book is addressed to Coates' 15-year-old son, readers can eavesdrop—perhaps listening with empathy, understanding the love that prompts this father to communicate honestly with his child about the injustices that all Americans *should* face but that some *have no choice but to* face because of the bodies they inhabit.

T. R. Johnson's chapter in this volume, "'Clarity' Really Means Rhythm," also emphasizes the relationship between writers and audiences and its implications for style. Addressing the conventional notion of clarity, Johnson reintroduces the concept of rhythm as helping to sustain a successful dynamic between readers and authors. As he argues, "we all know that what is meant by clarity is . . . a successful author-audience relationship," and "the key to this relationship can be captured in one word: rhythm" (chapter 3). Attention to patterns and cadences in writing that reflect elements of spoken discourse can help writers, including college students, craft discourse that generates, inflects, and sustains meaning by syncing with a reader's own expectations for repetition of sounds and units of language. Examples include emphasis, flow, alliteration, and parallelism, oral elements we generally neglect in many genres of writing.

Tom Pace's chapter, "Erasmus in the Professional Writing Classroom," offers a pedagogical approach that introduces students to the relationship between writers and readers, as mediated by genre and stylistic conventions. As Pace argues, "adhering to traditional textbook-based stylistic exercises in the professional writing classroom often does not prepare these students for what employers require of them in the workplace" (chapter 4). Instead, Pace's students, in an upper-level professional writing course, complete a number of genre-based projects ranging from memos and grant proposals to websites for local companies. The course provides scaffolding for each project that prompts students to pay attention to stylistic affordances and expectations. He states that in asking students to learn various stylistic strategies for workplace genres and to practice writing them in the classroom, they can then adapt these strategies to numerous rhetorical situations: "The assignments and their attention to style challenge students' preconceived conceptions of style and teach them numerous strategies for adapting these stylistic elements to both workplace and academic settings."

Indeed, for Pace, "teaching students various stylistic strategies for addressing workplace genres allows students to become better equipped to write for various audiences and purposes." This chapter represents our broader goal to move even further beyond the commonplace perception of style as simply correctness or adherence to rules, a view that many of Pace's students admit to holding at the beginning of the semester. The key goal for any college writing course, and perhaps especially upper-level courses in professional and technical writing, lies in helping students understand that style involves choices and active decision-making, as well as negotiations with readers and generic expectations. Pace shows the ways in which his students are effectively border crossers when it comes to writing in the disciplines and using style as the means by which they slip in and out of different territory in writing across curricular differences.

STYLE CONVEYS IDENTITY

Every time we write or speak, we define and redefine our identity through style. Michel Foucault (1994) explains an author's different identities as, for instance, the voice he or she uses in a narrative account versus the voice in the preface of a text. In each case, different "selves" are required. Foucault later says in an interview that identity is based on differentiation, creation, and innovation. The future of style in composition studies is tied to ever-changing identities and the way these identities are represented or performed stylistically. Style, we assert, can be seen as a common denominator for identity, constantly in a process of adaptation and reinvention.

These characteristics of stylistic identity are at the heart of T. R. Johnson's argument about rediscovering the oral rhythms within our unconscious minds. Arguing for a link between training in style, athletics, and musical training in Greece, Johnson probes something deep within the unconscious that brings about the same type of identity performance normally tied to innovation, transformation, and change. For Johnson, this fusion of identity and style, based on unconscious rhythms, is closely linked to writing:

> Given the deep roots of what we might today call a style-based pedagogy in the athletic and musical training of the ancient Greeks, the way the old oralist rhythms still haunt our most thrilling experiences of texts, one can't help but suppose that this territory is still with us at the level of the unconscious. In ways we only dimly understand, it continues to flash into view from time to time in contemporary discussions about how people should learn how to write.

Similarly, Cydney Alexis and Eric Leake (chapter 5) invoke theories of "possible selves" (imagining oneself in a role or occupation correlates with the ability to achieve it) to argue for a symbiotic merger of style and identity. As the authors foreground, style enables voices to speak that have not been heard before. What is fresh, original, innovative, and transformative finds voice through style because what needs to be said comes to the surface and insists on being heard. They write: "Style influences the ways people identify themselves as speakers and actors, as readers and writers. Research on possible selves and analysis of the stylized identities in popular portrayals of writers . . . help us focus on how the writerly self is made available and performed." On a practical level, Alexis and Leake see an important connection between possible selves and composition researchers: "How writing is styled and how writers are stylized on screen provides an entry point for writing studies scholars to understand the circulation of stereotypes around writing and the cultural availability of possible writer identities."

Laura Aull and Zak Lancaster (chapter 6) also make a strong argument for the importance of voice and identity in an emerging discursive style. They state: "Writers' stylistic choices . . . are driven largely by interpersonal considerations. These include the 'voice' or authorial persona the writer wishes to project; the relationship with the reader the writer seeks to create; and the writer's engagement and negotiation with others' views and voices in the discourse." The authors see these stylistic features as "resources for asking new questions about writing" and as a way in which style brings about change by "meeting the demands of other academic, disciplinary, and generic writing situations." Overall, the authors project a case for a dynamic style, mediated by voice and identity and constantly interacting with the rhetorical situation to produce discursive change.

Digital rhetoric and the digital humanities have given us the ability to produce new forms of meaning, with many different combinations of verbal, nonverbal, symbolic, and multimodal tools. We argue that style's future in composition studies contemplates its role as the arbiter of online expression, serving to coordinate, rearrange, and mediate among various modes of expression. Multimodal and visual elements produce new styles, while style offers options of ways in which these elements can be combined. Jimmy Butts (chapter 7) sees new forms of digital and multimodal expression as leading to what he says some may call a "stupid style." Claiming that "stupidity has its own power," Butts sees imperfection as part of stylistic innovation, urging everyone to embrace what might seem like error. He writes: "Language will always be deployed imperfectly, stupidly. One day, when we finally accept this, we can be kinder to each other as more hospitable audiences of language.

As such, a stupid style offers efficiencies, resistances, and sites of invention or of 'thinking otherwise.'" Butts thus sees advantages in multimodal and digital elements of style as opening up the effects of language and recognizing the stylistic importance in what might formerly have been considered "error" or, to use his word, stupidity, in writing.

Congruent with this new view, compositionists have started attending to the ways in which writers as well as speakers use language strategically in order to convey stances, construct identities, engage in social interactions, and craft personas for a range of situations. Just as people style their hair and clothes, they style their discourse to convey their attitudes toward the world while expressing or performing different elements of their identity. As Nikolas Coupland observes, style refers to "a way of doing something" (Coupland 2009, 1). It "marks out or indexes a social difference . . . a degree of crafting," and production of meaning. Someone may intentionally use an expression or part of speech to indicate their membership in a social group or to mark a level of status and authority. Or they might stylize their discourse to perform a persona.

This view toward style recognizes it as the "fleeting interactional moves through which speakers take stances, create alignments, and construct personas" (Bucholtz 2009, 147). When someone decides to incorporate a different dialect, vernacular, or slang into their writing, they're styling their discourse in order to construct a persona that achieves a specific effect on readers—one that the reader may engage with or reject. Even pronoun choice in a scholarly article qualifies as a stylistic decision, one in which the writer is actively trying to establish a relationship with readers and, as Olinger observes, "may index a particular class, ethnicity, gender, and/or locale" (2016, 125). Therefore, it is not for writing teachers to accept or reject the use of a particular nonstandard form but rather to understand why a student has chosen one form over the other and what meanings they intend to convey to us and other audiences. Once teachers understand and appreciate the indexical implications behind acts of language difference, they are in a better position to help students hone their writing across these different codes and modes—without imposing their own agendas.

The question of language change has been at the forefront of the field recently through the introduction of translingualism and code meshing as the blending, merging, and meshing of accents, dialects, and varieties of English (Young, Martinez, and Naviaux 2011). Bruce Horner and others have said a translingual approach sees difference in language as a *resource* for producing meaning in writing, speaking, reading, and listening. Suresh Canagarajah (2013) goes on to say that "speaking and writing are not acts of transferring ideas or information *mechanically*, but of achieving communicative objectives with art, affect, voice, and style."

We argue that all of these communicative objectives (art, affect, voice, and style) *are* style—whether different aspects of style or different ways we express or explain things stylistically. We recognize translingualism and code meshing as indispensable approaches to embracing language difference, and we also contend that the blending, merging, and effects produced by these resources are often achieved through stylistic choice. In the future, then, it is incumbent upon us to explore how style works in conjunction with a translingual approach to writing in order to express language difference in composition studies. As Bruce Horner and his coauthors argue in their opinion essay "Language Difference in Writing: Toward a Translingual Approach" (2011), "This [translingual] approach thus calls for *more*, not less, conscious and critical attention to how writers deploy diction, syntax, and style, as well as form, register, and media. It acknowledges that deviations from dominant expectations need not be errors; that conformity need not be automatically advisable; and that writers' purposes and readers' conventional expectations are neither fixed nor unified" (304). In this volume, Eric House experiments with his own translanguaging, code meshing, and the use of a "translingual style."

House's chapter uses hip-hop, which he calls "a valuable and generative space where discourses and language practices are continually negotiated (Petchauer 2012)," to argue for a "translingual style" that relies on "discourses of translingualism [to] describe difference as the norm in language practice (Horner and Lu 2013)." House uses his conception of a translingual style to make a generative argument for "inscrutability," a theoretical concept that, he argues, "invites critique and openness" by defying normative discourses. Ultimately, House sees the significance of inscrutability, viewed through the metaphor of the hip-hop cipher, as promoting difference in writing studies. He states, "An emphasis on an inscrutable style in rhetoric and composition might then teach us the nuances of difference and its impacts on the flows and movements in theories and pedagogies of writing." Indeed, the idea of an inscrutable style challenges us to re-see language as always emerging, continually innovating.

STYLE FORMS STRATEGY

For Jarron Slater (chapter 9), language change comes in a different form. He sees the classical notion of the sublime as enabling stylistic change through a transdisciplinary approach to language and discourse, one that brings audiences and speakers or writers together through a cooperation with each other he describes as "empowered" and "exalted." In the chapter, "Expectations of Exaltation," he proposes the notion of sublimity as originally introduced by Longinus and developed by Kenneth Burke. For Slater, sublimity "creates expectations of exaltation and then invites the audience to fulfill those expectations through their participatory and emancipated cooperation." His argument builds on Burke's definition of the sublime as "elation wherein the audience feels as though it were not merely receiving, but were itself creatively participating in the poet's or speaker's assertion" (Burke 1969, 57–58). According to Slater, "formal sublimity unbinds style because it shows how style, rhetoric, and poetics are not separate 'things' but are forever intertwined. Formal sublimity does not limit 'style' to a narrow 'canon' of rhetoric. Its very principle argues for *a priori* transdisciplinarity, one that has style having something to say on everything from the smallest syllable to the grandest reaches of the universe, and beyond." For Slater, the impact of style, and its effect on transdisciplinary change, is limitless. The use of figures, tropes, and schemes might aim not simply to embellish or amplify discourse in a conventional sense, but to draw in audiences as co-constructors of meaning.

Innovating style and composition studies has called on us as researchers to broaden our disciplinary identities, seeking to understand who else studies style and what methods and terms they use. Scholarship in sociolinguistics and discourse studies has expanded the horizons of stylistic study. As such, we have solicited work from scholars who cross disciplinary boundaries, drawing on corpus and discourse studies. Corpus studies by Zak Lancaster have already helped us investigate the accuracy of language patterns in textbooks such as *They Say/I Say*, specifically the extent to which they truly represent discourse conventions in academic writing. Laura Aull's (2015) work on first-year writing has also generated reliable, data-driven insights into students' acquisition of subjective pronouns, in order to counter myths about use of the first-person in academic writing. Further corpus investigations of style will help us learn more about the ways in which people use language interactively and indexically.

Contributions by Laura Aull and Zak Lancaster show the power of linguistic analysis to inform students' acquisition and navigation of academic discourse. In their co-authored chapter, "Stance as Style" (chapter 6), Aull and Lancaster demystify aspects of academic conventions by identifying "highly patterned stylistic features" and illustrating how "the unique stylistic qualities of academic prose become especially visible when seen through the lens of stance," which the authors define as "the writers' many 'micro' expressions of attitudes, evaluations, epistemic commitment, and interaction with the reader." Their chapter outlines three major stances that occur in academic prose along with corresponding features such as attitude markers, self-mentions, concessions, adversative connectors, hedges, and boosters. They show how instructors can introduce these terms to students, grounding their discussion in helpful examples of student writing and classroom activities.

Laura Aull's single-authored chapter, "A Civil Style" (chapter 10), also employs functional linguistics and discourse analysis in order to introduce a new term, "diplomatic evidentiality" (a civil style that, in Aull's words, features "both 'rhetorical listening'—a stance of openness in relation to other texts and views [Ratliffe 2005]—and a writer's own convictions, in that order"), into current approaches to civil discourse in college writing instruction. As Aull notes, research on civil discourse has curiously overlooked the role of actual language strategies and markers. Attending more closely to stance markers and evidentials, Aull claims, gives writers ways of "projecting honesty, modesty, and proper caution in self-reports, and for diplomatically creating research space in areas heavily populated by other researchers" (Swales, quoted in Aull 1990, 175). Here, teachers can see how style contributes to much more than adherence to rules or conventions. In fact, the choices they make in diction and sentence construction contribute to the overall stance and attitude that readers will perceive, which in turn affects their reception. Such work confirms and reminds us about the importance of language, tone, and voice and their role in mitigating or exacerbating conflicts—as when politicians and celebrities alike seem to enjoy exchanging barbs over social media, only elevating the toxicity of public discourse. By pointing to the importance of ethics and civility in the discursive realm, Aull helps the field reimagine a discourse, based on diplomatic evidentiality, that reinvents the very nature of argument, effectively rebalancing logos, pathos, and ethos within the rhetorical situation.

We have also worked to expand our understanding of writing and where it happens. Writing doesn't just occur in the academy, and stylistic innovations appear on the web every day through new words, new turns of phrase, and new grammatical constructions. To fully understand style, we need to study it in personal journals, newspapers, blogs, and social media. A turn toward quantitative, empirical data also characterizes the new direction in the study of style. Until recently, studies of style have been limited by a tendency to form a general impression of a writer's style, or to speculate about the effects of stylistic decisions on readers. Work on corpus linguistics offers new and better tools for studying meaningful patterns across large bodies of texts. Doing so allows us to make stronger, more reliable claims about the stylistic conventions within a certain discipline or genre. It also enables us to see with greater precision how writers negotiate, deviate, and innovate with regard to these expectations.

While discourse-based studies have always attended to the study of language in action, stylistic analysis adds a new dimension by showing how style, or stylization, is used to bring about a reversal in the very nature of discourse. What is notable here is that discourse, almost always closely connected to different genres, has been used to achieve specific effects. But style disrupts conventional genres, turning discourse on its head to expose inherent biases in language, gender, social interactions, and culture. It calls discourse into question and, in the process, engenders a new form of discourse inherently connected to, but changed from, its original forms. For Almas Kahn (chapter 11), legal discourse takes on new forms through the work of Applied Legal Storytelling (ALS), in which authors often begin with personal stories or vignettes for the purpose of "humanizing real-life actors in the legal system" through style, using tone, imagery, allusions, diction, and other features. ALS discourse gives new life to legal reasoning through its stylistic possibilities. In the case of a transgender bathroom rights case, Kahn argues, the judge cites a teen's "compelling statement" to a school board in the teen's YouTube video, bringing in visual and digital rhetoric, and forging a new, emergent form of legal discourse.

In "What Style Can Add to Genre" (chapter 12), Anthony Box suggests that strengthening connections between disciplinary writing and style can increase genre awareness. When writers are aware of the stylistic options available to them and can consciously choose them, they are better equipped to "question, interact with, and redefine the genres they participate in." However, style is often incorporated superficially in academic writing, out of habit rather than choice. As an example, Box analyzes the "faked coherence" present in metalanguage within samples of published prose. Instead, he argues, an internalized stylistic awareness can lead to variety, originality, and memorability.

STYLE CREATES AND TRANSCENDS BOUNDARIES

As style relates to both convention and deviation, it serves participatory, community-establishing functions, while also acting as gatekeeper.

Recent scholarship demonstrates how style reinforces and disrupts genre boundaries, disciplinary boundaries, and divisions between public and private. In an important article that drew a well-known response from Charles Bazerman, Anthony Fleury proposes that skills in public speaking are emblematic of styles of communication. He writes:

> Liberal education can be advanced through strategic use of core styles throughout the curriculum. Core styles of expression, exposition, and persuasion—which are foundational to but transcend disciplinary styles—provide tools for understanding, performing, critiquing, and resisting knowledge and identity production. A dialectic of Communication Against the Disciplines and CID [Communication in the Disciplines] would encourage in students multiple and diverse ways of thinking and doing. Approached this way, CXC [Communication Across the Curriculum] can help the student become a model citizen, able to not only argue well for a position but embody a democratic mix of multiple voices, to articulate the world from many positions. (2005, 72)

Even though Fleury was primarily addressing readers in communications studies, his remarks have been widely taken up in the field of rhetoric and composition. Bazerman, for instance, suggests that "advocates of the centrality of style, such as Fleury, may find ways of talking about how the styles that disciplines use to express their intellectual work are closely tied to the life, meaning, and accomplishment of these knowledge-creating communities" (2005, 89). Bazerman continues in a statement relevant to the current volume, stating, "This close connection between the styles of communication and the most fundamental projects, meanings, and vitality of the disciplines has made the study of disciplinary writing and the practice of writing across the curriculum deeply rewarding and engaging endeavors" (89). What is striking is the relevance of Fleury's remarks, not to mention Bazerman's, to what authors in this volume have contributed in this area, especially the emphasis on multiple voices coming from interdisciplinary stylistic approaches.

In "Points of Departure" (chapter 13), Jon Udelson addresses the recriminations some face in "trespassing" a disciplinary Maginot Line between creative writing and composition studies. In his chapter, subtitled "Composition and Creative Writing Studies' Shared Stylistic Values," he writes: "The ability to style one's writing by the common conventions of a particular discipline . . . aids in marking a writer as part of the discipline and the believed epistemological terrain it governs. From a disciplinary perspective, treading that terrain otherwise constitutes an act of trespassing." In a sign of the change signaled by the authors in this collection, Udelson aims to trespass, to usher in a new level of communication, erasing the truism that "[c]omposition cannot speak of creative writing because composition is still all too often thought of as the domain of 'general writing skills instruction' (Petraglia 1995), while creative writing exists in a domain beyond mere 'skill.'" Udelson invites trespass as a new way to erase the divide between the two fields and allow new possibilities to emerge across disciplines.

Mike Duncan (chapter 14) uses his skillful analysis to take up different disciplinary approaches and discover the truth about stylistic forgery in the New Testament. He writes: "Similar style could easily mean the opposite—a 'school' of forgers writing in that style, borrowing the *ethos* of the original. Accordingly, I argue that a stylistic imitator . . . wrote Acts—and that all the evidence arrayed in support of common authorship can be reversed to support two different authors." In suggesting that scholars look seriously at "critical factual inconsistencies," he argues that "ultimately, the initial sensing of 'something's off' may happen at the style level, but defensible proof of 'something's off' requires close reading of content and context."

William FitzGerald (chapter 15) offers the metaphor of the writing classroom as makerspace and style as craft to argue for renewed attention to the word in composition. Like all *makers*, writers must have comfort and fluency with the tools they use to create. Yet students often "arrive at college poorly resourced in terms of lexis." By increasing our attention to the word in composition pedagogy, we can "help students better access and leverage their stock of verbal resources." To make a case for a lexical pedagogy that interweaves style and invention, FitzGerald looks to the past, to the dominant narratives in our discipline that have either outright rejected style or emphasized sentences over words. The essay leaves us to imagine a pedagogical approach that treats style as "tinkering" and empowers students to explore, play with, and master the "material dimensions of words and the labor that adds to their value." Indeed, FitzGerald argues that we make space for style and style makes space for emergent and inventive meanings.

CONCLUSION

We argue that style stands at the future of composition studies. We see it as an open frontier that invites crossing divides, providing access, and celebrating difference. The contributions to this collection recognize style as inventive and innovative and prompt us to consider a number of ways to harness these attributes. They urge us to see style as a tool for engaging audiences through dynamic co-construction of meaning, recalibrating binaries, renegotiating identities, and traversing disciplinary spaces. We hope readers will come away from our collection with an understanding of how to use style for opening up new emergent approaches to writing, reading, thinking, and cross-disciplinary collaboration. We see style as contributing to the growth of the discipline, now and in the future. As editors, we focused our efforts on guiding individual contributors and on shaping the volume to help ensure its parts speak dialogically, collaboratively, collectively, and divergently and move across, between, among, and around questions, ideas, and meanings. The general public may still define style by way of conventional manuals like Strunk and White's influential but outdated *Elements of Style*. Even here, public intellectuals such as Steven Pinker (2015) have challenged conventional ways of thinking about style, moving discourse away from platitudes about correctness and convention and toward more nuanced approaches that embrace the inevitable mutability of language. While linguistic purists might bemoan the appearance of new words and phrases in the wake of momentous events and sociopolitical upheaval, contemporary stylisticians welcome them and see them as central catalysts for effective communication. As realities change, so must the styles we use to convey our perceptions of them. Nevertheless, the future work of rhetoricians will always involve efforts to counter the myth that style only involves following rigid rules about grammar and usage.

We see stylistically engaging writing in a broad range of genres and disciplines. Not only that, but style often plays a key role in the evolution of these written forms. Writers refashion these forms themselves, finding new ways to make meaning through manipulation of the existing stylistic conventions and constraints. In every case their stylings of discourse facilitate their intentions and reinvent the forms of writing they use. As much as any other canon or approach to rhetoric, style fosters agency and ingenuity in language. One shared goal among all teachers and researchers in our discipline lies in the value we see and promote in such autonomy and adaptability.

Every single chapter in this collection conveys one inflection of our central message about the inventive, generative potential of style. It may involve innovations on the sentence level or regarding word choice. More broadly, attunement to style offers new approaches to a variety of aspects within the discipline, from writing across the curriculum to the role of civil discourse in first-year composition. Just as changing knowledge in the discipline has influenced the way stylisticians think about language, we hope that new knowledge in style will give teachers and researchers concepts, frameworks, and strategies for attending to the stylistic dimensions of our shared endeavors, now and into the future.

REFERENCES

Aull, Laura. 2015. *First-Year University Writing: A Corpus-Based Study with Implications for Pedagogy*. New York: Palgrave Macmillan.

Bazerman, Charles. 2005. "A Response to Anthony Fleury's 'Liberal Education and Communication against the Disciplines': A View from the World of Writing." *Communication Education* 54 (1): 86–91.

Bergeron, Kat. 2006. "SLABBED! and Other Katrinaed Words; Katrina Patina." *Sun Herald* (Biloxi, MS), May 21, 2006. Sunherald.com.

Bucholtz, Mary. 2009. "From Stance to Style: Gender, Interaction, and Indexicality in Mexican Immigrant Youth Slang." In *Stance: Sociolinguistic Perspectives*, edited by Alexandra Jaffe. Oxford: Oxford University Press.

Butler, Paul. 2008. *Out of Style. Reanimating Stylistic Study in Composition and Rhetoric*. Logan: Utah State University Press.

Canagarajah, Athelstan Suresh. 2013. *Translingual Practice: Global Englishes and Cosmopolitan Relations*. London: Routledge.

Carillo, Ellen. 2010. "(Re)Figuring Composition through Stylistic Study." *Rhetoric Review* 29 (4): 379–394.

Carillo, Ellen. 2014. *Securing a Place for Reading in Composition: The Importance of Teaching for Transfer*. Logan: Utah State University Press.

Coates, Ta-Nehisi. 2015. *Between the World and Me*. New York: Random House.

Connors, Robert J. 2000. "The Erasure of the Sentence." *College Composition and Communication* 52: 96–128.

Coupland, Nikolas. 2009. *Style: Language Variation and Identity*. Cambridge: Cambridge University Press.

Duncan, Mike, and Star Medzerian Vanguri. 2013. *The Centrality of Style*. Fort Collins: The WAC Clearinghouse.

Fleury, Anthony. 2005. "Liberal Education and Communication against the Disciplines." *Communication Education* 54 (1): 72–79.

Foucault, Michel. 1994. *The Order of Things: An Archaeology of the Human Sciences*. New York: Vintage Books.

Halliday, M.A.K., and Christian Matthiessen. 2014. *Halliday's Introduction to Functional Grammar*. New York: Routledge.

Holcomb, Chris, and M. Jimmie Killingsworth. 2010. *Performing Prose: The Study and Practice of Style in Composition*. Carbondale: Southern Illinois University Press.

Horner, Bruce, and Min-Zhan Lu. 2013. "Translingual Literacy, Language Difference, and Matters of Agency." *College English* 75 (1): 586–611.

Horner, Bruce, Min-Zhan Lu, Jacqueline Jones Royster, and John Trimbur. 2011. "Opinion: Language Difference in Writing: Toward a Translingual Approach." *College English* 73 (3): 303–321.

Lancaster, Zak. 2016. "Do Academics Really Write This Way? A Corpus Investigation of Moves and Templates." In *"They Say / I Say."* *College Composition and Communication* 67 (3): 437–464.

Lanham, Richard. 2007. *The Economics of Attention: Style and Substance in the Age of Information*. Chicago: University of Chicago Press.

MacDonald, Susan Peck. 2007. "The Erasure of Language." *College Composition and Communication* 58 (4): 585.

Ochs, E. 1992. "Indexing Gender." In *Rethinking Context: Language as an Interactive Phenomenon*, edited by D. Alessandro and C. Goodwin, 335–358. Cambridge: Cambridge University Press.

Olinger, Andrea R. 2016. "A Sociocultural Approach to Style." *Rhetoric Review* 35 (2): 121–134.

Pace, Tom. 2009. In *Refiguring Prose Style: Possibilities for Writing Pedagogy*, edited by T. R. Johnson and Tom Pace.

Pinker, Steven. 2015. *The Sense of Style: The Thinking Person's Guide to Writing in the 21st Century*. New York: Penguin Books.

Ratcliffe, Krista. 2005. *Rhetorical Listening: Identification, Gender, Whiteness*. Carbondale: Southern Illinois University Press.

Ray, Brian. 2014. *Style: An Introduction to History, Theory, Research, and Pedagogy*. Fort Collins, CO: The WAC Clearinghouse.

Vance, John. 2014. "Pedagogy: Reconsiderations and Reorientations." PhD diss., University of Louisville, Louisville, KY.

Young, Vershawn Ashanti. 2004. "Your Average Nigga." *College Composition and Communication* 55 (4): 693–715.

Young, Vershawn Ashanti, and Aja Martinez, with Julie Anne Naviaux. 2011. "Introduction: Code-Meshing as World English." *Code-Meshing as World English: Pedagogy, Policy, Performance*. Urbana, IL: National Council of Teachers of English.

Zirin, Dave. 2007. "And Still They Rise: Confronting Katrina." *Rising Tide Blog*. The Rising Tide Conference 2. August 29, 2007.

SECTION 1

Style Mediates Relationships

1
CANS OF WORMS
Tracing an Undergraduate Thesis-Writer's Style Knowledge over Time

Andrea R. Olinger

> "The terms students used to characterize the kind of writing they did in FYC and other courses in the English Department included '**fluff**,' '**b.s.**,' and '**flowery**,' whereas in talking about the writing they did in other classes, students used descriptors such as '**concise**,' '**to the point**,' and 'not a lot of **flowery** adjectives.'" (Bergmann and Zepernick 2007, 125; bold added)

A key component of writing knowledge is the ability to identify and anticipate writing styles in particular genres and contexts. Yet discussions of style have been limited in or absent from recent studies of writing knowledge and transfer (e.g., Beaufort 2007; Nowacek 2011; Yancey, Robertson, and Taczak 2014). One reason for this neglect may be the imprecision of everyday style terminology. To some writing researchers and teachers, stylistic descriptors like "fluff" and "flowery" are adisciplinary, ageneric, and afunctional. For students taking a general-education writing course or progressing in their major, such superficial conceptions are ideally displaced by a more nuanced understanding of the situated nature of literacy practices, one educators typically convey and researchers explore through genre (e.g., Nowacek 2011; Tardy 2009). (See Aull and Lancaster, this volume, for a framework to move students beyond what they call such "generalized and vague" terms.)

Style may also be overlooked because it is frequently clustered with grammar and mechanics and therefore treated, within and without academia, as a basic, easily mastered skill. For example, in her chapter on writing-related knowledge, Nowacek describes how the students "think and talk" (2011, 99) about content, process, genre, and "mechanics and style" knowledge. Whereas the first three categories are addressed at lengths ranging from three-quarters of a page to three-and-a-half pages, "mechanics and style" is dispensed with in three sentences, and style is not defined. Not surprisingly, Nowacek's participants see style as self-evident.

Although genre is a rich site for investigating the situatedness of all aspects of writing, there is much to gain from probing writers' commonsense knowledge of style. Thaiss and Zawacki (2006) argue this in their research on how faculty across disciplines teach writing. In an analysis of rubrics for fifteen undergraduate degree programs, the terms "clear" and "appropriate voice" appear in more than 70 percent; "evidence," "organized," and "grammar" appear in over 90 percent (87). These overlaps manifest how stylistic concepts *seem* universal. In reality, Thaiss and Zawacki recount, the opposite is true: As "we . . . witnessed faculties arguing criteria, and as we read assignments and rubrics, we were more and more impressed by the variety of meanings and significances of these common terms. Not only did we uncover major differences in how faculty from different disciplines understood the common terms, but also we saw time and again faculty redefining 'evidence,' 'audience,' 'purpose,' 'style,' and other terms for first-year students, undergraduate majors, graduate students, and other constituencies" (88–89). Thaiss and Zawacki advise that faculty members clarify for themselves and students how their assignments and rubrics are a "deliberate blending" (146) of five phenomena:

- Generalized standards for academic writing
- Disciplinary conventions
- "Subdisciplinary" conventions
- Institutional and departmental cultures and policies
- Personal goals and idiosyncratic likes and dislikes (95)

They posit that undergraduates with more advanced knowledge of writing in their discipline will understand these factors "as components of an articulated, nuanced idea of the discipline," whereas undergraduates with less awareness may generalize "rules" from a few courses or may view every teacher as idiosyncratic (2006, 109–110). Arguably, students and teachers alike associate stylistic preferences with either universal rules or idiosyncrasy. Because style has been undertheorized or overlooked, researchers and teachers have been deprived of insight into how a writer's style knowledge might be a "deliberate blending" (146) of these preferences and the extent to which style knowledge changes over time.

As a remedy, I offer a case study of Corinne, a psychology major writing a senior thesis. Drawing on text- and discourse-based interviews with Corinne and two of her professors in different subfields of psychology, I trace Corinne's shifting views of the professors' stylistic differences as well as the constancy of her language-ideological notions of their styles as discrete and homogeneous. In capturing both the flexibility and fixity of her representations over time, I illustrate the value of collecting longitudinal data to explore style knowledge and, as Thaiss and Zawacki do, of foregrounding the notion of styles as blends.

Before I proceed, I should articulate what I mean by *style*. In a previous publication, I define *style* as the "dynamic co-construction of typified indexical meanings (types of people, practices, situations, texts) perceived in a single sign or a cluster of signs and influenced by participants' language ideologies" (Olinger 2016, 125). In other words, writers may associate one or more semiotic features (e.g., multiple adjectives, long or short sentences, even ways of dressing [see Alexis and Leake, this volume]) with indexical meanings like "concise" or "flowery." Styles may be composed of signs with conflicting or heterogeneous indexical meanings—for instance, a short sentence that uses metaphorical language might be simultaneously viewed as concise and flowery. Moreover, these meanings are not inherent in the semiotic features but are co-constructed by readers and other interlocutors, who may disagree—and these meanings may change. For instance, metaphorical language in a journal article might be viewed as fresh and boundary-pushing by the writer but as clichéd and inappropriate by a reader. Over time, the writer might agree with the reader—or disagree more strongly. Lastly, these meanings are shaped by language ideologies, whether standard language ideology or, in the case of the example, an ideology of the autonomous text, which might reject so-called flowery language for not contributing to referential meaning (Olinger, forthcoming). Importantly, however, language ideologies are "incomplete . . . attempts to rationalize language usage" (Kroskrity 2010, 192, quoted in Olinger 2016, 126); that is, writers may unconsciously contradict themselves in practice; the reader who bridles at metaphor in a journal article may unknowingly use metaphors in her own academic writing. Such misalignment indicates the need for researchers to pair writers' representations of their stylistic practices with textual analysis.

Overall, a sociocultural lens favors attention to ideology (the conceptions that, incompletely, drive people's preferences), the semiotic over the linguistic (as perceptions of styles may be influenced by signs of various types), co-construction (multiple meanings), and dynamism (shifts in meaning). In treating writing style more as verb than noun, this approach invites us to explore tensions and changes in writers' style knowledge and practice.

METHODS

This case stems from a qualitative study of how eight groups of eighteen academic writers—in such relationships as advisor/advisee and coauthor—understand and practice style in their disciplines. Corinne, a senior psychology major writing an honors thesis on narcissism and social rejection, was enrolled in a required three-semester thesis-writing course taught by a prior participant, Dan Simons. Dan is a cognitive psychologist and popular-science writer who coauthored a *New York Times* bestseller (Chabris and Simons 2010) and writes op-ed essays for national publications.

During the 2012–2013 year, Corinne and I met for a literacy history interview, three informal check-in conversations, and three text- and discourse-based interviews (Prior 2004), totaling just over four hours of audiorecordings. I also interviewed Corinne's advisor, Harold (a pseudonym), a clinical psychologist, about his work with Corinne (17 minutes/audiorecorded), and I interviewed Dan twice about his own writing and mentorship of Corinne and another undergraduate (104 minutes/audiorecorded). Drafts of Corinne's thesis informed the text- and discourse-based interviews. Corinne shared around fifty texts, including outlines and section drafts, which often contained notes from her meetings with Harold or comments from Harold or Dan.

In the first semester of Dan's course, Corinne's junior spring, students produced a twenty-page literature review. In the second semester, senior fall, students began writing their methods sections, conducting their research, and condensing their literature reviews into the introduction sections of their theses, which would resemble a journal article. In the third semester, senior spring, students completed their theses and presented posters. Throughout senior year, Corinne worked on the draft primarily with Harold, with occasional feedback from Dan.

In our first interview Corinne remarked on differences between Dan's and Harold's writing styles and how she negotiated them. We returned to this topic in all of her interviews and in my conversations with Dan and Harold. As I began data analysis, I looked for similarities and differences between their representations and practices. The sections below trace how, over the three semesters Corinne spent working with both professors, she alternately professed and wavered from language-ideological notions of their styles as stable and homogeneous.

LEARNING TO SEE "CANS OF WORMS"

When the course began, Dan distributed a writing guide he had created, "Musings on Writing" (Simons 2012). Per his website, the guide is for "scientific writing, but the same principles apply to most non-fiction (including journalism)" (Simons n.d.). The eight-page document offers "broad principles of effective writing," including suggestions for an engaging opening—"Entice your readers. Establish a controversy, present a real-world conundrum, or reveal a mystery. All are more effective than simply stating your topic because they develop a narrative thread, one that compels readers to seek a resolution" (Simons 2012, 1)—a list of thirty-one "common mistakes and pet peeves"; and a "revision worksheet" that distills the guide to a checklist. In the first semester of the course, Dan had students consult the guide as they revised their own writing and complete the checklist as they reviewed classmates' drafts.

That semester, Corinne wrote a portion of the literature review. After receiving feedback from Harold, she revised it accordingly. To this five-double-spaced-page draft, Dan and the course's teaching assistant added thirty-seven comment bubbles, culminating with the charge that Corinne "use the revision worksheet more systematically" by editing for items such as passive voice, "X has Y that" structures, and uses of "I think." Dan wrote:

> I've inserted a number of comments throughout, but I stopped at the end of the opening. You need to use the revision worksheet more systematically before submitting your drafts. The paper has a TON of passive voice, "many X has Y that" structures, and other minor wording issues that are in the search/destroy part of the worksheet (e.g., the word "very," many "I think" and "I believe," etc.). I'd like to see you put more effort into the revision process before submitting the next paper draft. That will give you an opportunity to do a re-thinking with the next iteration.

Alarmed, Corinne met with Dan and discovered that, as she wrote to me, "this semester was supposed to be an 'exercise' in using Dan's writing style" ("Harold notes" [document in author's possession] 2012). She inferred that she would switch to Harold's style during senior year, when the actual experiments would be run and the thesis would be written under Harold's oversight. To avoid inviting conflicting feedback, Corinne decided to withhold her literature review from Harold for the rest of the semester. She revised the introduction to her literature review using the comments she had received from Dan. In a comment bubble on her revision, he praised her "nice job of cleaning up some of the wording issues we discussed."

Corinne explained that Dan "emphasized not writing in the journal-style format"—that "he wanted a lot more narrative and a lot more, um you know, less use of jargon, kind of more trying to make it accessible to the—to a person who isn't even in a psychology field" (interview, November 2, 2012). She enjoyed writing in Dan's style, citing its emphasis on being brief and "colloquial," which "allowed me to have a little bit more freedom with how I wrote and how I organized my thoughts." However, "basically none of that—none of his style really applies anymore this semester when I'm actually writing an introduction that I'm intending to put in my thesis" (interview, November 2, 2012). And over a week later, she noted that "obviously if we ended up submitting it to a journal, then we would just have to look at whatever style was used by the journal. And that won't be Harold's or Dan's or anything. So that'll just be a whole new can of worms" (interview, November 14, 2012).

This language-ideological notion of Dan's and Harold's styles as discrete silos—or "can[s] of worms"—shapes how she conceives of their stylistic preferences. When Corinne emailed me some of her drafts, she enclosed a table representing "how Dan and Harold differed in writing style" (email, November 4, 2012; see table 1.1). According to the table, Dan and Harold differ on "show, not tell," the use of "I," the use of jargon, and sentences that start with "X has Y that" but share preferences for brevity, clarity, and avoiding verbosity. The table reveals Corinne's awareness that different styles can achieve the same goals.[1]

SEEING AND ENACTING TENSIONS WITHIN STYLISTIC PRACTICE

According to Thaiss and Zawacki, an advanced writer understands that, and how, writing expectations are a "deliberate blending" (2006, 146) of general academic, disciplinary, subdisciplinary, local/institutional, and personal preferences. This knowledge applies to style as well. Although the representations "Dan's style" and "Harold's style" project that Corinne views them as clusters of idiosyncratic preferences, Corinne did demonstrate an awareness of at least one way in which they blend multiple categories. In our first interview she identified a tension between Harold's preference for concision and a subdisciplinary preference for how to characterize the traits she was studying. I asked if Harold, like Dan, had any pet peeves. She responded that he did: when she had used the terms "vulnerable narcissists" and "grandiose narcissists" in an early draft, Harold favored "individuals with vulnerable narcissist personality traits." She explained to me that a "vulnerable narcissist" does not exist; instead, per her thesis, "narcissistic personality traits fall along two separate dimensions," a vulnerable and a grandiose narcissism dimension (Corinne, final thesis, 2013). Corinne revealed that

Table 1.1. The table Corinne created for me to differentiate Dan's and Harold's styles.

Dan	Harold
Use "narrative style"; wanted us to "show it," not "say it."	Do not use "narrative style." Harold wanted me to "say it," not "show it." Perceived "showing" and not "saying" (i.e., using narrative style) as "gimmicky." Harold also thought that "showing," as opposed to "saying," something detracted from writing clearly and poignantly.
Don't use "I" (e.g., "I believe," "I think").	Use "I." Harold would say, "It's *your* research, and this is what *you* think will happen in your study, so use 'I believe/hypothesize.'"
Don't try to "sound science"; eliminate "jargon" ("*show* it, don't *say* it").	Sound sciencey! Harold wanted me to write in "journal article style" and encouraged the use of jargon because it made my paragraphs and sentences more brief and clear. He said that individuals who read journal articles will know what the jargon means. He didn't want me to spend several sentences "showing" (i.e., *describing* what I am referring to) what I could have just said with one "jargon" word.
Don't start sentences with "X has Y that" (e.g., "Research has shown that . . .").	Use "X has Y that" (e.g., "Research has shown that . . ."; "Researchers found that . . ."). Harold believes I need to use these sentences to justify the points I proposed in my literature review. His philosophy is, "If you don't have support, you don't a have a study."
Use active voice.	Harold never explicitly mentioned that he preferred active voice and never caught or commented on passive voice (like Dan did—see Dan Revisions I) when I used it. I assume he prefers active voice because using passive voice makes your sentences less clear and wordier.
Be brief and clear.	Be brief and clear.
Don't be verbose.	Don't be verbose.

avoiding "vulnerable/grandiose narcissist" was "hard because it makes it more wordy, which is what I'm trying—which is what he doesn't like and what I don't like" (interview, November 2, 2012). She speculated, "[S]o I guess his preference for not labeling someone is kind of overshad—is kind of preceding or superseding his preference for, um, succinctness [*she laughs, and I join her*]" (ibid.). Here, Corinne identified a tension between general academic values for "succinctness" and the subdisciplinary value to represent the trait accurately and ethically. Embracing the "more wordy" option, she prioritizes her alignment with her own subdiscipline. She thereby reveals a nuanced understanding that such homogeneous and monolithic representations as "Harold's style" can in fact encompass competing stylistic influences.

Not surprisingly, Corinne's writing embodies heterogeneity: even when tasked to write in "Harold's style," Corinne borrows from the semiotic features she associates with Dan's. To illustrate how Corinne enacted both styles, I have copied the first two paragraphs of the final

Table 1.2. The first two paragraphs of Corinne's literature review paper, spring 2012, and the first paragraph of her thesis, spring 2013 (right)

Opening of Corinne's Literature Review Paper	Opening of Corinne's Thesis
Imagine you gave an evaluated presentation and received negative feedback. You likely would view your presentation more negatively. But would the negative feedback change how you evaluate yourself? Our personalities affect how others perceive us and how we perceive ourselves. For example, personalities affect the emotions we experience when receiving criticism from others (i.e., social criticism). An individual's self-belief is one personality characteristic I am interested in examining.	People vary in the degree to which they have a grandiose self-view, need admiration, and exploit others for personal gain. Clinicians call people who possess these traits "narcissistic." There is emerging evidence, however, that narcissistic personality traits fall along two separate dimensions: a vulnerable narcissism dimension and a grandiose narcissism dimension (e.g., Miller & Campbell, 2008). Of particular relevance to the present study, both vulnerable narcissism and grandiose narcissism share an inflated self-view (e.g., Besser & Priel, 2010; Dickinson & Pincus, 2003). However, one conceptualization of the differences between vulnerable and grandiose narcissism is that those with high levels of vulnerable narcissism need approval from others to reaffirm their grandiose self-view, whereas those with high levels of grandiose narcissism do not (Raskin, 1991; Rhodewalt & Pederson, 2009). Thus, a major distinction between grandiose narcissism and vulnerable narcissism may be in their differential responses to the feedback they receive from others.

version of her literature review paper and the first paragraph of the final version of her thesis (table 1.2).

Following the advice in Dan's writing guide to "entice your readers," Corinne opens her literature review paper by directly asking readers to imagine and place themselves in a scenario. By contrast, she begins her thesis by describing the traits of narcissism and situating them in literature. The first two sentences, however, are likely influenced by Dan, with whom she has now worked for over a year: "narcissist" is defined without jargon—a move that may not be necessary for her audience—and, per one of Dan's preferences, the word "people" is used instead of "individuals." The final version in Harold's style is thus more hybrid than Corinne might have imagined when she pronounced, in November of her senior year, that "none of [Dan's] style really applies anymore" (interview, November 2, 2012). This exemplifies one of the important qualities of language ideologies: that awareness is always partial and never completely describes practice. Corinne may perceive styles as neat containers, but, to push her "cans of worms" analogy further than she intended, stylistic practice is more like a bundle of squirming worms of different shapes and sizes—composed of heterogeneous semiotic material that may have clashing and changing interpretations. Below, I show how Corinne's language-ideological notion of their styles as cans—homogeneous and discrete—is disrupted throughout the year yet still quite present during our final interview.

STYLE REPRESENTATIONS IN FLUX

The differences between Dan's and Harold's styles as categorized in Corinne's table seem fixed. However, as Corinne and I met over the course of her senior year and she continued to get feedback from Dan and Harold, her understandings grew to incorporate new information about their preferences. In Corinne's view, Harold's style began to appear more "sciencey" at one point and both more and less narrative at another point. Because stylistic meanings are not inherent in the text but are co-constructed by other readers and interlocutors, these changes of mind are wholly unexceptional and reveal the dynamism of style.

Harold's Style Becomes More "Sciencey"

In her table, Corinne indicates that Dan prefers active voice and that Harold probably prefers active voice "because using passive voice makes your sentences less clear and wordier." But during an interview a few weeks after emailing me the table, she reversed her view. Discussing the differences between Dan's and Harold's feedback, she commented, "I also realized as I was reading back through some of Harold's papers that he likes to use passive voice 'cause it sounds kind of more sciencey and research, whereas Dan likes active voice" (interview, November 14, 2012). When I asked if Harold addressed this with Corinne or if she inferred it herself, she replied, "I just assumed he had used active voice because by nature you'll—it's less wordy, but—Dan had pointed out that Harold likes to use passive voice and when I was looking through some of Harold's comments when Harold would rewrite a sentence, I was like, oh, wow" (ibid.). Although Corinne was surprised that Harold would prefer wordier language, she reasoned that this preference fits his "sciencey and research" style, which, according to her table, includes jargon and constructions with more words (like "X has Y that" structures). Interestingly, her explanation does not reference the functions of passive voice (e.g., controlling information flow) but instead invokes the ideological notion of stylistic consistency—of styles as composed of homogeneous elements. This indicates a change from just weeks before, when Corinne assumed that Harold did not use passive voice, because being "brief" and "clear" would supercede his desire to "sound sciencey."

Harold's Style Becomes More and Less Narrative

By the time Corinne and I spoke a few months after she sent me the table, she had begun to realize that Harold embraced a more "narrative" style after all. Her reasoning was twofold: first, Harold used a metaphor, that of scientific writing as telling a "story"; second, he faulted her abstract as "dense," a trait Corinne associates with Harold's "sciencey" style. When I asked whether Dan used the actual term "narrative style," she confirmed and elaborated:

> And I guess I'm realizing this more about Harold now, he calls it a "story" so—he says, in your thesis, in your, specifically in the abstract, you want to tell a story and he felt like my abstract was too dense—heh so I was like I think I'm doing it, and then I realize I don't—um—and I—had thought that because Harold has a very kind of stereotypical academic style, um I thought that he wouldn't have ever been concerned with like the denseness of my abstract, but he was actually really concerned that I wasn't telling a story, and that I was focusing too much on the details and not enough about the main picture. So then I'm like, wait, maybe he's more similar to Dan than I kinda initially thought. (interview, February 5, 2013)

Because she had seen Harold as practicing a "stereotypical academic style"—and, after the discovery of passive voice, one that she now viewed as even more so—she had assumed that he would neither notice nor mind "denseness." Corinne subsequently reported that Harold had advised her to show "the forest, not the trees." This directive, she felt, was uncharacteristically "creative." For Corinne, "narrative style" had expanded to encompass not only the written artifact—text that is not "dense"—but also a way of conceptualizing and talking about writing, such as creative expressions and concepts like "story" and "show the forest, not the trees."

But this expansion, we immediately discovered, did not necessarily entail further stylistic freedom. After Corinne mentioned Harold's use of "story," I replied that "story," although a synonym for "narrative," could mean "main point." She agreed and continued:

> And I also think that when Dan says "narrative," he—he thinks of more um, like anecdotal hypothetical examples, which is what he used all the time in his books. Well he used real-life examples in his books, but it—whereas in journal articles that's called gimmicky. If you used like a quote from a popular article, or if you make up a hypothetical example, like I've—I've seen manuscripts submitted, and then I've seen the

comments, and one person had a quote at the beginning from a character in her—her article was on narcissism and she had a quote from Barney from *How I Met Your Mother*, and of course the comment was the—"the first quote that you had in your introduction was gimmicky and we don't like it." (interview, February 5, 2013)

Corinne defined Dan's use of narrative to mean "anecdotal hypothetical examples" or "real-life examples"—both of which she said appear in his popular-science book *The Invisible Gorilla*, and the first of which she used to open her spring 2012 literature review paper, written in "Dan's style" (table 1.2). She then implied that such narrative practices are not appropriate for journal articles, extrapolating from when a manuscript that began with a TV show quotation was called "gimmicky" by a reviewer.

These examples illustrate the fluidity of representations like "narrative" and "sciencey and researchy"/"stereotypical academic": they may expand and contract to accommodate semiotic elements with disparate indexical meanings. Initially, "narrative style" embraced metaphor use in talk and the conception of scientific arguments as "stories"; later, "narrative style" involved, and dismissed, the use of a real-life or hypothetical anecdote and a quotation from a TV show. "Narrative style" thus becomes both something Corinne should emulate—by telling a story in the abstract and avoiding "denseness"—and something "gimmicky" that she should eschew.

During our last interview, after we discussed articles that Corinne would be working on with Harold and graduate research assistant "Melanie" (a pseudonym), I asked if the TV show quotation was from one of Melanie's manuscripts. Corinne corroborated this, and I added, "But I assume that was *not* on the coauthored one" (i.e., a manuscript Melanie and Harold were coauthoring that had been rejected by several journals). Corinne answered that the quotation *was* in the coauthored manuscript. "So Harold allowed that—little thing?!" I asked. Corinne responded, "He *totally* di—I mean maybe like, maybe he initially didn't, but Melanie is, um, how should I put this, like ballsy? So she'll—I can totally see Harold saying 'don't do this' and she saying 'I'm going to do it' and Harold's like 'okay whatever'" (interview, June 10, 2013). Here, we see the power of language ideologies in shaping representations of styles. Even I, the writing researcher who should arguably know better, assumed universal agreement on what "narrative" or "stereotypical[ly] academic" style looked like: if a journal reviewer found the epigraph "gimmicky," I inferred, Harold would not have allowed it. Corinne seconded this and speculated that Harold likely protested but was simply overruled.

"Narrative style," "stereotypical academic style," and even "Harold's style" and "Dan's style": these sound like stable constructs composed of neatly aligned features. Hypothetically, a "stereotypical academic style" would appreciate a "dense" abstract and reject a TV show quotation. In line with the sociocultural approach limned above, however, these styles comprise a dynamic, heterogeneous bundle of multisemiotic elements. Harold's "stereotypical academic style" is inspired by metaphors and other creative elements like "story" and "show the forest, not the trees," but—Corinne guesses—it pronounces TV show quotations gimmicky. It scorns dense prose, but—in embracing constructions like "individuals with vulnerable narcissist personality traits"—it admits wordiness if accuracy and ethical representation require it. Moreover, if we asked Harold, Melanie, other lab members, or even Dan about the indexical meanings they read into particular semiotic features, they may disagree with Corinne, the reviewer, or one another. Such is the clashing, conflicting, dynamic picture of style that a sociocultural lens reveals.

CONCLUSION

Did Corinne's understanding of writing style mature? Surprisingly, it is hard to find clear development. At the start of her senior year, Corinne articulated a view of Dan's and Harold's styles as discrete and homogeneous, but she also understood that Harold's style was shaped by heterogeneous influences—namely, subdisciplinary and general academic preferences. Over the course of the semester, her representations of Dan's and Harold's styles continually shifted, demonstrating the fluidity of the categories. And yet at our final interview, she reasserted the categories' distinctness. When I asked her what she found the most challenging about writing her thesis, she cited learning "the scholarly journal style," a "very efficient way of writing" that allowed no "flowery" language or "hypothetical examples." "It was definitely hard for me to learn," she admitted, "because I usually tend to be pretty verbose" (interview, June 10, 2013). Shortly after, I asked whether Dan or Harold was the more influential mentor or if both affected her equally. She credited Harold, explaining that "Dan's style is, um, not very journally at all" and "I really couldn't combine the two" (interview, June 10, 2013). In addition to maintaining this view of the different styles as separate "cans of worms," Corinne's use of "verbosity" aligns with general academic preferences and effaces the subdisciplinary. Like the stylistic terms quoted at the start of this chapter, "verbosity" is arhetorical, ageneric, and solely formal, and it partakes of the language-ideological notion of good writing as universal. Corinne's statements and my own assumptions about universal agreement around narrative style demonstrate that these conceptions endure alongside fluid and even contradictory stylistic practices (see also Olinger, forthcoming). Longitudinal research on writers' representations of style surfaces these tensions in ways that data collection at a single point in time—via focus group, single interview, or survey—often cannot.

Representations of style abound in writing research, and the stylistic terms people use to describe their writing deserve further research. Exploring these representations in individual writers over time can illuminate what semiotic features are being linked to these descriptions, how and from where the associations emerged, and how they have changed or are changing. Beyond demonstrating the value to researchers, however, this case study challenges teachers to develop pedagogies that help writers critique their commonsense understandings of styles and notice the heterogeneity of and tensions in stylistic practice—worms and all.

NOTE

1. Both professors observed differences similar to what Corinne noticed. For instance, Dan said he wrote "in a more narrative style" and was "more likely to use prose that you'd see in a newspaper than [Harold] would be" (interview, March 28, 2013). Harold commented that Dan has "a somewhat atypical" style, "one that I like actually, but tends to be more, uh, informal and more written for, um, general audiences." Harold stated that whereas Dan prefers to begin a paper "with something to grab your attention," he "focus[es] on clarity and brevity but not necessarily grabbing someone's attention" (interview, June 26, 2013). They declared, however, that the similarities between them were actually greater, and they wondered if Corinne was overestimating the differences.

REFERENCES

Beaufort, Anne. 2007. *College Writing and Beyond: A New Framework for University Writing Instruction*. Logan: Utah State University Press.

Bergmann, Linda S., and Janet Zepernick. 2007. "Disciplinarity and Transfer: Students' Perceptions of Learning to Write." *WPA: Writing Program Administration* 31 (1-2): 124–149.

Chabris, Christopher, and Daniel Simons. 2010. *The Invisible Gorilla: And Other Ways Our Intuitions Deceive Us*. New York: Broadway.

Nowacek, Rebecca S. 2011. *Agents of Integration: Understanding Transfer as a Rhetorical Act*. Carbondale: Southern Illinois University Press.

Olinger, Andrea R. 2016. "A Sociocultural Approach to Style." *Rhetoric Review* 35 (2): 121–134.

Olinger, Andrea R. Forthcoming. "Self-Contradiction in Faculty's Talk about Writing: Making and Unmaking Autonomous Models of Literacy." *Literacy in Compositon Studies*.

Prior, Paul. 2004. "Tracing Process: How Texts Come into Being." In *What Writing Does and How It Does It*, edited by Charles Bazerman and Paul Prior, 167–200. Mahwah, NJ: Lawrence Erlbaum Associates.

Simons, Daniel. n.d. Personal website. Accessed May 3, 2018. http://www.dansimons.com/index.html.

Simons, Daniel. 2012. "Musings on Writing." Accessed May 3, 2018. http://www.dansimons.com/resources.html.

Tardy, Christine M. 2009. *Building Genre Knowledge*. West Lafayette, IN: Parlor Press.

Thaiss, Chris, and Terry Myers Zawacki. 2006. *Engaged Writers, Dynamic Disciplines: Research on the Academic Writing Life*. Portsmouth, NH: Boynton/Cook Heinemann.

Yancey, Kathleen Blake, Liane Robertson, and Kara Taczak. 2014. *Writing across Contexts: Transfer, Composition, and Sites of Writing*. Logan: Utah State University Press.

2
"HERE'S WHAT I WOULD LIKE FOR YOU TO KNOW"
Epistolary Style as an Invitation to Read and Write Metonymically

Melissa A. Goldthwaite

In reporting on her collaborative research project, the Stanford Study of Writing, Andrea Lunsford notes that students are "writing more than ever before in history"—and that "the whole world can be [their] audience" (quoted in Haven 2009). Although the potential for a large audience may be inspiring to some writers, it can be confusing or even debilitating to others, especially when writing about important cultural issues or engaging in public debates. How can writers tailor their tone, message, style, and sources to an unimaginably large and multiple audience, especially one that may be divided? Without a sense of a specific audience, writers often either use meaningless generalities ("in today's society") or take a defensive stance in relation to those who might disagree. Epistolary writing, however, invites readers to practice what Krista Ratcliffe calls "listening metonymically" to "a text or a person . . . associated with—but not necessarily representative of—an entire cultural group" (2005, 78). Epistolary writing allows writers to write metonymically, as well, to address one person (or small group), even as they seek to communicate with a larger, more diverse group.

Analyzing the stylistic moves made in epistolary writing can help students consider the ways audience shapes writing and reading. In this essay I analyze two common forms of epistolary writing: letters of advice (Chimamanda Ngozi Adichie's *Dear Ijeawele, or A Feminist Manifesto in Fifteen Suggestions*) and an epistolary memoir (Ta-Nehisi Coates's *Between the World and Me*). I chose these texts not only because they offer examples of two different stylistically rich approaches to epistolary writing but also because of the authors' contributions to contemporary conversations about gender and race. In analyzing these texts I consider the interplay of pronoun usage, sentence type and variation, repetition, imagery, and juxtaposition, seeking to show how each author's use of style and epistolary form can encourage metonymic listening. I then offer prompts that help students write to a specific audience in a way that a larger audience can hear. In doing so, I offer a pedagogy that encourages writers to listen rhetorically through stylistic analyses of epistolary nonfiction and to use the stylistic strategies they learn to then write about the issues and challenges most important in their lives and communities.

EPISTOLARY AUDIENCES ADDRESSED AND INVOKED: STYLE, METONYMIC LISTENING, AND EAVESDROPPING

In *Rhetorical Listening: Identification, Gender, Whiteness*, Krista Ratcliffe develops a theory of rhetorical listening. She expresses a concern that individuals often have difficulty "imagining simultaneous differences and commonalities," a problem echoed in "larger cultural discourses," especially about gender and race (2005, 2). She offers the idea of listening metonymically as a means of resisting gendered and racialized silences that are dysfunctional, uncomfortable, and unproductive (79). Metonymy is a form of metaphor in which a person, place, thing, or concept is referred to by something closely associated with it. According to Ratcliffe, "Metonym signifies figurative juxtaposition; it assumes that two objects do not share a common substance but are rather merely associated" (98). Building on this explanation, she asserts, "Thus, the trope of listening metonymically assumes that a text or person does not share substance with all other members of its/his/her cultural group but, rather, is associated with them" (98). In emphasizing association rather than essentialism, Ratcliffe offers metonymic listening as a trope for avoiding "unfair generalizations and stereotyping" (99), especially about race and gender.

Ratcliffe argues that readers can listen metonymically in order to create a place of pause and reflection in which it's possible to recognize both differences and commonalities, and she explains that such "recognition implies a complex understanding of how gender and race become embedded within our bodies via cultural socialization and identifications and also how they intersect with other cultural categories, such as nationality and age, at particular historical moments to construct our personal and cultural functions and dysfunctions" (2005, 93–94, 96). This intersectional approach to listening and understanding encourages thoughtful response rather than shutting down or becoming defensive.

Ratcliffe's theory of metonymic listening seems especially promising in understanding epistolary reading and writing. For writers, an epistolary form provides the focus of addressing a specific audience—someone who is known. It allows the writer to construct an audience in time and place and to address that audience in a way that is personally and historically situated. Further, such a concept of metonymic listening may encourage the writer to understand that she or he is associated with different groups but does not represent all others associated with a particular group or identity.

For readers, epistolary writing provides a space to pause and reflect—to listen as someone else is addressed. Ratcliffe presents "eavesdropping" as a way of intentionally positioning oneself on the edge of one's knowing in order to overhear and to learn from others and oneself (2005, 105). She offers eavesdropping as a *choice* readers and listeners can make in a variety of situations. But "eavesdropping" is especially pertinent to epistolary writing because the author is invoking a different audience, often by name, explicitly putting readers in the position of eavesdroppers. Readers are always, often unconsciously, negotiating their identifications and disidentifications—the ways they are or are not the intended audience for a piece of writing. Epistolary writing, however, makes that negotiation more explicit, encouraging readers either to identify with the audience being invoked or to consciously inhabit the role of eavesdropper.

In "Audience Addressed/Audience Invoked: The Role of Audience in Composition Theory and Pedagogy," Lisa Ede and Andrea Lunsford discuss the "integrated, interdependent nature of reading and writing" (1984, 156). They argue that "writers create readers and readers create writers" (169), showing that the relationship between audiences addressed ("those actual or real-life people who read a discourse") and audiences invoked ("the audience called up or imagined by the writer") is complex (156). Yet the strategy of invoking a specific audience can serve both writers and readers. It can authorize writers to speak from a situated place and to an imagined audience who can receive what the author has to say. Depending on who that invoked audience is, it might also allow the writer to write more openly, less defensively. This strategy can also be useful for readers—inviting identification in some places but also creating an awareness of difference. From the start, the reader is aware that he or she is not fully the intended audience, and with that knowledge the reader can intentionally inhabit the role of eavesdropper, listening metonymically in order to understand self and others by exploring not only similarities but also differences.

AUTHORIZED TO ADVISE: CHIMAMANDA NGOZI ADICHIE'S *DEAR IJEAWELE, OR A FEMINIST MANIFESTO IN FIFTEEN SUGGESTIONS*

> *"I had done a lot of watching and listening, and I had done even more thinking."*
> —Adichie (2017, 3)

Epistolary writing positions readers as eavesdroppers, as those listening to a seemingly private correspondence—even though that correspondence, if published, is public. Letters of advice further disrupt the public/private binary. A productive tension between public and private is evident in Adichie's *Dear Ijeawele, or A Feminist Manifesto in Fifteen Suggestions*, a short book in which Adichie offers advice on how to raise girls to be feminists. Consider the tensions evident in just the title. "Dear Ijeawele" suggests the intimacy of an audience of one, yet this personal salutation is followed by "or A Feminist Manifesto in Fifteen Suggestions." A manifesto is a public declaration of opinions and objectives that suggests proclamation and pronouncement, yet Adichie softens the resoluteness by also including the term "suggestions" in her title.

In the introduction to her book, Adichie explains that she was asked by a childhood friend to "tell her how to raise a baby girl a feminist" (2017, 3). In response, she wrote her friend a letter. The book, "a version of that letter," responds to an exigency, her belief that it is "morally urgent to have honest conversations about raising children differently, about trying to create a fairer world for women and men" (4). Although the actual readers of this book may not be Ijeawele and may not have a young daughter named Chizalum or a husband named Chudi, they may share a sense of purpose in creating a fairer world. The specific examples drawn from Ijeawele's life and culture may be different from the readers' experiences, but the advice can still resonate with readers. Importantly, the invitation to give advice authorizes the writer; it creates a space for her to share her opinions and beliefs. She does not have to try to convince someone who is hostile to feminism. Since her advice is sought out, she need not temper it.

Stylistically and in terms of arrangement, Adichie highlights general advice. She structures the book as a list of numbered suggestions. Most often, she renders the suggestions in imperative sentences, commands such as "Be a full person," "Ask for help. Expect to be helped," "Give yourself room to fail," "Don't assume that you should know everything," "Take time for yourself. Nurture your own needs" (2017, 7–10). The subject of these commands is understood (you); on one level, readers understand that Adichie is addressing Ijeawele—and not a general reader—but to the extent that readers identify with Ijeawele (those who are mothers raising daughters will likely identify most closely) they are included in the audience. Still, the advice Adichie gives in the above-quoted section can be taken by a broader audience as well.

Adichie does provide variety in terms of types of sentences after initial commands. While the general commands invoke a distant audience, many of Adichie's declarative sentences show her connection with Ijeawele and create a more conversational tone. She writes, for example, "It doesn't surprise me that your sister-in-law says you should be a more 'traditional' mother and stay home" (2017, 8). Here, Adichie couches a "traditional" expectation (that mothers should stay home with their children) in a personal example. After telling Ijeawele that having a dual-income family is actually part of Igbo tradition—and that the sister-in-law would know this "if reading books were not such an alien enterprise to her"—Adichie acknowledges that her "snark" was meant to cheer Ijeawele (9). Her humor is meant to help diffuse the annoyance Ijeawele feels toward her sister-in-law, yet this humor also serves another purpose. One danger of giving advice (or writing manifestos), of using imperatives, is being overly didactic, which can create a hierarchy where the one giving advice is above the person being advised. Adichie lessens the potential negative effects of didacticism by alternating sentence types, creating a conversational tone, and showing her sensitivity to Ijeawele's feelings and relationships.

In using this specific example, Adichie also avoids the more general and distancing "some people"—as in "some people will tell you that mothers should stay home to rear their children." By using a specific example—and humor—Adichie shows she's being attentive to her audience's actual concerns, concerns that may be shared by a broader audience.

Throughout the book, Adichie alternates between imperative sentences that invoke a general audience and specific details directed to Ijeawele. For example, after her second suggestion, "Do it together," she extends her general advice with interrogative and declarative sentences that relate specifically to Ijeawele's experience: "Remember in primary school we learned that a verb was a 'doing' word? Well, a father is as much a verb as a mother. Chudi should do everything that biology allows—which is everything but breastfeeding" (2017, 11). The focus on her friend's family creates a sense of intimacy, yet it also relieves Adichie of having to detail the ways her advice may not apply in every situation. She does acknowledge that "do it together" might not be an option if Ijeawele were a single mother, but she reaffirms her advice by reminding

Ijeawele that she should not act as a "single mother" unless she truly is one (13).

Invoking Ijeawele as audience allows Adichie to explore Nigerian culture, even as she gives advice that can be applicable across cultures. Her third suggestion is "Teach her that the idea of 'gender roles' is absolute nonsense" (2017, 14). In this section her use of metaphor and adjectives strengthens such advice. She refers to "the straightjacket of gender roles" (17–18). While Adichie may be referring to gender roles as constraints, the metaphor also evokes a sensory image of a person bound and unable to use his or her limbs because someone else believes that person might be a danger to self or others. Adichie is using this metaphor in relation to gender roles restricting children, which heightens the pathos of the metaphor.

Adichie also colors her position on the "nonsense" of gender roles by using adjectives. She describes going to a store to buy Chizalum an outfit and finding "pale creations in washed-out shades of pink" in the "girls' section," "vibrant shades of blue" in the "boys' section," and "an array of bloodless grays" in the "gender-neutral section" (2017, 15–16). She bought blue, thinking it "would be adorable against [Chizalum's] brown skin—and photograph better," showing a range of reasons why one might choose a particular color (16), perhaps encouraging a broader audience to think about why they choose particular colors, especially for children.

Throughout the book, Adichie chooses examples from more than one culture. She refers to Nigerian social media debates about whether women must cook for their husbands; she also discusses clothing color, toys, and specific behaviors that tend to be gendered by people from many different cultures. By sharing examples of both Nigerian and American acquaintances, Adichie allows readers to listen metonymically, to consider what is similar and different across cultures.

In some chapters she writes specifically about Igbo culture—as well as images of blackness and Africans. In a section on appearance, she tells Ijeawele not to "link hair with pain" (2017, 44) and instead make "Chizalum's hair loose—big plaits and big cornrows, and don't use a tiny-toothed comb that wasn't made with our hair texture in mind" (45). Her use of the pronoun "our" links Adichie, Ijeawele, and Chizalum; their commonality, in this case, is based on hair texture. Readers may or may not share that commonality, but they can listen metonymically, perhaps gaining an understanding of ways products or even expectations about hair and appearance can be exclusionary.

In urging Ijeawele to surround Chizalum "with a village of Aunties, women who have qualities you'd like her to admire," Adichie lists the names of African women—Ama Aita Aidoo, Dora Akunyili, Muthoni Likimani, and others—"who are sources of feminist inspiration" (2017, 47). These examples ground the text with historical and cultural specificity. These examples are geared toward Ijeawele, valuing her culture. For a broader audience, such specificity might help them learn more about a different culture, especially if they seek out more information on the African women she names. Adichie, though, provides little of that information, which perhaps serves different purposes for a broad audience. One positive purpose might be that each reader can make her or his own list of sources of feminist inspiration. Or, if readers do not know about the women Adichie lists, they may ask themselves *why* and learn something about the limits of their own knowledge.

Although the advice can be abstracted and understood by a larger audience, Adichie crafts her specifics and examples with one family in mind. In doing so, she does not need to imagine cultural, class, or regional situations that differ from her own or that of her friend. Still, she acknowledges her limitations. For example, Adichie writes assuming that Chizalum is heterosexual—and that "she might not be, obviously"—and explains that heterosexuality is what she feels "best equipped to talk about" (2017, 55). Her advice is limited by her assumptions and experience, but the acknowledgment of that assumption also foregrounds the fact that every perspective is limited. A limited perspective, though, can be broadened by listening to the stories, examples, and ideas of others—and of seeking to foster, in Ratcliffe's terms, "cross-cultural communication in places of identification, disidentification, and non-identification" (2005, 78).

Adichie's last suggestion—"Teach her about difference. Make difference ordinary. Make difference normal" (2017, 61)—takes the form of most of her other advice: short, imperative sentences. More than a third of her suggestions begin with the word "teach," emphasizing the action she wants audiences to take. Perhaps ironically in this final section, she urges Ijeawele: "Teach her never to universalize her own standards or experiences. Teach her that her standards are for her alone, and not for other people" (62). Just as there is a tension between public and private in this book of epistolary advice, there is also a tension between providing clear advice to others and not universalizing one's own standards. Adichie, however, shows the compatibility of both in what she "hopes" for Chizalum: "[T]hat she will be full of opinions, and that her opinions will come from an informed, humane, and broad-minded place" (63). Through listening to the experiences, hopes, and advice of others, perhaps readers and their opinions will become more informed, humane, and broad-minded as well.

REMEMBER, KNOW, STRUGGLE: TA-NEHISI COATES'S *BETWEEN THE WORLD AND ME*

> "There is no them without you, and without the right to break you they must necessarily . . . tumble out of the Dream" (2015, 105).
> —Coates

In *Rhetorical Style: The Uses of Language in Persuasion*, Jeanne Fahnestock writes, "Skillful rhetors alter the footing, the participation status between themselves and audience members. . . . Texts are best seen as constantly changing the footing, the status, the relationship, between speaker and listener, writer and reader" (2011, 288). In epistolary writing, the audience invoked may remain stable (a specific person addressed at a particular time in history, for an identified purpose), but the audience addressed (actual readers) shifts over time and depending on who is reading. Further, the audience hailed and constructed by the author stylistically—in Coates's memoir through pronouns, repetition, sentence structure, imagery, and juxtaposition—shifts and is negotiated in the way Fahnestock describes, revealing how "I" and "you" may be "identities constructed for the occasion" (280). How do actual readers negotiate the shifting ground of identification, disidentification, and nonidentification in reading epistolary writing? What happens when the writer partitions the audience—*distributio*—by "naming a group in the presence of other groups" (295)? Can a group "purged" from the intended audience still listen metonymically and intentionally eavesdrop in ethical ways?

Memoir, a historical account written from personal remembrance, provides an interpretation of the writer's experience. In an epistolary memoir, the interpretation of experience is shaped by the audience invoked. In *Between the World and Me*, Coates addresses his fifteen-year-old son Samori, making the exigency clear early in the memoir:

> I am writing you because this was the year you saw Eric Garner choked to death for selling cigarettes; because you know now that Renisha McBride was shot for seeking help, that John Crawford was shot down for browsing in a department store. And you have seen men in uniform drive by and murder Tamir Rice, a twelve-year-old child whom they were oath-bound to protect. And you have seen men in the same uniforms pummel Marlene Pinnock, someone's grandmother, on the side of the road. And you know now, if you did not know before, that the police departments of your country have been endowed with the authority to destroy your body. It does not matter if the destruction is the result of an unfortunate overreaction. It does not matter if it originates in a misunderstanding. It does not matter if the destruction springs from a foolish policy. (2015, 9)

This long passage illustrates the themes and style Coates uses throughout his memoir: the centrality of black bodies, strong verbs to show the violence committed against black bodies (choked, shot, murder, pummel), how experience leads to knowledge ("you have seen" and "you know now"), anaphora (here, the repetition of "It does not matter") to heighten emotion and emphasize main points. Coates points to the injustices and violence his young son has seen and shows the long history of such violence. He uses both anaphora (repetition at the beginning of successive sentences or clauses) and epistrophe (repetition at the end of successive sentences or clauses) to emphasize the effects: "All of this is common to black people. And all of this is old for black people" (9). Although Coates specifically addresses his adolescent son in this passage—and in the book as a whole—readers (if they watch or read the news) will be aware of such violence. And if readers were not aware, Coates brings this awareness through the details, names, and verbs.

That this experience and history is "common" and "old" does not mean looking away; in fact, Coates tells his son—and the reader, "You must never look away from this" (10). Readers cannot look away because Coates's use of a combination of strong verbs, sensory images, and lists has an accumulative effect, forcing the reader to face the violence committed against black bodies. Racism, he shows through these stylistic elements, is not an abstraction; rather, "racism is a visceral experience" that "dislodges brains, blocks airways, rips muscle, extracts organs, cracks bones, breaks teeth" (10).

Coates tells Samori that "the question of how one should live within a black body" in the United States is the question of his life, one he seeks to answer through reading, writing, music, arguments, education, and experience (12). Of course, the stakes are different for different audiences, different bodies. Although most readers should be aware of the violence, not all readers will identify with this statement: "the police departments of your country have been endowed with the authority to destroy your body" (9). "Your body" refers specifically to Samori but also to others who "live within a black body" (12). Samori and others who live within black bodies are the audience invoked, yet they are not the only audience who needs to face the violence Coates recounts because America, Coates argues, has been built on that violence.

Early in the memoir, Coates partitions his audience, creating an us/them binary, even as he destabilizes this binary; he writes that "white America's progress, or rather the progress of those Americans who believe that they are white, was built on looting and violence" (6). In referring to those who "believe that they are white," Coates alters the footing of at least one segment of his audience (those who believe that they are white), forcing readers to question the notion of race. He shows that racial categories are not inevitable, that "race is the child of racism, not the father" (7). This father/child analogy and his repetition throughout the memoir of the phrase "believe that they are white" destabilizes the binary between black and white. He asserts that the belief in being white is hopeless, tragic, deceitful, and "a modern invention" since those who believe themselves to be white "were once something else," wearing labels defined by religious affiliation or country of origin rather than skin color (7).

Although Coates questions these categories and labels intellectually, he continues to emphasize the bodily effects of such categories and beliefs. To stress the corporeal effects of racism, he again uses sensory images, strong verbs, and lists (and here the alliterative "l" sound): "the belief in being white" was achieved "through the pillaging of life, liberty, labor, and land; through the flaying of backs; the chaining of limbs; the strangling of dissidents; the destruction of families; the rape of mothers; the sale of children" (8). His sentence structure, again, highlights violence, showing bodies being acted upon in horrific ways.

Coates's pronoun use and careful labeling may also alter the footing of other segments of his audience; for him, there are differences, too, among those who live in black bodies. Consider, for example, this passage in which he recounts his and his family's resistance to traditions many people, regardless of race, practice: "We spurned the holidays marketed by the people who wanted to be white. We would not stand for their anthems. We would not kneel before their God" (2015, 28). Often in his memoir, "we" refers to those who live in black bodies and "they" refers to those who believe themselves to be white. Here, though, Coates refers to "the people who wanted to be white," which might also include some of those who live in black bodies. Throughout, he shows the violence inherent in the "Dream of acting white, of talking white, of being white," a Dream not determined exclusively by skin color (111).

Coates contrasts the "Dream of being white" with "the Struggle," and he identifies himself and Samori with the latter. He tells his son, "The Struggle is in your name, Samori—you were named for Samori Touré, who struggled against French colonizers for the right to his own black body" (68). For many readers the Dream may not seem entirely negative; Coates expresses the Dream metaphorically: "It is perfect houses with nice lawns. It is Memorial Day cookouts, block associations, and driveways. The Dream is treehouses and the Cub Scouts. The Dream smells like peppermint but tastes like strawberry shortcake" (11). Those who desire or have or believe in these things must contend, though, with the violence Coates associates with them. He follows the seemingly pleasant metaphors with this assertion: "the Dream rests on our backs, the bedding made from our bodies" (11). Later in the text he uses another metaphor, saying that the Dreamers accept violence against black bodies as "the cost of doing business" and "accept our bodies as currency" (131). He extends the metaphor by explaining a corrupt economic system in which black bodies throughout history have been a "windfall," "down payment," "second mortgage," and "lucrative investment"; "our bodies," he writes, "have refinanced the Dream of being white" (131–32). Coates's use of "our bodies" excludes "the Dreamers," partitions the audience, purges those who believe they are—or those who want to be—white from the audience.

In "Between the World and the Addressee: Epistolary Nonfiction by Ta-Nehisi Coates and His Peers," Emily J. Lordi analyzes the "performance of in-group intimacy" many black epistolary writers use in writing about racial oppression (2017, 436). She shows how Coates and other writers of color "working in an embattled political moment" use the epistolary form to "address the effects of racial oppression" without focusing on "those who perpetuate and benefit from it" (445). In fact, Coates skillfully partitions the audience in a way that sidelines white readers (or those who believe they are white or those who want to be white), placing them in the position of eavesdroppers. It is not Coates's job or his purpose to "awaken" the Dreamers; he tells Samori, "[Y]ou cannot arrange your life around them and the small chance of the Dreamers coming into consciousness" (2015, 146). More pointedly, he urges Samori: "do not struggle for the Dreamers" (151).

How might "Dreamers" struggle themselves in reading Coates's text? In developing her theory of rhetorical listening, Krista Ratcliffe offers the strategy of eavesdropping. Although eavesdropping suggests listening to the private conversations of others (and, therefore, may have negative connotations), Ratcliffe posits eavesdropping as an ethical stance, "a tactic for listening to the discourses of others, for hearing over the edges of our own knowing, for thinking what is commonly unthinkable within our own logics" (2005, 105). It may be "unthinkable" for some readers to recognize complicity in systemic violence, to see themselves in the Dreamers Coates describes. Ratcliffe's strategy does not demand that eavesdroppers accept and agree with all that they hear or read, but it does ask listeners to avoid defensiveness and to seek to learn. Ratcliffe argues that "rhetorical eavesdropping entails positioning oneself to overhear both oneself and others, listening to learn, and most importantly, being careful . . . not to overstep another's boundaries or interrupt the agency of another's discourse" (106). Coates sets high stakes for the Dreamers' awakening: "The Dreamers will have to learn to struggle themselves, to understand that the field for their Dream, the stage where they have painted themselves white, is the deathbed of us all" (2015, 151). Although the stakes are high—the deathbed for all—it is not his or Samori's responsibility to help the Dreamers in their struggle. It's the responsibility of the eavesdropper to learn without interrupting. Samori—and perhaps others who live in black bodies—is still the audience invoked.

Throughout his memoir, Coates shares the knowledge he has gained through experience and uses his memories to guide his son. Readers who listen metonymically and those who eavesdrop may be guided as well, gaining a better understanding of their own identifications, disidentifications, and nonidentifications with the experiences Coates relates. Because the book is addressed to Coates's fifteen-year-old son, readers can eavesdrop—perhaps listening with empathy, understanding the love that prompts this father to communicate honestly with his child about injustices that all Americans *should* face but that some *have no choice but to* face because of the bodies they inhabit. Perhaps, in places, the use of second person—the repetition of "you"—places the reader imaginatively in a different body, even temporarily, to feel sadness, rage, fear, and the effects of violence. But readers, especially those who do not live in black bodies, must also contend—at least metonymically, by association—with their own complicity in the Dream.

Coates writes about what he remembers, what his son may or may not remember, what his son must remember. He admits what he doesn't know—and what he does know—acknowledging that he and his son have lived different lives: "I don't know what it means to grow up with a black president, social networks, omnipresent media, and black women everywhere in their natural hair" (2015, 21). Yet he follows this statement with "What I know," showing the connection between father and son: "[F]or all our differing worlds, at your age my feeling was exactly the same" (21). Coates uses antithesis and parallel structure often in the memoir to show both differences and similarities, reaffirming his central purpose: "My work is to give you what I know of my own particular path while allowing you to walk your own" (39). The grammatical balance provided by parallel structure shows the equal importance of Coates sharing his wisdom *and* allowing Samori to learn from his own experience.

Coates provides not only his personal history but also the history of black Americans, urging his son through anaphora and imperative sentences to "never forget" that history: "Never forget that we were enslaved in this country longer than we have been free. Never forget that for 250 years black people were born into chains—whole generations followed by more generations who knew nothing but chains" (70). He repeats the image of chains to reinforce the sense of confinement.

Confinement can take many forms. Coates recounts being stopped by police with no explanation. As he sits in the car, terrified, waiting for the police to return, he replays the violence committed against others, believing that he too is "in their clutches," that police could do whatever they please with his body (2015, 76). That same year, Coates's friend Prince Jones was killed by police. Throughout the section in which Coates recounts Jones's death, his response, the funeral, and the reports that came out after the shooting, he points to what he remembers and what he doesn't and also to what is known. He structures this information through anaphora, repeating "I think" when he recounts learning about Jones's death and repeating "We know" in describing what happened to Jones (77, 80). By repeating "we know," he makes both Samori and other readers witness to the facts of Jones's death.

Coates then urges his audience—again through anaphora and lists—to think of all that was put into Jones's life. He recreates Jones's life and relationships through common images: music lessons, football games, soccer balls, science kits, and more (2015, 81). Coates then follows ten consecutive sentences that begin with "Think of the . . ."—listing what was poured into Jones's life—with this metaphor: "And think of how that vessel was taken, shattered on the concrete, and all its holy contents, all that had gone into him—sent flowing back to the earth" (82). He figures Jones's body as a fragile vessel and the seemingly mundane experiences of his life as holy.

The memories Coates shares with his son are infused with the importance of remembering in order to know something deeper. In recounting a time his young son was pushed by a white woman, Coates opens the story with "Perhaps you remember" (2015, 93). He recounts his own rage, his confrontation, a man coming to the woman's defense—and the only thing that could pull him back from that rage: "I remembered someone standing off to the side there, bearing witness to more fury than he had ever seen from me—you" (94). He shares this memory to address his own regret that in seeking to defend his son, he endangered him (95), yet Coates also points out the injustices that led to such endangerment (99), providing historical context for even the most personal memories.

He does this, too, when he recounts taking his son to Civil War battlefields, acknowledging what his son "may well remember," what he doesn't know if he remembers, and questioning, "Do you remember?" (2015, 99, 101). These gestures toward memory serve the purpose of reminding both his son and a larger audience what they should know: that the richest Americans made their money off of "stolen bodies" (101). In recounting this history, Coates repeats the phrase "our bodies" multiple times, reminding his son of his corporeal connection to a past lived out in the present (101). Later in the book, he recounts another memory—this one of visiting a mother whose son was killed for playing his music loudly—again asking his son, "Do you remember?" (111). Whether or not Samori remembers this particular experience, the recollection allows Coates to bring this knowledge (yet another instance of senseless violence) to readers.

Often, Coates's lessons to his son are embedded in memories and stories, but there are times, too, when he makes his points explicit, directing his audience's attention. After writing about slavery, the Civil War, and police violence, he writes, "Here is what I would like for you to know: In America it is traditional to destroy the black body—*it is heritage*" (2015, 103). Coates explicitly calls out certain beliefs and memories for his son to remember; these shared experiences draw father and son together and help educate a broader audience. In eight consecutive sentences, all beginning with the word "Remember," Coates directs his son: "Remember that you and I are brothers, are the children of trans-Atlantic rape. Remember the broader consciousness that comes with that" (128). Father and son are united through their bodies, their consciousness, their place in history, their memories, and their struggle. Coates urges his son: "Struggle for the memory of your ancestors. Struggle for wisdom. . . . Struggle for your grandmother and grandfather, for your name" (151). This struggle is personal, familial, cultural, and historical.

Through sharing memories (ones that Samori might remember but that a broader audience would not otherwise have access to), placing those experiences in historical context, providing an interpretation, and uniting in struggle, Coates broadens the consciousness not only of his son but also, potentially, of a larger audience. But expanded consciousness for many readers must involve something different from what it involves for Samori. Near the end of the book, Coates argues that the Dream destroys not only black bodies but also the earth, that the Dreamers "plunder not just the bodies of humans but the body of the Earth itself"—and that the earth will get its own "vengeance" (2015,

150). Coates tells Samori that they cannot stop the Dreamers, that the Dreamers "must ultimately stop themselves," and that Samori should not struggle for them or pin his "struggle on their conversion" (151). While Coates provides his son—the audience he invokes—with a list of what he must remember and what he must struggle for, he provides a broader audience with a context, an interpretation, and, for some, a sense of culpability. But more than that he reminds Dreamers of their own responsibility. What the reader does with what is given, though, is up to him or her. Readers who listen metonymically can pause and reflect and sort through their own identifications, disidentifications, and nonidentifications and perhaps come away with a new understanding.

CONCLUSION: AUDIENCE OF ONE, AUDIENCE OF MANY

Adichie writes to a mother about raising a daughter; Coates writes to his son about being a black man in America. Adichie's feminist manifesto would likely take a different tone if it were addressed to men, just as Coates's memoir would be changed if it were addressed to the Dreamers. The audience the writer imagines shapes what is written—and how. It shapes the writer's authority, ideas, examples, diction, tone, sources, allusions, and more. No writer can write effectively and persuasively to everyone at once; no writer can speak to audiences across generations without some elements of his or her work being open to critique. But writers can choose an audience—a friend, a child—that allows them to write something they need to say. And readers can listen rhetorically, pausing, seeking to understand moments of identification, disidentification, and nonidentification. They can eavesdrop intentionally and ethically, attentive to when they are the audience for a specific text and when their footing shifts or even when they feel "purged" from the audience. I am not a young Nigerian mother, not a fifteen-year-old black son. But in listening to these texts, eavesdropping from the position of a different culture or gender, paying attention to the substance of style, I can learn to be more attentive to others, to their experiences and cultural logics, and to my own, recognizing simultaneous differences and commonalities.

As a writing teacher, I can ask my students to do the same: to be attentive to style, to differences, to commonalities, to critiques. I can also provide strategies for writers to say what they need to say—whether to an audience of one or many. Here, in closing, are some prompts for epistolary writing to help students seek an audience willing to listen rhetorically.[1]

- What is the story you need to tell or the argument you need to make? Who would listen most intently? Who would ask the kinds of questions that would help you clarify your ideas? Write with that person in mind.
- Think of a time you've been asked a significant question, one that required a thoughtful response. Think of the person who asked the question and recall the experiences you share or knowledge you have of that person's life. Address that person as you answer the question.
- Write a letter to someone who has critiqued you, an action you have taken, or a belief you hold. What common ground do you share with that person or group of people? Use that common ground to help establish your ethos. What sources hold authority for both you and your audience? Use those sources as you respond thoughtfully to the critique.

NOTE

1. These prompts can be used in both creative writing and composition classrooms; for more on bridging composition and creative writing pedagogies, see Jon Udelson's chapter in this volume.

REFERENCES

Adichie, Chimanda Ngozi. 2017. *Dear Ijeawele, or a Feminist Manifesto in Fifteen Suggestions.* New York: Alfred A. Knopf.

Coates, Ta-Nehisi. 2015. *Between the World and Me.* New York: Spiegel & Grau.

Ede, Lisa, and Andrea Lunsford. 1984. "Audience Addressed/Audience Invoked: The Role of Audience in Composition Theory and Pedagogy." *College Composition and Communication* 35 (2): 155–171.

Fahnestock, Jeanne. 2011. *Rhetorical Style: The Uses of Language in Persuasion.* New York: Oxford University Press.

Haven, Cynthia. "The New Literacy: Stanford Study Finds Richness and Complexity in Students' Writing." *Stanford News*, October 12, 2009. https://news.stanford.edu/news/2009/october12/lunsford-writing-research-101209.html.

Lordi, Emily J. 2017. "Between the World and the Addressee: Epistolary Nonfiction by Ta-Nehisi Coates and His Peers." *CLA Journal* 60 (4): 434–447.

Ratcliffe, Krista. 2005. *Rhetorical Listening: Identification, Gender, Whiteness.* Carbondale: Southern Illinois University Press.

3
"CLARITY" REALLY MEANS RHYTHM
Toward a Psychoanalytic Poetics of Prose

T. R. Johnson

It don't mean a thing, if it ain't got that swing.
    —Duke Ellington

Those who know the most about the past know the most about the future.
    —Theodore Roosevelt

In trying to determine the context for the second epigraph above, I learned that, in fact, I was wrong, for Roosevelt did not quite say those words. Rather, he said something far less memorable: "I believe that the more you know about the past, the better you are prepared for the future." The difference is more important than might first appear. I like my version a lot better than TR's, so I've decided to let it stand—and, yes, I'm having fun now.

Thus, the unconscious speaks, and it does so with considerable clarity, which is not to say that its meanings are simple and straightforward but rather evocative, engaging, multiplicious. Stay tuned—more to follow in the near future.

Now, the future worries me quite a bit, and in the broadest of ways: climate change, coastal erosion, and general environmental degradation; white male reaction to the social progress made by those they've traditionally organized their identities against; the diminishing power of the free press and other essential institutions of democracy; and the endless array of nightmares that might follow the synergistic combination of these trends, particularly as they might bear down on my particular little stake in the global economy, the academic humanities, to say nothing of the possible fates of friends and loved ones who grow more vulnerable with each successive wave of public acquiescence to the breakdowns that

DOI: 10.7330/9781646420117.c003

have followed the election of 2016. The upshot: I'm anxious to prepare as best I can for what's coming.

And that means, in part, that I need to follow Roosevelt's advice and learn as much as I can about the past. What an irony, though, that I always misremember his famous line, that I always turn it into something more elegant, more punchy, more rhythmic. I find it easy to remember the revised version of his remark that found its way into my ear—and nearly impossible to hold onto the klunky version that he actually spoke. And therein lies an important lesson about writing, one that holds, for me, the keys to whatever future the field of composition studies might have.

Most simply, language is memorable and valuable to the degree that it has rhythm. I first arrived at this notion some twenty-five years ago when I was teaching a few sections of the standard first-year writing course as an adjunct faculty member at a small community college in my hometown. I was told to teach my students about thesis sentences, as that seemed to be the key way to get them to produce more coherent papers. I had not yet hit upon Joseph Williams's *Style: Ten Lessons in Clarity and Grace* (1981), so couldn't show my students the more sophisticated tools he offers for revising texts to heighten their focus. Thus, I worked on the mostly futile task of getting them to see that a thesis sentence needs to "grab the readers' attention." This means, I told them, that the sentence needs to be an especially "clear" iteration of what the paper will be about. And so I came up with a strange little torment for my students to push them in this direction: "A piece of prose that we find particularly meaningful," I told them, "is relatively easy to memorize." I looked around the room, saw their eyes widening, and went on, "Loose BS is almost impossible to memorize." Thus began what my students started calling the "memorization quiz" that formed a key step in their drafting process: they knew they had a draft that was ready for a reader's feedback only when they could recite the draft's opening paragraph from memory, in front of their peers. This exercise seemed to work well in getting them to write better thesis sentences, and their papers as a whole seemed to get a bit better once they experienced the content of the paper as "meaningful," as actualized communication before me and their immediate peer collective in the classroom.

More to the point, my students faced a certain pressure to write in a way that shared in the spontaneity, directness, and rhythmic punchiness that characterizes natural, oral dialogue all the time. What I was doing with this memorization quiz probably echoes some of the several territories that Peter Elbow recently engaged in *Vernacular Eloquence: What*

Speech Can Bring to Writing (2012), and I think Elbow would agree that this characteristic of our experience of prose—the more rhythmic, the more easy to memorize, and the more meaningful—tells us something important about "clarity," something that we should rally around by way of preparing for the inevitable crisis-of-relevance that those most hostile to our work seem increasingly likely to trumpet ever more loudly in the coming years.

I'm making two very different points here, so let me slow down and make each of them with greater care and in more detail, then contextualize these matters more fully in theories of writing instruction. First, about the dynamic between rhythm and what we traditionally call "clarity": no one still believes that language can be literally "clear," that it can offer a reliable, pure, neutral representation of objects that are "out there" in the world; rather, we all know that what is meant by clarity is, as Richard Lanham (1974) put it, a successful author-audience relationship. This assertion, however, begs the question of what makes such a successful relationship. I know that such dynamics are endlessly complex, and mostly unconscious, but I have some ideas about ways a certain set of psychoanalytic concepts can help us to understand them. More simply, I follow a long line of rhetorical theorists who claim that the key to this relationship can be captured in one word: rhythm.

Rhythm: when we first learn to walk, what we've learned is, in essence, to control and limit the experience of falling by playing with possibilities of balance and repetition, our weight tilting out precariously over one foot, as we then kick our other foot out in front of the first one to catch our weight as it rolls yet farther out over that first one, next balancing that second move yet again by throwing in turn that first foot yet farther, repeating and repeating as confident movement gradually becomes an unconscious routine of steady, controlled, rhythmic, stylized semi-falling.

But our sense of rhythm goes far deeper than the ability to walk, as the inevitable ebb and flow of our breath—the vital sign—always defaults to a steady repetitive balance. In fact, I've often thought that's part of why people enjoy smoking, for the smoke makes breath visible, not merely as a tight, fleeting column, say, of the sort one sees on a freezing morning; rather, as it hangs in a shaft of light, curling, drifting, it offers a glimpse of the ocean of air currents that surround us and that our breath shares in, twisting and lifting, like a spectral living image of thought itself, an opportunity for consciousness to become momentarily conscious in a very immediate way *of itself,* an apotheosis that energizes and focuses the mind, potentially ad infinitum—a life project that the mystics of India call *pranayama*. The more one becomes conscious of one's breath, the more one can bring it back to its easy, natural rhythm. As smokers often observe, smoking relaxes them, and I think what they describe goes beyond the satisfaction of a chemical addiction. More precisely, our breath deviates from steady, easy rhythm only under duress, only as an expression of tension, and as tensions resolve, steady rhythm returns. And again the more conscious we are of this, the more readily breath can steady itself, and also the more deeply—potentially *ad infinitum*. Again, the deliberate study of this rhythm and its cultivation, this, for some, can become a life-long discipline, the fourth of the eight limbs of Ashtanga yoga.

Rhythm permeates our experience in other ways too, organizing, for example, the muscular movements of digestive and sexual processes. Of course, at the center of lived embodiment is the heartbeat, and I assume that the very first stirring of consciousness in the human embryo is the sound, just above the thin membrane that will become the child's skull, of the steady thump of the mother's heart. Rhythm, in short, is a primordial, even inaugural affair of human subjectivity—or, more precisely, given the proximity of the mother's heart to the embryonic brain, of intersubjectivity, part of the body's "hard-wired" experience of an always radically social reality. And, as such, our capacities for perceiving and expressing it are deeply rooted in the unconscious—and psychoanalytic concepts, in turn, are invaluable tools, therefore, for identifying and enhancing these capacities.

Before moving into psychoanalysis, however, consider the most substantial precedents for what I'm proposing among theorists of writing instruction. In *Style: An Anti-Textbook*, Richard Lanham offers a deft deconstruction of the age-old binary of poetry-versus-prose (1974, 95–114), the distinction between them being, finally, one of mere typography, what my students today would call visual layout, which has relatively a superficial and recent relation to the way human beings experience language. Both poetry and prose, after all, are modes of language, and language always functions in time, unfolding meanings incrementally, moment by moment—precisely as this very sentence that you're reading right now is doing, as it tacks on this clause by way of pointing to itself as its own illustration and likely, by now, trying your patience just a tad, as it borders on the excessive, and, in so doing, threatens to strain the established rhythms of this text, undermine my ethos, and exasperate you.

The strain of that preceding sentence suggests that good writing, successful writing, is writing that manages well the energy that inheres around this temporal movement of language. That last paragraph, in short, took too long to wrap up. As Peter Elbow puts it, in one of his richest but too seldom discussed works, "The Music of Form" (2006), to learn to write successfully is to learn to play with language in these terms, speeding a passage up or slowing it down or managing to end it altogether in a resounding resolution or dragging it out mischievously as I appear to be doing again. What Elbow is talking about, of course, is the artistry of rhythm.

But here's the tricky part: as Lanham points out, in order to study the rhythm of a piece of prose, you have to read it out loud, something hardly anyone in English departments wants to do anymore. Ask students to read aloud in class, says Lanham, and they seem as though they've been hit with lockjaw (1974, 100). Following Lanham, I would suggest that to read aloud before an audience is to evince a certain attitude toward the text at hand, toward the people who are listening (or not listening), toward the wider social- and institutional-context, even toward one's self. To read aloud is to reveal a lot—to stand, in effect, naked. More elaborately, to read aloud is to struggle with the array of disconnections and alienations that define contemporary adult life, particularly in a consumer society, which prevents in endless ways, as Marxists would say, full access to sources of knowledge, value, and power, to say nothing of a healthy, functional, self-aware, and sustainable subjectivity that can play well with others. These disconnections and alienations can be thought of as scars, as festering wounds, forever sore, the disfigurings of a crushed and closeted *soul*.

Nowhere are these symptoms more vividly or more elaborately displayed than in Wyndham Lewis's *Time and Western Man* (1993), in which he suggests that the whole business of civilization is to transcend time—music, for example, that quintessential expression of the temporal dimension, having never functioned other than to summon "men to the slaughter or to the rut." Lewis, were he to work among theorists of writing instruction today, would likely champion, as the best path for the future of our field, the realm of visual rhetoric (see also Duncan, this volume), and while I have no quarrel with those who would draw our attention to the visual dimension of our relationships with text, the ear, and all that it evokes, strikes me as having been underappreciated. If you're not so sure about this, listen to your students when you ask them to read their work out loud in front of the class. Chances are you don't often try to do this, because it lays bare a certain lifelessness and, like the lurching and murmuring of zombies, seems not an especially promising way to spark conversation. Our students' resistance to reading aloud and the broader skepticism among theorists about the value of the radically social, even intersubjective power of rhythm strikes me, again, as a sign of deep alienation, and moreover as supremely reactionary and repressive, not simply wrong-headed, and, if not mitigated with the kinds of pedagogy and scholarship I'm advocating here, likely to injure or impoverish us yet further.

Not surprisingly, Wyndham Lewis was sharply critical not only of music but also of psychoanalysis as being, like music, a key source of the "primitivism" then coming into vogue. Conversely, in 1931 he published a book that was not at all critical of the figure after whom he named it—the book is titled *Hitler*. Coupling this book with Lewis's well-known anti-semitism and homophobia contextualizes his broader squeamishness regarding the intersubjective power of rhythm: the ear, for him, is the gateway to the animal kingdom, to the darkest, primitivist anarchy, the enemy of civilization.

In contrast, of course, I would argue that this is the domain of "clarity," of successful author-audience dynamics, a relation analogous to the erotic (the Christian term is "love," the Freudian term is "desire"); contra Lewis, I maintain that it cannot be purged from civilization, nor is such a purge the primary means by which civilization constitutes itself. More likely, it is civilization's cornerstone and foundation. Therefore, the burgeoning subfield of visual rhetoric notwithstanding, we should contemplate the ear, and all that it represents, as offering among our best prospects for future inquiry. A fine example of what that might mean, pedagogically, can be found in Melissa Goldthwaite's essay in this volume, for the particular nature of listening, as she would teach it, is precisely what I mean by focusing on the ear—that is, such a classroom is fostering an analytic frame of mind, even approaching that special kind of listening we associate with a particular brand of analysis—*psychoanalysis*.

To say it another way, "a change," as the famous song has it, "is gonna come," new meanings will continue to proliferate (they always do), new collectives and conflicts will follow in turn, always, and, as heady and challenging as all of this is, we therefore ignore the dynamic, temporal dimensions of language—the ear—at our peril. Most to the point, the conceptual tools of psychoanalysis, as powerful as they are, can well equip us, so to speak, to face the music.

The most explicit study of this territory that I've ever found is in Julia Kristeva's first major work, *Revolution in Poetic Language* (1984), wherein she delineates a dynamic between what she calls the semiotic chora and the symbolic order. The semiotic chora precedes the human subject's transition into language, social codes, and differentiations between identities; it is the realm of bodily impulse and literal pulsation, of the infantile experience of sheer, physical continuity between his or her own body and that of the mother, particularly the breast, and, for that matter, with all food and physical instantiations of caregiving, as well as with their harrowing, momentary absence. When the child migrates into the realm of differentiation—between self and other, between words and things, and between words themselves (which have meaning only by differing from each other)—the semiotic chora is by no means extinguished; rather, it endures beneath or behind or within the individuated ego and its language, registering and guiding our experience of sound in particular; for the chora knows that sounds are transpersonal waves of energy, floating through things and, in a sense, partially uniting them, at least momentarily, in the way that smoke, in the example a moment ago, visually manifests the movements of the air we propel with our lungs and permeates the space where it occurs. As the realm of pulsation and sound and physical connectedness, the semiotic chora plays a key, though largely unconscious, role in our experience of language: when words line up in a way that sends chills down our spines or triggers an intense identification with the imagined voice delivering them to us, a deeply felt starburst of "clarity," all of these are instances of the semiotic chora in action, registering or conjuring what we call the poetic, that which our desire, though mostly unconscious, forever seeks. I think that such moments, to borrow Jarrod Slater's terms from his essay that appears in this volume, are marked by exultation, and that these experiences of intersubjectivity, these dissolutions of the borders of self and other, Slater would suggest, echo what Longinus meant when he talked about the sublime.

And, very importantly, this terrain is intrinsically revolutionary with regard to the ego's fantasy of discrete individuation, autonomy, and mature control over its immediate environment. By breaking up, at least temporarily, the boundaries of the ego, letting the semiotic chora crash forth like an ocean wave, poetic language threatens, and at times overturns, all of the other social structures that are rooted in the ego and its economic machinery of values, such as hierarchies of class, race, ethnicity, age, gender, and sexuality, all of which start to wobble as new mass movements and collective solidarities threaten to spring up in their place. Hence the role of slogans in any revolutionary movement, and the requirement that effective slogans be built out of subtle poetic repetitions and balances. Even a demand as simple as "Make America Great Again" is brimming with internal echoes and phantom rhymes, as in the long vowel sound in "make" and "great," the alliteration on "m" in the first two words that sets the stage for the alliteration on "r" in the second and third words, and the way the fourth word constitutes a rhythmic repetition of the same iambic beat that appears twice in the second word. Such simple music—even if only fleetingly and in limited ways—dissolves the ego and binds individuals, registering thus as a thrilling reversal of alienation, a tiny rumble toward mass movement. Of course, any such movement can turn into a movement against those who, for whatever reason, seem not "to get it," and/or the movement can become a mad gallop off a cliff, possibilities that cry out for the counterforce of a yet greater poetry (which, in essence, is the cry this essay seeks to register).

In any event, at a much smaller scale, this is what happens in all instances of "clarity"—a subtle music weaves its spell and softens the boundaries of the ego, opening the way for the sensation of intersubjective connection, ultimately of the sort that happened, for the first time, when we listened to the beat of our mother's heart just above our heads.

A long tradition in the field of rhetoric has understood stylistic ornament in these terms. Consider the way Kenneth Burke talks about "identification" in *A Rhetoric of Motives* (1969), a term that means, in this context, the writer's success in connecting with an audience: one of the chief ways a writer manages to do that is by creating subtle formal flourishes, instances of elegant repetition or balance, what Burke calls a "form" or an instance of rhythm, whereby the audience begins, even if unconsciously, to notice certain patterns and, as Burke puts it, to read with a distinctly "collaborative expectancy." Here's how Burke himself describes it in *A Rhetoric of Motives*:

> [I]magine a passage built out of a set of oppositions ("*we* do *this*, but *they* on the other hand do *that*; *we* stay *here*, but *they* go *there*; *we* look *up* but *they* look *down*," etc.). Once you grasp the trend of the form, it invites participation regardless of the subject matter. Formally, you will find yourself swinging along with the succession of antitheses, even though you may not agree with the proposition that is being presented in this form. . . . [I]n cases where [you, the reader, are not yet fully persuaded of the matter at hand] a yielding to the form prepares for assent to the matter associated with it. (1969, 58)

Burke's idea here goes to the heart of what we mean by "clarity," which he frames in terms of an "identification" of audience with author. In short, to write "clearly" is to stir this "collaborative expectancy" and to satisfy it, and the more artfully and subtly and insistently one can do that, the more one moves beyond mere "clarity" and into the domain of the poetic.

These ideas find yet richer delineation in what we've come to understand about the residues of oralist culture within literacy. Oral cultures, as Walter Ong (1982) famously explained, must organize their information about their own histories in ways that are easy to remember. This is the primary task of the rhapsodes of ancient Greece, who would sing their community's history at sacred holiday rituals to anchor the community's collective experience of itself. Here is how Ong summarizes the rhapsodes' verbal performance:

> In an . . . oral culture, to solve effectively the problem of retaining and retrieving carefully articulated thought, you have to do your thinking in mnemonic patterns, shaped for ready oral recurrence. Your thought must come into being in heavily rhythmic, balanced patterns, in repetitions and antitheses, in alliterations and assonances, in epithetic or other formulary expressions. (1982, 34)

Of course, oralist cultures also hinge on the fact that words, when spoken and heard without any sort of recording technology at hand, cannot travel great distances or survive over time. As such, they function only in binding people together in the immediate, concrete, present situation. Such instances of intersubjective binding are precisely what Burke will call "identification" and what, when we're reading something that seems especially "clear," comes ghosting down to us from our oralist ancestors, an atavistic system of feeling summoned up from the depths of our cognitive structures. This same intersubjective connection is nurtured by what Kristeva (1984) calls the semiotic chora, and what psychoanalytic thought in general associates with the unconscious.

So essential is this sounded, oralist dimension of our experience of written prose that, as Stephen Katz (1996) notes, even when we're silently reading, our vocal chords can be shown to register subtle movements, as if we were indeed reading out loud and trying, in contemporary parlance, to settle into a groove—and thereby surrender to the passage at hand as "clear," a passage we can dance along through without stumbling. Katz has titled his book on the subject *The Epistemic Music of Rhetoric*, arguing throughout that rhetoric should be understood as a temporal art that works on our affective register and, as such, something much more closely akin to music and to live oralist performance than contemporary writing teachers have imagined, even though the ancients grounded their practice in it.

More specifically, those who taught the arts of rhetoric in antiquity—the sophists—were particularly attuned to the way this work entailed practice with the figures and patterns of oralist performance, transposing those rhythms into the realm of writing to capture the older musical magic that brings people together and to combine that magic with the new powers of print to travel and endure. The sophists, in fact, often came to ply their trade as pedagogues in the wrestling schools, argues Debra Hawhee (2004), for it was there that students were drilled in the stock set of moves that enabled them to best an opponent. Sophists in turn presented their lessons in parallel ways, as practice in a stock set of moves—the figures and patterns of the oralist rhapsodes. As the students studied the old poems and memorized them, their teachers would often accompany this practice by playing a harp. This study of poetic forms, happening so close by the study of the stock maneuvers of the wrestlers, also involved learning rhythms and scales from the live musical performances that were underway well within earshot. Hawhee quotes Plato's *Protagoras* thus: "[A]s the boys' souls familiarize themselves with the rhythms and scales . . . [they grow more] efficient in speech and action" (97). The training with language, with music, and with athletics in general were all of a piece, all sharing in preparing the student for a life of honorable civic engagement. In artworks depicting these scenes, the images nearly always include musicians, suggesting that the training of young people nearly always involved live musical performance (135). As Hawhee explains, the sophistic training in rhetoric was modelled closely on training for sports and music and was rooted in what she calls the three R's: rhythm, repetition, and response. Here is how she put it:

> [E]ach gymnasium had at least one aulos player associated with it. It was the aulos player's job to set the rhythm for all gymnastic exercises. . . . Given the proximity of athletic and rhetorical training . . . it is also likely that the music flowed into recitations and sophistic lectures, producing an awareness of—perhaps facilitating—the rhythmic, tonic quality of speeches. . . . [M]usic's role in the gymnasium was to introduce a rhythm, to provide a tempo to the practice, regulation, and production of bodily movements. (136–138)

Hawhee lingers at length over the meaning of the Greek word "rhythmos," but settles ultimately on the idea that it refers to movement that unfolds over time in a regularly recurring pattern, and this orderliness that comes to anchor one's character is essential to the larger project of character building—of preparation for civic life—at the center of classical pedagogy.

Given the deep roots of what we might today call a style-based pedagogy in the athletic and musical training of the ancient Greeks, the way the old oralist rhythms still haunt our most thrilling experiences of texts, one can't help but suppose that this territory is still with us at the level of the unconscious. In ways we only dimly understand, it continues to flash into view from time to time in contemporary discussions about how people should learn how to write. Today, for example, the interest in what's known as hip-hop pedagogy would seem the most direct descendant of the classical scene, as in Marc Lamont Hill's *Beats, Rhymes, and Classroom Life: Hip Hop Pedagogy and the Politics of Identity* (2009). I would argue too that a great deal of this interest in the rhythms of language undergirds Joseph Williams's classic *Style: Ten Lessons in Clarity and Grace*, thus:

- In the chapter on the concept of emphasis, he explains how best to end sentences with words worthy of the special, natural thrust that readers always experience there.
- In the chapter on coherence and cohesion, he shows how sentences that open with words or phrases that repeat ones that came just before can bind readers more closely to the movement of a piece of writing, the web of repetition creating a rhythmic continuity commonly called "flow."
- In the chapters on clarity, he explains how sentences that observe, in the position of subject and verb, the basic dynamic of concrete characters and the actions they perform, honor the essential two-part rhythm of narrative, so vital to human cognition.
- In the chapter on parallelism that attach such positive value to the repetition of syntactic structures, he shows how these rhythms undergird what we call elegance and grace.

In a very different register, Stephen King, in his book *On Writing* (2010), suggests that paragraphs should be understood as "beats"—that is, discrete units of information—and these beats need to be arranged in careful patterns, patterns that can be subtly disrupted or altered for certain effects. What King has in mind likely has something to do with the notion of timing that we associate with the best comedians, the creation of a repetitive pattern such that the art of delivery—subtle delays, disruptions, and foreshadowings—means teasing the audience's tendency to collaborative expectancy and identification, and timing, in turn, comes to mean letting the right word land, eventually, on the right beat. I think that narratives of suspense probably also play with our inclination to "collaborative expectancy" and identification in similar ways.

More immediately within the domain of the writing classroom, whether we're exploring with our students a repetitive pattern for a sequence of paragraphs or the way syntactic structure can be repeated for an elegant instance of parallelism at a key juncture in an argument or, at a still smaller scale, the way a pattern of vowel and consonant sounds can be repeated to create a yet more "micro" experience of rhythm, all of these summon the power of the old oralist rhapsodes up from the depths of the cognitive patterns of the unconscious to create an experience of "clarity."

We've already noted Kristeva's notion of the semiotic chora as a musical domain of bodily energy that can disrupt or even temporarily demolish the individual ego and create the sensation of connection to another person, and, as such, it is clearly a version of what psychoanalysis more broadly calls the unconscious. This strikes me as the key to the future of composition: the work of thinking psychoanalytically about how to access the rhythmic inclinations of the unconscious, to allow that extraordinary musical power to inform our experience of language, for this, in essence, is the key to what we've superficially known as "clarity."

After all, many who don't work in composition studies assume that our purpose, above all, is to figure out how to get students to write more *clearly*. All the other stuff that crops up in the pages of *College Composition and Communication* and *JAC* and *Pedagogy* and *Written Communication* and *Rhetoric Review* and so on is, for these nonspecialists, fairly bizarre fluff, utterly beside the main point, utterly irrelevant to our primary raison d'être. What do business leaders want English 101 to accomplish? What do law school professors want their students to have learned from us? What, for that matter, do all of our colleagues in other departments want us to achieve? What do the parents who are paying our students' tuition hope their kids glean from the required composition course? Why, in fact, is the frosh writing course so important as to constitute virtually a nationwide requirement, a rite of passage, comparable in scale to no other course in the US collegiate curriculum? Because, quite simply, this course is where, it is hoped, students will learn the most important thing that college can teach them, without which little else is possible: to write clearly.

Whatever else we might be interested in, no matter how abstract and intricate our ruminations on the implications and permutations of this imperative, all of that, as Stephen King puts it in *On Writing*, will appear to the wider public and the government officials who sign off on the funding for all that we do, as only so much "woolly-headed bullshit" (2010, 170). If students aren't writing a lot more clearly after they've taken our courses, the funding that props up our research journals, that staffs our programs, that supports our scholarly work, will, in the coming decades, if not years, slow to a trickle then altogether die.

In short, we fail to come up with a reliable strategy for fulfilling our essential purpose at our peril.

The future of composition studies therefore is in its remotest past, buried in what I want to call the wrestling music that suffused the sophists' scene of writing instruction. In planning and carrying out our future, we should proceed as archaeologists of the rhetorical psyche, exhuming from the unconscious our inheritance, this legacy, this buried musical treasure chest. We have at our disposal a number of useful treasure maps, for as early as the mid-1960s, Janet Emig (1964) urged writing teachers to see the two different ways the unconscious could inform the composing process (one analogous to Mozart, she says, the other to Beethoven), and some four decades later Mark Bracher (1999) devoted an entire book to the way unconscious conflicts can undermine the writer. Soon thereafter, Nancy Welch (1997), still more ambitiously, showed how the dynamics between the real, the symbolic, and the imaginary could be understood to expand and energize the practice of revision, and I myself, a few years ago, published a book that sketches the way the Lacanian psychoanalytic system known as the four discourses can help writing teachers locate the unconscious and tap into its musical powers (Johnson 2014). But this small library is just a start—let their works-cited sections unfold as the proverbial royal road to the splendors of the ancient rhythms, for they are our unconscious, our future.

REFERENCES

Bracher, Mark. *The Writing Cure: Psychoanalysis, Composition, and the Aims of Education.* Carbondale: Southern Illinois University Press.

Burke, Kenneth. 1969. *A Rhetoric of Motives.* Berkeley: University of California Press.

Duncan, Mike. 2011. "Questioning the Auditory Sublime: A Multi-Sensory Organic Approach to Prose Rhythm." *JAC* 31 (3–4): 579–608.

Elbow, Peter. 2006. "The Music of Form." *College Composition and Communication* 57:4 (June): 620–666.

Elbow, Peter. 2012. *Vernacular Eloquence: What Speech Can Bring to Writing.* Oxford: Oxford University Press.

Emig, Janet. 1964. "On the Uses of the Unconscious in Composing." *College Composition and Communication* 15: 6–11.

Hawhee, Debra. 2004. *Bodily Arts: Rhetoric and Athletics in Ancient Greece.* Austin: University of Texas Press.

Hill, Marc Lamont. 2009. *Beats, Rhymes, and Classroom Life: Hip Hop Pedagogy and the Politics of Identity.* New York: Teachers College Press of Columbia University.

Johnson, T. R. 2014. *The Other Side of Pedagogy: Lacan's Four Discourses and the Development of the Student Writer.* Transforming Subjects: Psychoanalysis, Culture, and Studies in Education. Albany: State University of New York Press.

Katz, Stephen. 1996. *The Epistemic Music of Rhetoric: Toward the Temporal Dimension of Affect in Reader Response and Writing.* Carbondale: Southern Illinois University Press.

King, Stephen. 2010. *On Writing: A Memoir of the Craft.* New York: Scribner.

Kristeva, Julia. 1984. *Revolution in Poetic Language.* Translated by Margaret Waller. New York: Columbia University Press.

Lanham, Richard. 1974. *Style: An Anti-Textbook.* New Haven: Yale University Press.

Lewis, Wyndham. 1993. *Time and Western Man.* Los Angeles: Black Sparrow Press.

Ong, Walter. 1982. *Orality and Literacy: The Technologizing of the Word.* Abingdon: Routledge.

Welch, Nancy. 1997. *Getting Restless: Rethinking Revision in Rhetoric and Composition.* Portsmouth: Heinemann.

Williams, Joseph M. 1981. *Style: Ten Lessons in Clarity and Grace.* Glenview, IL: Scott, Foresman.

4

ERASMUS IN THE PROFESSIONAL WRITING CLASSROOM
Workplace Genre, Designing and Writing for the Web, and the Future of Style

Tom Pace

INTRODUCTION

Professional writing instructors who dive into the thorny business of teaching style to their students are well aware of the dilemma that often awaits them: addressing issues of style appears to run counter to teaching course content. In his essay on style and the professional writing classroom, Buehl (2013) insists that students should engage in a multiplicity of styles in science-based writing classrooms, noting that "[s]tudents planning to compete for jobs as writers and editors must develop stylistic fluency—a meta-mastery of style—if they are to adapt successfully to the rhetorical situations they will face in ever-evolving workplaces" (Buehl 2013, 280). Yet, addressing style in the professional writing classroom remains a confounding and fraught challenge for many instructors. On the one hand, getting students to understand concision, brevity, and clarity is a stylistic concern that connects directly to issues of audience, genre, and content. For example, Horning (2006) argues that for many professional writing students, learning how to revise the stylistic features of workplace writing by becoming more critical users of toolbox features such as grammar check, spell check, and other computer characteristics leads directly to revising content and allows students to, as Horning writes, mimic professional writers to "make skilled use of the dictionary, grammar handbooks, and pre-writing tools like outlines or webbing to help them produce clean, well-structured sentences and paragraphs that are error-free and clear" (Horning 2006, 12). On the other hand, extended instruction in those areas separates form from content, with many instructors often privileging form *over* content. In their study of memo writing in the professional writing classroom, Amare and Brammer (2005) argue that many professional writing instructors tend

DOI: 10.7330/9781646420117.c004

to be more critical of style issues in their students' writing, while employers and the students themselves focus more on the document's content. In doing so, Amare and Brammer show how adhering to traditional textbook-based stylistic exercises in the professional writing classroom often does not prepare these students for what employers require of them in the workplace (Amare and Brammer 2005). This research, then, suggests that a tension exists between how professional writing teachers should best balance style and content in their courses.

As far back as 1512, in his textbook *De Copia*, Erasmus recognizes this dilemma, but he addresses it by separating form from content not for purposes of meaning but for pedagogical reasons. In general, Erasmus views style as a canon of rhetoric where students gather a variety of expressions, words, and other variations of language use and use them to discover meaning as well as to vary what to say and write as the situation dictates. Noting that meaning can never be separated from form, he nevertheless writes in *De Copia* that "I intend to separate them as a teaching procedure, doing it in such a way that I lay myself open to the charge neither of drawing hair-splitting distinctions, or of being careless about details" (Erasmus [1512] 1978, 301). In short, challenging students to collapse the supposed divide between form and content in the professional writing classroom, while at the same time teaching them to build a reservoir of stylistic strategies, may require us as instructors to separate it first during instruction, a move many of us find counterintuitive to our position as rhetoricians.

Milic (1965) echoes this method for separating form and content as a theory for teaching style in his essay "Theories of Style and Their Implications for the Teaching of Composition." Milic identifies three theories of style: "rhetorical dualism," the theory that ideas exist outside the boundaries of language and "can be dressed in a variety of outfits, depending on the need for the occasion" (67); two, "individualist or psychological monism," the idea that "style is the man" (67); and three, "Croacean aesthetic monism," the idea that style and content can never be divided, that there is "no style at all" (67). Of these three, Milic prefers the classical "rhetorical dualism" that pedagogically teachers must start with form as an avenue toward content. As such, Milic and Erasmus both provide professional writing classrooms a theory for teaching style as an avenue toward broader rhetorical communication.

In this chapter I argue that a pedagogy of style based on Erasmus's insistence to use style as an entrée into workplace communication allows professional writing students to produce successful professional documents by connecting stylistic concerns with professional audiences and genres. In doing so, I draw from *De Copia*, in which Erasmus stresses the need for students to vary and enrich language. Here, students can build a stockpile of future stylistic strategies for professional writing purposes. To show how students can start with form and proceed to content, in learning about workplace genre and non-scholarly audiences, I also describe assignments from my professional writing classroom to show how such a pedagogy of style helps demystify such rhetorical challenges as addressing workplace genres, as applying sentence-level strategies, and as designing text for the web. I draw from drafts of my students' assignments to show how this pedagogy leads to more rhetorically savvy projects. This chapter, then, draws from an important part of style's past and applies it to the production of emerging texts that point to style's future. Conceiving of the professional writing classroom as explicitly stylistic encourages students to take various sentence-level and design elements and use them as avenues into learning about workplace genre and audience.

ERASMUS AND DEBATES ABOUT FORM AND CONTENT

Erasmus is an important figure in this study because he, perhaps more than almost any other figure, united style with content in early modern rhetoric, a period in rhetoric's history where style appeared at the forefront of the five rhetorical canons. His thinking about the role of style during the early modern period, therefore, connects to our period's own concerns about the production of professional workplace documents. His textbook *De Copia* is divided into two sections: Book I features a variety of figures, tropes, and other methods for amplification, and Book II includes a variety of subject matter intended for the student to discover ideas. Based on Quintilian's idea of *facilitas*, or "fullness of expression," *De Copia* expects students to learn different things to say on a certain subject and then practice saying the same thing in many different ways. It goes well beyond merely decorating ideas and forms the very essence of language use. Early in his book, for instance, Erasmus suggests that learning different styles for different rhetorical considerations allows the writer to acquire style and avoid repetition. "Variety is so powerful in every sphere that there is absolutely nothing, however brilliant," Erasmus writes, "which is not dimmed if not commended by variety" (Erasmus [1512] 1978, 302). As such, Erasmus stresses the importance of avoiding repetition by developing different strategies for different rhetorical contexts. For the purpose of instruction, though, Erasmus separates form from content, equating style with ornamentation: "But to return to the main point, style is to thought as clothes are to the body. Just as dress and outward appearance can enhance or disfigure the beauty and dignity of the body, so words can enhance or disfigure thought" (306). Here, Erasmus warns his students of the possible dangers of too much ornamentation or stylistic flourish. It is this metaphor of style as the dressing up of thought that has, in many ways, dominated the way many students come to view style.

Erasmus, in so doing, suggests an inherent tension between expression and content: "Such considerations have induced me to put forward some ideas on *copia*, the abundant style, myself, treating its two aspects of content and expression, and giving some examples and patterns" (Erasmus [1512] 1978, 295). It seems apparent, then, that expression and content are divorced in Erasmus's world. But, later, he modifies this argument by insisting on the *twofold* nature of copia.

> It might be thought that these two aspects are so interconnected in reality that one cannot easily separate one from the other, and that they interact so closely that any distinction between them belongs to theory rather than practice. Even so, I intend to separate them as a teaching procedure, doing it in such a way that I lay myself open to the charge neither of drawing hair-splitting distinctions, nor of being careless about details. (301)

This passage is significant because Erasmus recognizes the connection between expression and content, yet he separates the two not for purposes of meaning but for pedagogical reasons. As an example of this kind of pedagogy, and to reinforce his insistence on variety, Erasmus tells his reader that he draws from Quintilian an exercise where he asks students to take poetry and rewrite it into prose and to take prose and rewrite it as poetry (303). An analogous exercise in the professional writing classroom might be to ask students to take a paragraph of information and rewrite it as a bullet-point list and vice versa. Erasmus understands that for students to attain the copiousness that he stresses is so vital to effective rhetorical communication, it may become necessary for teachers to split the two in an effort to achieve fullness of expression—as the above exercises require—so that student will have a stockpile of ideas and ways to express those ideas. Once students put these ideas into practice, Erasmus argues, students begin to see the benefit of abundant variety of language for different rhetorical situations, insisting that we should be aware of every stylistic trick, "store it in our memory once observed, imitate it once remembered, and by constant employment develop an expertise by which we may call upon it instantly" (303). In doing so, *De Copia* provides professional writing teachers with a historical forerunner to cutting through a reductive either-or division between form and content by teaching students various stylistic strategies that can be used in multiple workplace genres and contexts.

THE PROFESSIONAL WRITING CLASSROOM

For over six years, I have taught an introductory course, Writing in the Professions. The course, the gateway for my English department's professional writing track, explores rhetorical principles and strategies for planning, writing, and revising workplace documents. In the course student writers explore the importance of writing to a particular audience, the role of purpose and genre in workplace writing, the simplifying of complex information, the principles of document design, and the role of project management. We also spend quite a bit of time working on stylistic concerns in their writing. Specifically, we focus on understanding the differences between passive and active voice, the uses of and differences between the imperative and declarative voice, the practice of "chunking" bits of information into easily digested paragraphs for better reader understanding, the role of parallel construction in sentences and bullet points, and the various sentence-level strategies for achieving cohesion, coherence, and clarity in their documents. I attempt to teach these principles and strategies of style in the context of their assignments and to challenge students to see how issues of workplace style lead to their learning about audience, purpose, content, and, especially, genre.

Much of this course focuses on the variety of genres students will encounter in the workplace. Debates about how to introduce professional writing students to workplace genres is nothing new. In her book *Writing in the Real World: Making the Transition from School to Work*, Beaufort (1999) investigates how students best acquire genre knowledge, whether by becoming immersed in them or through explicit classroom teaching. She conducts an ethnographic study of writers at a nonprofit organization who had to learn three new workplace genres: press release, letter of request, and grant proposal. Researching how adult writers learn new genres in the workplace, Beaufort argues that "[u]nderstanding the social action the genre represents within the discourse community is . . . crucial" (111). She finds that content and procedural knowledge work together, that depth of knowledge grows over time, and that genre knowledge is based on participation in the community (103–137). Beaufort concludes her argument by suggesting that while acquiring genre knowledge is mostly tacit, writers learn new genres by combining both immersion and explicit classroom instruction. Thus, in my professional writing course, the major assignments allow for this combination of tacit and explicit instruction.

I set up these assignments so that students learn about generic conventions and their accompanying stylistic expectations. I begin teaching each assignment not by addressing the material they will write about—the content—but rather I teach them first the various stylistic elements and conventions of the various workplace genres, perhaps reinforcing an understanding of the interplay between style and genre that Andrea Olinger explores in her essay (this volume). In other words, we start with the forms, and then students adapt those forms and elements to the rhetorical situation of their task. The major projects they complete in the course fall along two lines: one, they complete three major individual writing projects; two, they work in small groups during the second half of the semester and complete a larger project for a local industry. At the end of the semester, representatives from the company visit the class, and each group gives a 20-minute presentation. Each assignment I ask students to complete, including the group project, usually revolves around learning a different professional genre. Over the years of teaching the course, some of the assignments have changed, but in general the course invites students to write the following genres: memoranda, executive summaries, instructions, usability reports, brochures, progress reports, websites, and proposals.

Students receive mostly explicit instruction in genre and style by examining models and determining how to use those models for the assignment under consideration. Introduction to various genres also comes in the form of the group project the students complete for a local company. Recent genres students have completed for these companies include proposals, PowerPoint slides, white papers, budget reports, media kits, and marketing plans, among others. In doing so, students learn genre and style by immersing themselves in the workplace culture of the company and by gaining a more tacit understanding of the genre and the stylistic strategies needed to achieve understanding. For instance, when planning PowerPoint slides for an outside client, my students learn about the efficacy of limiting text and bullet points, focusing on keywords and phrases that connect to their project and to their audience. In short, most of the lessons on style I teach my students in this course grow out of their learning multiple generic conventions. Like Amare and Brammer, my class begins with addressing stylistic conventions of the genre before addressing the content they write about in the documents. One example comes from a recent project when I asked students to write a progress report. We began by reading about and examining various models for their style and generic conventions as a method for deciding the content of the reports. Students would then tweak and massage the material to fit the conventions of the genre. Challenging my students to engage in multiple genres for various audiences—both in class readers and readers from outside businesses—puts into practice Buehl's insistence that professional writing students must "develop stylistic fluency" (2013, 280). To that end, Erasmus's insistence to separate form from content as a pedagogical necessity in order to teach students how to gather multiple stylistic strategies in order to develop their own sense of *facilitas* allows professional writing teachers to find flexible ways of teaching style—such as my focusing on simple words and phrases for PowerPoint slides or my starting with the stylistic and generic structure of a progress report before addressing content—that take into consideration sentence-level conventions for workplace genres, document design, and writing for the web.

PROFESSIONAL WRITING ASSIGNMENTS AND STYLISTIC PROFICIENCY

Now, I would like to share some of the work my professional writing students performed when incorporating stylistic strategies in their multiple assignments that led some of these students to see style not only as a key component of rhetorical thinking but as a way toward crafting their writing to fit the needs of workplace audiences and genres. These examples demonstrate the role focusing on stylistic features of workplace genres can have for different kinds of professional writing students, bolstering their transformation from students who rarely—if ever—wrote such genres or considered much about style to writers who, through both tacit and explicit instruction, became more aware of the relationship between the style various workplace documents demanded and the audiences and purposes for which they wrote. Teaching students various stylistic strategies for addressing workplace genres allows students to become better equipped to write for various audiences and purposes, to put into practice what Buehl calls for—a pedagogy that "helps students develop stylistic proficiencies, making them more effective communicators and more marketable professionals" (2013, 292). To show how my course helps professional writing students use stylistic strategies for workplace communication, I reflect on how my student writers, in their responses to the course assignments, led them to grow more proficiently in their sentence-level development and in their ability to apply stylistic strategies to writing and designing for the web.

Sentence-Level Concerns

Much of the time my professional writing course focuses on various sentence-level strategies to help students not only develop a writing style more appropriate for multiple workplace genres but to get students to see style as a broader feature of rhetoric and of audience-based communication. When introducing elements of style to my student writers, I connect it to issues of audience, reminding them that the goal of workplace writing is often to take complicated material and present it clearly to a reader who then needs to do something with that content, not an academic audience. When addressing the first assignment, for instance, most students have a difficult time making that shift from writing for an academic audience to writing for a workplace reader. To assist, I teach the following strategies to help them achieve clarity in their workplace assignments: use the active voice as much as possible; identify the subject and verb and place them as close to the front of the sentence as possible; connect material from the end of a sentence to the beginning of the next sentence to achieve cohesion from sentence to sentence; focus on a main idea to achieve coherence in paragraphs or "chunks" of text; and use principles of grammatical balance in sentences and lists.

For instance, an early assignment in my class asks students to write a one-page memo to an employer whose company may be funding their coursework, in which they define professional writing as rhetorical and argue that the company should continue to fund their education. Many students struggle with their early drafts, in part because they are still trying to reach an academic audience, not a workplace one, and in the process tend to write long, confusing sentences, assuming that is something most academic readers expect. One student, Theodore, wrote the following in his first draft under the "Discussion" heading of his memo:

> Individual arguments consist of a message that a speaker persuades to an audience for a particular purpose, highlighting Aristotle's Rhetorical Triangle, where each point on the triangle collaborates. For instance, a doctor lectures to a group of doctors about his/her new cancer research developments and explains the significance of his/her research by sharing a story about a friend dying from cancer. A message's purpose appeals to an audience through three categories: ethos (the speaker's credibility), pathos (the message's emotional appeal), and logos (the logical appeal).

Theodore's memo is clumsy. He never clarifies the connection between rhetoric and the workplace writing, nor does he show how understanding rhetoric makes for more effective workplace communication. The examples he uses come from a general example of a doctor, not the specifics of his workplace. The section also continues with more information and examples about the three modes of persuasion, none of it pertaining to the employer audience or to the memo's purpose. By the time Theodore submitted his final memo in his final portfolio, he had revised it several times, drawing from the stylistic advice we addressed in the class. In doing so, Theodore was able to connect the stylistic elements to an audience different from the one he originally addressed. Theodore spent less time defining rhetoric to show me, his instructor, he knew the term, and he eliminated the general allusions to other professions, such as his example about a doctor's lecture:

> In this memo, I explain the purpose of my coursework by highlighting the significance of rhetoric in the workplace. Having employees trained in rhetoric leads to a more productive work environment, allowing your company to succeed internally and externally.

Here, Theodore narrows his focus from an academic audience to a workplace one, drawing on many of the stylistic elements we addressed in class: chunked text, few sentences per paragraph, putting subject and verb closer together, and use of the active voice. Of course, these guidelines are not unheard of in most professional writing classrooms, and most professional writing textbooks offer guidelines on how to achieve these elements in their writing. At worst, overreliance on teaching these issues in a professional writing setting can neglect broader rhetorical matters and course content and lead to what Buehl calls a "monochromatic" style, instead of the "polychromatic" style he insists we should be teaching our students (2013, 280).

When teaching these elements, though, I find myself needing to separate the style from the form in order to show students how they can craft their sentences in ways to achieve the stylistic clarity necessary for professional writing, echoing Erasmus's call for separating form from content for pedagogical purposes. Far from turning my students' style into a single, "monochromatic" entity, introducing them to a range of stylistic strategies leads them to develop *facilitas*. For her group's final project, another student, Hannah, drafted much of the executive summary, and her prose echoed this focus on rhetorical awareness, audience, and *ethos*. For the group project, students completed work for a local company in which they analyzed websites from competing companies and wrote a proposal with suggestions for how the company can improve services. The executive summary Hannah wrote for her group's proposal was concise and used workplace stylistic conventions such as chunked text, bullet points, subheadings. Here is one of her paragraphs from the executive summary in which she offers final recommendations:

> We recommend that [NAME OF COMPANY] streamline the search process for managed Ethernet switches on the [NAME OF COMPANY] website. Excessive information bogs down the user, and it might deter them from making a purchase. We also recommend that [NAME OF COMPANY] define equivalent terminology for the sake of comparing competitors like [NAME OF COMPETITOR]. Greater accessibility and clarification of highly technical language will make the site more attractive to the average user.

Hannah's prose features active voice, cohesion from sentence to sentence, and a brief number of sentences in each chunked paragraph, elements that allowed her to begin with the stylistic elements of workplace genres (in this case the executive summary) and adapt those to fit her rhetorical situation (clients from an outside company looking for strategies to improve customer service). While most workplace genres we address in the classroom may not call for the fullness of expression Erasmus envisioned in *De Copia*, the ability to say something in a variety of ways becomes very useful in professional writing settings. Indeed, teaching these sentence-level guidelines can lead students to see the relationships between style and genre, in the case of Hannah and her executive summary, and style and audience, in the case of Theodore's memo.

The memo assignment is a good example of how students use various stylistic elements and connect them to the conventions of workplace genre. The memo, I tell my students, should be no more than a page long and adhere to the generic conventions of most memos: *To*, *From*, and *Subject* headings; identify the main point in the opening sentence; contain short paragraphs that are single-spaced, bullet lists, and subheadings to organize essential points. Thus, when I teach the generic conventions of the memo to my students, I identify at the same time various stylistic elements, model them for the students, and show them how to use them to convey complex information clearly. Mostly, I unpack for them the importance of using the active voice, cohesive elements between the end of one sentence and the beginning of the next, brief chunks of information rather than long paragraphs, and subheadings. Most students find that in needing to convey complex information clearly to an outside audience, such as the rhetorical nature of workplace communication to a boss who may not know what rhetoric is, a reliance on active voice, on cohesive and balanced sentences, and on coherent paragraphs is necessary. In reflecting on the need to focus on reducing complex information to short, digestible chunks, most students noted how it challenged them to clarify their sentences more than they had done in other writing contexts. Hannah, for instance, in her final portfolio, reflected on how playing with and revising the various stylistic elements of the memo led her to become a stronger writer:

> I benefited tremendously from the rhetorical memo assignment, which showed me how to communicate effectively with professionals. . . . I found that I was most satisfied with the cohesion and flow of my memo as a whole, the evidence that I used to support my claims about rhetoric, and the overall strength and persuasiveness of my argument for continued funding. . . . I improved upon my conciseness and wordiness, my audience appeal, and my usage of appropriate word choice.

Hannah notes the importance of learning various stylistic strategies for workplace genres and how those issues of style lead to stronger writing by allowing her to connect style to larger issues of audience and purpose. Below is an example from her final workplace memo. Like Theodore, Hannah's first draft tried too hard to define rhetoric for an academic audience and was wordy and lacked focus. After receiving feedback from her peer review group and from me, she began to use the stylistic conventions of workplace writing to focus her memo toward the workplace audience. Here is an example that comes from the "Discussion" section of the memo in which Hannah connects the importance of understanding rhetoric to effective workplace writing:

> My professional writing class defines rhetoric as the way in which language persuasively reaches and influences an audience. My professor challenged us to recognize that attention to rhetoric by tailoring my terminology to the individual client. I can also focus my attention on technical wording or simple language, which will convey the appropriate style in all workplace exchanges.

By using elements of style as an avenue toward effective workplace writing, Hannah focuses her attention to her workplace audience and, using language that features active voice, cohesion from sentence to sentence, and clear language, shows how rhetoric affects professional communication. In the process, these elements of style taught her the conventions of the workplace memo. In short, both Theodore and Hannah took lessons on clarity, active voice, balance, and other stylistic principles and were able to apply them to writing workplace genres in a way that allowed them to focus on elements of audience and purpose, in ways that suggest that by teaching them conventions of a workplace genre, we are teaching them style, and that by teaching them workplace style, we are teaching them genre.

Designing and Writing for the Web

Another assignment in my professional writing class that provides opportunities for instructors to reimagine instruction in style as a place for student writers to develop *facilitas* and to learn about generic conventions is writing for the web. Writing for the web allows professional writing students to combine both sentence-level elements and elements of document design to flex their stylistic muscles. In my class the web writing assignment is a three-week assignment in which I tell each student to imagine themselves in their first professional writing job as a writer for the tourism board in one of the fifty states. Each student is assigned a different state. I give a piece of paper to each student with a list of random facts and information about their state. Their job is to take that copy and develop a website and rewrite the copy for that website, so that it is appropriate for the intended user of the site. After they design their website, they write a two- to three-page reflection to me in which they provide a rationale for why they chose the audience they chose and how the stylistic features of the site are appropriate for their rhetorical situation. To prepare them, we read Carolyn Miller's essay "Genre as Social Action" to learn how genres arise out of recurring rhetorical situations. Then, as a class, we analyze numerous examples of state tourism websites to look for repeating stylistic features and elements—both sentence-level and design, such as divisions by towns and regions, links for things to do in that state, links for additional help, and links for international users. In addition, students note that most of these websites rely on short, one- to two-sentence paragraphs, on the use of second person, on embedded links, and on easily scannable prose. We make a list of those various features and conventions and talk about how they would fit in their own websites. In other words, we treat the tourism websites as genres and examine their recurring features and conventions as matters of style: chunked text that is scannable, use of the imperative voice, balanced sentences and lists, inclusion of links within the prose, subheadings, large background pictures and other visual elements, drop-down menus, among many others. For instance, one state site we examined, Vermont's, alters between second person and the imperative. The following examples are indicative of the entire site: "Embark on a Vermont Grape and Wine Council tasting tour that's bound to please every palate" and "You'll find a range of locally-owned restaurants, featuring locally-sourced food, antiques and art galleries . . ." Most of these verbal elements are set against a background of screen-sized images of Vermont, its restaurants, and farms. We also examine who the intended audiences may or may not be for the different tourism sites we analyze.

Typically, students point out in class that many of the sites are for general travelers from around the globe, which is why each site provides features to read their sites in multiple languages. Other students note that some of the pages focus exclusively on families, while others may focus on single travelers or couples without children. In order for students to connect their stylistic choices to their audience, I ask students then to choose an intended user for their site and structure and craft the site around the needs of that user. In all, these sentence-level and design elements allow students to develop *facilitas* by combining explicit and tacit instruction in web-based genres.

Consider my student Nate. Like most students in the class, Nate had little to no experience with workplace writing. Like Theodore and Hannah earlier with their memos, Nate's experience in the class led him to become more aware of non-academic style and gave him practice writing and designing for non-scholarly audiences. Nate's website, for instance, revolved around a food tour of Wisconsin. After researching the food and culture of Wisconsin, Nate divided his site into sections called "Beer," "Cheese," "Fresh Produce," and "Classes/Tours." For each section, he kept his language simple and mostly in the imperative mood and second person ("Indulge in the tastes of Wisconsin" and "Reserve your spot today. Spaces are limited" and "Refresh yourself as you sample farm fresh tastes"). He also used large background pictures of the Wisconsin landscape, cheese farms, breweries, and other inviting locales to balance with the verbal elements of his page. For example, the list of cheese farms and factories is set against a background of cheese curds and cheese platters in a style that does not take the user's eye away from the verbal elements. Elements of document design, not unlike the sentence-level elements, become part of the stylistic choices students make in their work.

Another student, Naomi, suggests that the web assignment led to a greater understanding not only of design and writing for the web but for workplace writing in general. Writing for the web, she wrote in her reflection, taught her to "deliver a message in an ideal manner to a large audience." For her website, Naomi drew South Carolina and had to design her site for a specific user—golfers. Her site focused on different golf destinations and travel packages for golfers headed to South Carolina. In her website reflection, Naomi told me that she wanted to "make the website less like a general tourism site and more like a place for those to go if they wanted to learn more about golf in South Carolina." Later, she observed how this change in focus and audience allowed her to pare down the text and keep her site simple and clean.

"To correct myself from creating a large webpage with many chunked paragraphs filled with too much information on this topic, I decided to make a bulleted list of the activities, each with an embedded link." As a result, her site was sparse, simple, neat, and effective, relying on images and few verbal elements. But, the verbal elements she did use were highly useful and easy to read for her intended audience. On her page for "Courses," a page where she listed a number of golf courses for users to learn about, her first link provides a broad series of courses based on the city in South Carolina. Her second link narrows the search by featuring only the top-ranked golf courses from the previous year. Finally, her third link highlights only ten golf courses for users to explore, while also providing the option to search by city. In the end, her website found a remarkable balance between providing sufficient information for users and using sparse and simple language.

Naomi's website and subsequent reflection are interesting here for two reasons: one, she shows rhetorical awareness of genre when she notes that her site will be less like a tourism site and more like a site for experienced golf travelers, suggesting that she is aware that styles may need to change when the genre may need to change; two, her choice to use bulleted lists and embedded links rather than chunked paragraphs suggests further that her choices in style change as her audience changes. In other words, for Naomi, writing means to be adaptable and to use various stylistic elements as the situation calls. Her site features fewer verbal components than many of the other student websites, but they are appropriate and effective. Echoing Erasmus's insistence in *De Copia* to be able to say something in a number of different ways, Naomi shifts her style from chunked paragraphs to bullet lists to convey information to her audience. Later, in her final semester portfolio, Naomi reflected that the web assignment was particularly useful to her development as a writer. "Issues of style can change when writing for the web, as you may have to alter your writing to suit an audience on a different platform for a different purpose." She then connected these ideas to different rhetorical situations when she wrote in her portfolio about some writing she had done for a campus organization that promotes awareness of women's rights and for her semester internship. Naomi's response here connects, again, to two main ideas this chapter has addressed: one, connecting her work in EN 250 to her work for a campus organization and for her internship suggests that her learning of websites as genre echoes Beaufort's argument that learning genre requires both tacit learning on the job and explicit learning in the classroom; two, Naomi's response reinforces Erasmus's call for copiousness in words and thought and that learning style is about developing adaptive strategies from one rhetorical situation to another.

CONCLUSION

This chapter has drawn from an important era of style's past and applied it to the production of emerging texts that point to style's future. Asking students to learn various stylistic strategies for workplace genres leads students to be able to adapt these strategies to numerous rhetorical situations, putting into practice Erasmus's insistence to develop *facilitas* and copiousness of language and thought. Drawing from Erasmus's suggestion to divide form from content pedagogically in order to teach style can be consistent with a pedagogy of style that addresses style as a larger part of workplace communication—audience, purpose, and genre. The assignments and their attention to style challenge students' preconceived conceptions of style and teach them numerous strategies for adapting these stylistic elements to both workplace and academic settings. Instructors, then, should not hesitate to address issues of professional writing style for fear of seeming to treat style as separate from the content of the course but rather find solutions in the push and pull of separating style from content as well as treating it as a significant part of the broader rhetorical situation. At the same time, professional writing assignments that lead students to learn various sentence-level and document design stylistic strategies within the context of workplace genre illustrate the importance of style in professional writing classrooms. Drawing from an important part of style's past—Erasmus—and connecting it to the twenty-first-century professional writing classroom provides a new direction for style, one that broadens our understanding of style to include not just sentence-level issues but issues of genre, document design, and writing for the web. Style, therefore, conceived of in as broad a method as I have suggested here allows writing instructors to view style not just as a crucial part of the professional writing classroom but perhaps as *the* central component of the professional writing classroom.

REFERENCES

Amare, Nicole, and Charlotte Brammer. 2005. "Perceptions of Memo Quality: A Case Study of Engineering Practitioners, Professors, and Students." *Journal of Technical Writing and Communication* 35 (2): 179–190.

Beaufort, Anne. 1999. *Writing in the Real World: Making the Transition to School and Work.* New York: Teachers College Press.

Buehl, Jonathan. 2013. "Style and the Professional Writing Curriculum: Teaching Stylistic Fluency through Scientific Writing." In *The Centrality of Style*, edited by Mike Duncan and Star Medzerian Vanguri, 279–308. Fort Collins, CO: Parlor Press.

Erasmus, Desiderius. (1512) 1978. "Copia: Foundations of the Abundant Style." In *Collected Works of Erasmus*, edited by Craig R. Thompson, 280–660. Translated by Betty I. Knott. 42 volumes. Toronto: University of Toronto Press.

Horning, Alice. 2006. "Professional Writers and Revision." In *Revision: History, Theory, and Practice*, edited by Alice Horning and Anne Becker, 117–141. West Lafayette: Parlor Press.

Milic, Louis. 1965. "Theories of Style and Their Implications for the Teaching of Composition." *College Composition and Communication* 16 (2): 66–69, 126.

Miller, Carolyn. 1984. "Genre as Social Action." *Quarterly Journal of Speech* 70 (2): 151–167.

"Vermont." n.d. Accessed September 5, 2018. https://www.vermontvacation.com.

SECTION 2

Style Conveys Identity

5
THE STYLIZED PORTRAYAL OF THE WRITING LIFE IN SPIKE JONZE'S *HER*

Cydney Alexis and Eric Leake

In "Remembering Writing, Remembering Reading" (1994), Deborah Brandt makes a statement that should have inspired a wealth of research: though the identity label of "reader" is readily available to all, the identity label of "writer" is more elusive. She provided many reasons for this, including systemic, institutional, cultural sponsorship of reading, generally perceived to be a positive act with discernible benefits by most of the public, contrasted with writing, an act pursued by children in secrecy and silence, apart from their parents, teachers, and peers. Alexis elsewhere has questioned how writing is differentiated, arguing that writing's fairly recent association with fiction and poetry and attachment to the word "creative" in defining a discipline has cordoned off the possibility of writing as an identity label for the millions and perhaps billions who write for a living, including academics, ghostwriters, and workplace writers (2017). For example, an article in *Writer's Weekly* estimates that 50 percent of all published fiction employs a ghostwriter, line editor, or book doctor (Suzanne 2001). (See Jon Udelson in this volume on how style might bridge divides between composition and creative writing.) Yet because much writing is viewed neither as real labor nor as creative, much writing work is invisible as the identity of writer is kept out of reach.

That writing is often devalued as an occupation or activity while it is simultaneously lauded as a specific profession for a small segment of the population—fiction writers and poets—makes it unsurprising that despite the untold number of people who daily write vocationally and avocationally, there are so few representations in popular culture of those who write in ways that reflect the preponderance of writers. The representations we do have are generally limited to white fiction and poetry writers and teachers inspiring students, frequently underprivileged students of color, to write (examples include *Dangerous Minds*,

Finding Forrester, and *Freedom Writers*). In addition to this, both in popular culture and in the popular imagination there is a strong mythology that writing is solitary, the product of a gifted, haunted (generally white) genius. Popular representations are important because, as Bronwyn Williams and Amy Zenger argue, portrayals of literacy in popular culture "recreate and reinforce pervasive concepts and perceptions of literacy, perceptions that inevitably influence both how we teach reading and writing and how our students respond to print literacy and to writing classes" (2007, 5). These popular and pervasive renderings don't match the complex understanding of the writing process researched and understood by writing studies, and they don't fully represent who writers are or who may become a writer.

In this chapter, rather than focusing exclusively on style in prose, we investigate style in a popular culture rendering of the figure of the writer. After viewing Spike Jonze's film *Her*, we were struck by the film's stylization of the work and private life of its protagonist, Theodore Twombly (Joaquin Phoenix), a ghostwriter of love letters. *Her* is the rare film that centers on a workaday writer; rarer still, it lauds the creativity of such a profession. The film presents a vision of the future of composition, at home and in the workplace. It offers the chance, then, both to analyze a popular culture product for how it understands writers and writing through its mise-en-scène and stylistic imagination, and to attend to how it at once addresses style, composition, identity, and writing labor. Why does this matter? It matters, we argue, because through popular culture people learn what it is possible for them to be, do, and achieve. The possible selves literature that we review in this chapter makes this abundantly clear: the mere ability to imagine oneself in a certain role or occupation or achieving a particular goal correlates with the ability to achieve it (Markus and Nurius 1896; Oyserman, Gant, and Ager 1995). Popular culture renderings of writers pass on possibilities (or lack of them) to those who encounter them. These become central conceptions of who writers are, and as the depictions circulate they gain authority. As Barry Brummett observes, "The cultural authority that was once located at a mother's knee is now found on a screen" (2008, 7). It is important that these renderings are in accordance with the understandings about writing and writers as developed through writing studies over more than one hundred years of research.

Just as culture valorizes the "creative" writer, its stories generally turn their attention to these writers as well. *Her* provides an opportunity to read what we can discern about public understanding and portrayals of the writing life through the film's stylistic crafting. We argue that how people imagine writers and writing, for themselves and for others, is intricately bound with questions of style in who writers are and how they act against a larger social backdrop. *Her* foregrounds these concerns through its richly detailed writer's world. Representations in popular culture can teach us much about stylization and possibilities of writerly identities. As Brummett contends, "Style is so central to popular culture that the rhetoric of style and the rhetoric of popular culture are practically the same thing. One might say that thinking in terms of style is a way to think about popular culture" (2008, xiii). To this, we would like to add that to think about both style and popular culture is to think about what the mass media indicates is possible to do and achieve. How writing is styled and how writers are stylized on screen provide an entry point for writing studies scholars to understand the circulation of stereotypes around writing and the cultural availability of possible writer identities.

STYLES, IDENTITIES, AND POSSIBLE SELVES

Style and identity are interwoven but under-researched within composition. While his definition of style emphasizes written discourse, Paul Butler acknowledges competing conceptions that view style as "the unique expression of an individual's personality," overlaying style and identity (2008, 3). Within the rhetorical tradition, the qualities of speech have long been associated with the qualities of the speaker, as in Quintilian's definition of effective rhetoric as "a good man speaking well" (Ellis 1946, 85). For a more comprehensive view aligning style and identity, we again look to Brummett, who understands style as

> [a] complex system of actions, objects, and behaviors that is used to form messages that announce who we are, who we want to be, and who we want to be considered akin to. It is therefore also a system of communication with rhetorical influence on others. And as such, style is a means by which power and advantage are negotiated, distributed, and struggled over in society. (2008, xi)

Style then may be regarded as an expression of identity. Within composition, the various identities of students and writers, as well as of teachers, are frequent areas of attention although rarely in terms of style. In a classic essay on the challenges of reading male narratives, for example, Lad Tobin focuses on an essay by Tim, a student whose particular male identity is represented in part by his baseball hat, a choice of style. Commenting on the significance of the cap, Tobin writes, "I've noticed a busy intersection between the caps, talk about the caps, the identification of problematic male students, and the resistance of many teachers to male narratives" (1996, 168). He adds, "By wearing the cap during class, the student crosses certain lines of decorum, propriety, and control, and thereby asserts his individuality" (169). Tobin notes that the cap also represents social affiliation, allowing the student to conceal himself through group connections. We may read the cap as an expression of style and identity, in line with Brummett's conception of style. Tobin's reading of the cap affects his reading of Tim's narrative, as performances of identity and writing are intertwined. Tobin is put off by Tim's style, his performance of identity, both personal and affiliative, in appearance and in writing. In this case as in others, identity and style are not merely personal but constructed and performed through the available social and cultural materials, against a social backdrop, including representations that circulate through popular culture and are readily available to wear and present.

To better understand the relationship of identity, style, and how popular representations of the figure of the writer influence conceptions of writers and writing, we turn to related research in the sciences and social sciences on possible selves. The possible-selves literature demonstrates that the ability to imagine oneself occupying a role or achieving a goal correlates with achievement and with motivation to attain the goal (Markus and Nurius 1986). This holds for diverse outcomes such as academic achievement (Oyserman, Gant, and Ager 1995) and career aspirations (Markus and Nurius 1986; Lips 2000). In an attempt to address, understand, and remedy the gender gap in pursuit of STEM and related careers, scholars have demonstrated that popular representations of individuals in STEM fields in film and television have played a significant role—among other factors such as personal motivation, mentor encouragement, and family and social support—in the ways the public understands these roles and even the numbers of men and women who enter these majors in college and ride the "science pipeline" into these professions (Google and Gallup 2015; Steinke 2005, 2017; Steinke et al. 2007). The research does not attend to style, but the representations of individuals in the STEM fields are clearly concerned with style if we approach style as ways of announcing who we are, what we do, and who we want to be. Hence the lab coats and glasses worn by so many of the scientists in television shows and movies or the tweed worn by university professors. We build on the findings of possible-selves research to demonstrate the importance of turning to popular representations of writers and writing in order to understand writing's possibilities, as well as the stylized images, stereotypes, and biases about writing that circulate more broadly in culture.

Since Markus and Nurius's 1986 article "Possible Selves," research has flourished that has demonstrated that our internalized senses of what we would like to become, and our ability to imagine these future desired selves, play a strong role in achieving those selves; they "provide the essential link between self-concept and motivation" (954). Markus and Nurius elaborate that "the pool of possible selves derives from the categories made salient by the individual's particular sociocultural and historical context and from the models, images, and symbols provided by the media and by the individual's immediate social experiences" (954). These "models, images, and symbols" are, of course, necessarily concerns of style as they circulate in the media. In this way, personal experience—whether influenced by sociocultural context or one's lived experience and interactions with others—determines one's outlook of what's possible. As they detail through research they conducted on hundreds of individuals and an exhaustive review of relevant literature, possible selves can be positive or negative, can allow for possibility or constraint of life choices, and work as a sort of affective filter through which experiences are read and future self possibilities are determined. The media is one source from which possibilities related to selfhood are derived, and the ways that those selves are styled inform the ways that they are understood and considered available.

A wealth of studies has indicated the importance of possible-selves perspectives. Studies have found that adult occupational attainment is linked to one's belief in abilities in adolescence (Schoon 2001); that having a positive self-schema around math and science, for example, impacts taking courses in those areas, performance on tests, and seeing career possibilities in these areas (Lips 1995); and that female college students in math-intensive fields have trouble linking self-concept to math if they associate math with masculinity (Nosek, Banajii, and Greenwald 2002). Elizabeth Brown and Amanda Diekman found that women associated more future possible selves with family and caregiver roles than did men and that both men and women report anxiety around having careers or taking on roles that are not congruous with cultural definitions of masculinity and femininity. We include this sampling to indicate that in the sciences and social sciences, a substantial body of scholarship has linked the ability to conceive of possible selves with performance in all kinds of arenas and that in much of this research, cultural stereotypes, in this case often related to gender and gender roles, impact perceived abilities in relation to who somebody may become and what they may do. With its attention to cultural representation and questions of style, composition could do well to focus on some of the same questions of possible selves in relation to writers and writing.

STYLE AS SUBSTANCE IN *HER*

In *Her*, Jonze presents a gorgeous and intricately stylized film set in a futuristic landscape, one that provides a tableau through which to analyze both traditional and provocative understandings of writers and writing. Through our analysis we wish to argue that it is important to persistently combat simplistic and troubling portrayals of writers and the writing life if we wish to advocate for the public to have a more comprehensive understanding of writing and a view of writer as an available identity. This understanding is important not just to bring new writers into the trade but to positively affect the identities of those who find themselves within it. Simultaneously, through *Her*, we would like to argue that an important place to turn in order to understand what a text says about writing is to attend to its style. For as Brummett contends, regarding style as surface or as trivial is misguided, for in late capitalist society, style is at the heart of all our actions and movements or, as he argues, "the key to constructing a rhetoric for the twenty-first century" (2008, xiii). Richard Lanham similarly calls for a greater attention to style as the driver of a new economy of attention. Whereas substance—or as Lanham calls it, "stuff"—has long been privileged over style, Lanham flips those: "If attention is now at the center of the economy rather than stuff, then so is style. It moves from the periphery to the center. Style and substance trade places" (2006, xi–xii). There is plenty of substance available, so style becomes a determining factor in what matters. Like Brummett, we view style as "an aesthetic unity of behavior and expression," as "substance," as a "set of signs," and as a "language" (2008, 41, 10, 7, 4). We will, accordingly, read *Her*'s language and signs to take the temperature, so to speak, of how writing is envisioned as a cultural activity now and how it is projected into the future.

Her undertakes an envisioning of the future of writing through the ghostwriter character of Theo. In the world of *Her*, style is central to workplace writing, as is also argued in this volume by Tom Pace (chapter 4). Jonze, through Theo, presents the writer as a highly stylized and nostalgic figure. Theo's is a futuristic, individualized, and yet highly corporate style, one that is mirrored in his work and personal surroundings. The ghostwriting office space has an open-plan, contemporary layout with colorful desks in close proximity to one another, and the space is naturally lit by light that floods through multicolored window panes. This stylized interior contributes to the ethos of those who work and write there. The city is stylized as an amalgam of many of the world's cities, including Los Angeles and Shanghai: it has clean, sharp lines; people are orderly and organized; and technology hangs out in many public spaces through the presence of ubiquitous digital devices, both personal and those used for marketing (Murphy 2013). Theo's apartment is technologically advanced and reflective of his high earning potential, as it is clearly a downtown apartment with floor-to-ceiling and wall-to-wall windows; it is also, however, stripped down, minimalistic, barren, either a nod to his recent divorce or a comment on the thing-less-ness of futuristic culture. Theo stands out with his mustache, minimalistic hipster shirts, and high-rise pants, a style that both harkens back to the 1950s yet also signals a stylistic sea change favored by many of the people we see flooding this city's storyworld, which we mention because the fashion choice stood out, was commented on widely by reviewers as anachronistic, and yet was a defining feature of the clothing style presented by the film, part of its aesthetic language. Theo's identity as a writer, as well as the meaning of the writing that he does, is constructed against this stylish backdrop.

Let us look at an example of that style in writing. The film opens with a close-up on Theo's face as he dictates a letter. We notice his trendy acetate glasses, his hipster mustache, and the emotions that register on his face as he speaks, although at the moment we are unsure exactly to whom he is speaking. He begins, "To my Chris":

> I've been thinking how I could possibly tell you how much you mean to me. I remember when I first started to fall in love with you like it was last night. Lying naked beside you in that tiny apartment, it suddenly hit me that I was part of this whole larger thing, just like our parents, or our parents' parents. Before that I was just living my life like I knew everything, and suddenly this bright light hit me and woke me up. That light was you. I can't believe it's already been 50 years since you married me. And still to this day, every day, you make me feel like the girl I was when you first turned on the lights and woke me up and we started this adventure together. (*Her* 2013)

Theo ends the letter, "Happy Anniversary, my love, my friend til the end. Loretta," and then, as we see a copy of the handwritten letter drafted on his computer screen alongside digital photos of a couple labeled "Chris" and "Loretta," we begin to understand the writing labor Theo is doing in words both his own and for somebody else. The letter works because of Theo's style, because of the emotions that it expresses and evokes. A sense of romantic nostalgia and a bespoke quality, key markers in Theo's style, are present throughout the letter: in the salutation to "my" Chris; in the listing of generations from parents to parents' parents to connect with the past; in the short central sentence, "That light was you," that adds emphasis through its brevity; in the setting off and underscoring of "every day"; and in the emotional momentum that builds in the rush of the last sentence, ending with the idea of love, friendship, and marriage as an adventure together. The style of the letter matches Theo's style as a writer. He is presented as somebody who is careful in his neatly trimmed facial hair and selective in the corresponding colors of his clothing. He is sensitive; as he leaves work, Theo requests that his phone play a melancholy song. Although Theo is young, in his check shirt, solid-colored jacket, and high-waisted brown woolen pants, he appears both of his time and of an earlier one. His nostalgic orientation, along with his attention to detail and his sensitivity, is evident in Theo's style, his self-presentation, his writing, and how he relates to others, which is also done through writing. The film closes with Theo writing another letter, one addressed to his ex-wife, in which he apologizes to her and lets her move on while he expresses an abiding love for their past relationship. That letter fits Theo's nostalgic romantic style too, and its writing is another kind of emotional labor. The film is bookended by these letters.

Theo as "writer" is interesting on many levels, most notably because his position as a ghostwriter of love letters envisions a future of writing quite different from the present day, in which, as Brandt argues in *The Rise of Writing*, ghostwriting is a source, for many, of discomfort and tension. Brandt defines ghostwriting as "taking on substantial parts of a composing process for which someone else, not you, will be credited—whether by byline, signature, institutional title, or oral delivery, or in some other way" (2015, 31). As she notes, "ghostwriting can both artfully exploit and at times offensively violate normal assumptions about writing and reading" because "beliefs and values developed as part of mass reading literacy have come to saturate social systems, affecting the sense of how things work, or should work" (33). Some of these assumptions in modern-day culture are that one's love letters should be personally written, as they are records of an individual's selfhood, love, and commitment. There is not, with the exception of greeting cards, a mainstream culture of ghostwriting love letters. It is in line with Brummett's (2008) assertion that both consumption and style (the latter as the outward form that manifests selfhood) are at the heart of late capitalist societies, that Theo's writing is an acceptable form of labor. Whereas people used to define themselves through what they produced, now, Brummett writes, "We are increasingly what we buy or own," which the film extends from the writing of letters to the purchase of letter writing (68). Theo's employer, BeautifulHandwrittenLetters.com, is in the writing style business, where style becomes substance. Anybody can write an anniversary letter, but it is the style in Theo's writing that makes it meaningful, valuable, and even lauded. Lauded because toward the end of the film, we learn that Theo's work has been published as a collection in book form and received praise not only from the individuals in the corresponding relationships but also the publishers. In book form the letters are re-stylized and aestheticized. The appeal of the book, and of Theo's work more broadly, is its epistolary style in addressing specific and general audiences, a style detailed in this volume by Melissa Goldthwaite (chapter 2). Brandt asserts that ghostwriting is about scarcity of literacy, skill, and time, about how literacy is mobilized in service of another with more power and less time, or in service of those without skill. *Her*'s depiction of ghostwriting proposes another sea change: the scarcity of romantic literacy in the futuristic landscape. This lends additional significance to Theo's divorce, the dissolution of his best friend's marriage, the cavernous, empty spaces in his office and home, and the metallic coldness of the urban landscape Jonze imagines. Theo's work as a ghostwriter presents writing in which style is substance, as the question is not the authenticity or legitimacy of the authorship but the effect of the evocative expression, carefully styled through Theo's collaborative composition. His writing bridges rhetoric and poetics in a style akin to what Jarron Slater in this volume describes as sublime (chapter 9). Theo's writing creates and fulfills desires for emotional expression and collaboration among writers and readers, in this case among Theo, his patrons, and the intended recipients of his cards and letters.

It is tempting to read Theo as the only "writer" in this film. However, we view Samantha, an operating system (OS1) that Theo purchases and is his primary love interest, as a writer in her own right whose labor, which is levied in service of Theo, communicates volumes about the gendering and subjugation of secretarial/ghostwriting labor, the power dynamics involved with ghostwriting, and the way the public conceptualizes what writing is and is not and who writers are. Throughout the course of the film, Samantha writes and edits his correspondence, serves as his intellectual companion, and is responsible for the publication of his collected letters. As a surprise, she culls from his writings a sample of letters, edits and proofs them, and submits them to a publisher, who accepts them for publication. Theo's letters were composed based upon the stories and artifacts of other lives, and they were edited and arranged and pitched by Samantha. Samantha's role as writer, however, is eclipsed by how the film treats Theo's collected writings, by its lack of explicit commentary on Samantha's labor. If we minimize Samantha's role to mere scribe, and the film in large part does, we risk reifying the historic rendering of women's collaborative work with their male counterparts invisible.

To return more explicitly to style, we cannot ignore Jonze's stylization and gendering of Samantha. As an operating system, Samantha does not come with a name. She chooses the name Samantha after Theo asks her if she has one. With this name, and the feminine, sexualized voice selected for Theo after he answers an extremely brief series of questions, Samantha becomes, for Theo and the viewer at least, a gendered woman. This effect is intensified due to the voice Jonze selected for Samantha, one recognizable to audiences, that of Scarlett Johansson. The character of Samantha becomes stylized once she is identified with a gender and a name. Reviewers frequently reduce Samantha's characterization to the power of the voice, her central style element, and neglect some of the tough realities of the love relationship that Theo and Samantha develop. Peter Bradshaw calls "the voice" "warm, witty, and sensual" (2014). Manohla Dargis under the title "Disembodied, but Oh What a Voice" and writes: "The voice brightly greets him in the morning and, with a sexy huskiness, bids him goodnight in the evening. The voice organizes his files, gets him out of the house, and, unlike some multitasking females, doesn't complain about juggling her many roles as his assistant, comfort, turn-on, helpmate, and savior" (2013). At once, these reviewers are correct in that the voice is the main way Samantha is characterized for the viewer and are also at risk of trivializing not only Samantha's role but important questions the film raises about the role of technology in the near future. To complicate things more, one effect of using Johansson's voice is that her body comes along with it; we imagine Samantha's body into being, because of our previous exposure to the actress. The style of the voice cannot be disassociated from the person. Although she lacks a physical body, Samantha is *embodied* through her voice, her expression of emotions, her human associations, and her role in the narrative, a performance of embodiment like that identified by Almas Khan in this volume (chapter 11). Samantha and Theo's relationship asks us to consider tough questions about artificial intelligence and about love, such as whether a love such as this, one that in many ways equates style with substance, can ever truly be "real." The relationship is real enough to Theo and to Samantha, who seeks a surrogate body in order to allow her to feel embodied and to allow Theo the experience of sex with physical contact. It also, however, raises questions about authenticity and style, about what counts as real. Theo ghostwrites for couples. Samantha ghostwrites for Theo. Theo sees his ghostwriting as meaningful; on the other hand, he balks at sexual surrogacy as compromising the relationship.

As writers, Theo and Samantha use writing to realize who they are, Theo through his final letter to his ex-wife and Samantha in how she composes herself. Writing is also how they relate to each other. Later in the movie, as she becomes faster and she and Theo are growing apart, Samantha describes the feeling of losing her connection to him as similar to spending time with a favorite book:

> It's like I'm reading a book, and it's a book I deeply love, but I'm reading it slowly now so the words are really far apart and the spaces between the words are almost infinite. I can still feel you and the words of our story, but it's in this endless space between the words that I'm finding myself now. (*Her* 2013)

That Samantha would relate her relationship with Theo to reading a novel is telling, as it demonstrates how central writing and reading are to the movie in maintaining and defining characters and relationships. The film opens and closes with scenes of Theodore writing, first somebody else's letter and later his own, and it suggests that what's important in relationships can be understood through the writing that maintains and defines them. The writing in *Her* is pervasive. Even in a technologically advanced future, people write and connect through their writing. The centrality of writing in these relationships highlights the significance of style in relating, that relationships are questions of *how* things are done, how people go about relating, which makes them also questions of style. Indeed, relationships in the film, especially Samantha and Theo's, are shown to be essentially performances. Judith Butler defines performance as an "expectation that ends up producing the very phenomenon that it anticipates" (2010, xv). The relating anticipated the relationship that it becomes, and how it does so—and how it is constituted—is a matter of style. In the ways that the characters write and relate, in how they perform their relationships, those relationships become real.

STYLE AND THE WRITERLY SELF

As we have argued in this chapter, the importance of style extends beyond written discourse. Style influences the ways that people identify themselves as speakers and actors, as readers and writers. Research on possible selves and analysis of the stylized identities in popular portrayals of writers, such as we have done here with *Her*, help us focus on how the writerly self is made available and performed. They also tell us how style remains central to writing and identities, as distinctions between substance and style blur. Lanham would have us keep them in dual focus, oscillating between style and substance in looking *at* and looking *through*, because style and substance are always in cooperation and flux. "Style is always turning into substance and back again," he writes (2006, 163). "Push style to its extreme and it becomes substance" (255). In our analysis we attempt to track a similar change, as stylistic representations of writers become the substance of writerly identities. Rhetoricians and compositionists generally are comfortable recognizing the social-epistemic role of language, that we use language just as language uses us. Brummett suggests the same for style: "[S]tyle performs us as much as we perform any given style" (2008, 3). To recognize this function of style is to put it at the core of who we are, what we do, and how we do it, including as writers. Identities are always stylized and formed in relation to the styles and identities of others as circulated through public spaces, including popular culture. If writing always is to some degree a performance of the self, then writing always is to some degree also a concern of the stylized writer. Williams and Zenger write that just as no one doubts the importance of popular culture in contributing to conceptions of gender or class or other facets of identity, "We should not doubt, then, that such media are influencing perceptions and practices of writing and reading" (2007, 7). We extend their argument to include representations of the stylized writer as always a factor in how people think of themselves as writers, how others think of them as writers, and how they write, with style. Just as style is an unavoidable feature of all writing, so is it an unavoidable feature in the identifications of all writers.

REFERENCES

Alexis, Cydney. 2017. "Let's Banish the Phrase 'Creative Writing.'" *Inside Higher Ed.* January 3, 2017. www.insidehighered.com/views/2017/01/03/we-should-stop-distinguishing-between-creative-and-other-forms-writing-essay.

Bradshaw, Peter. 2014. "*Her*—Review." *The Guardian.* February 13, 2014. www.theguardian.com/film/2014/feb/13/her-review.

Brandt, Deborah. 1994. "Remembering Writing, Remembering Reading." *College Composition and Communication* 45 (4): 459–479.

Brandt, Deborah. 2015. *The Rise of Writing.* Cambridge: Cambridge University Press.

Brown, Elizabeth, and Amanda Diekman. 2010. "What Will I Be? Exploring Gender Differences in Near and Distant Possible Selves." *Sex Roles* 63, nos. 7–8: 568–579.

Brummett, Barry. 2008. *A Rhetoric of Style.* Carbondale: Southern Illinois University Press.

Butler, Judith. 2010. *Gender Trouble.* New York: Routledge Classics.

Butler, Paul. 2008. *Out of Style: Reanimating Stylistic Study in Composition and Rhetoric.* Logan: Utah State University Press.

Dangerous Minds. 1995. Directed by John N. Smith. Buena Vista Pictures.

Dargis, Manohla. 2013. "Disembodied, but, Oh, What a Voice." *New York Times.* December 17, 2013. www.nytimes.com/2013/12/18/movies/her-directed-by-spike-jonze.html.

Ellis, Carroll Brooks. 1946. "A Good Man Speaking Well." *Southern Journal of Communication* 11 (4): 85–89.

Finding Forrester. 2000. Directed by Gus Van Sant. Columbia Pictures.
Freedom Writers. 2007. Directed by Richard LaGravenese. Paramount Pictures.
Google and Gallup. 2015. "Images of Computer Science: Perceptions among Students, Parents, and Educators in the U.S." services.google.com/fh/files/misc/images-of-computer-science-report.pdf.
Her. 2013. Written and directed by Spike Jonze. Warner Brothers Pictures.
Lanham, Richard. 2006. *The Economics of Attention: Style and Substance in the Age of Information.* Chicago: University of Chicago Press.
Lips, Hilary. 1995. "Through the Lens of Mathematical/Scientific Self Schemas: Images of Students' Current and Possible Selves." *Journal of Applied Social Psychology* 25 (19): 1671–1699.
Lips, Hilary. 2000. "College Students' Visions of Power and Possibility as Moderated by Gender." *Psychology of Women Quarterly* 24 (1): 39–43.
Markus, Hazel, and Paula Nurius. 1986. "Possible Selves." *American Psychologist* 41 (9): 954–969.
Murphy, Mekado. 2013. "Below the Line: Designing '*Her.*'" *New York Times.* December 18, 2013. carpetbagger.blogs.nytimes.com/2013/12/18/below-the-line-designing-her.
Nosek, Brian, Mahzarin Banaji, and Anthony Greenwald. 2002. "Math=Male, Me=Female, Therefore Math [Not Equal to] Me." *Journal of Personality and Social Psychology* 83 (1): 44–59.
Oyserman, Daphna, Larry Gant, and Joel Ager. 1995. "A Socially Contextualized Model of African American Identity: Possible Selves and School Persistence." *Journal of Personality and Social Psychology* 69 (6): 1216–1232.
Schoon, Ingrid. 2001. "Teenage Job Aspirations and Career Attainment in Adulthood: A 17-Year Follow-up Study of Teenagers Who Aspired to Become Scientists, Health Professionals, or Engineers." *International Journal of Behavioral Development* 25 (2): 124–132.
Steinke, Jocelyn. 2005. "Cultural Representations of Gender and Science: Portrayals of Female Scientists and Engineers in Popular Films." *Science Communication* 27 (1): 27–63.
Steinke, Jocelyn. 2017. "Adolescent Girls' Stem Identity Formation and Media Images of Stem Professionals: Considering the Influence of Contextual Cues." *Frontiers in Psychology* 8: 1–12.
Steinke, Jocelyn, Maria Lapinski, Nikki Crocker, Aletta Zietsman-Thomas, Yaschica Williams, Stephanie Evergreen, and Sarvani Kuchibhotla. 2007. "Assessing Media Influences on Middle School-Aged Children's Perceptions of Women in Science Using the Draw-a-Scientist Test (Dast)." *Science Communication* 29 (1): 35–64.
Suzanne, Claudia. 2001. "The Good Life of Ghostwriting." *Writer's Weekly.* October 3, 2001. writersweekly.com/this-weeks-article/the-good-life-of-ghostwriting-by-claudia-suzanne.
Tobin, Lad. 1996. "Car Wrecks, Baseball Caps, and Man-to-Man Defense: The Personal Narratives of Adolescent Males." *College English* 58 (2): 158–175.
Williams, Bronwyn, and Amy Zenger. 2007. *Popular Culture and Representations of Literacy.* New York: Routledge.

6

STANCE AS STYLE
Toward a Framework for Analyzing Academic Language

Laura L. Aull and Zak Lancaster

INTRODUCTION: ANALYZING LANGUAGE IN ACADEMIC WRITING

A central goal for teaching style is to provide students with an analytic framework for exploring how language-level details create stylistic effects within rhetorical contexts. Without such a framework, student and instructor discussions of style can remain generalized and vague. They can remain, for example, at the general level of "flows vs. choppy," "formal vs. informal," "personal vs. impersonal," and "lively vs. dull," without drilling down to the details of language—that is, to specific words, phrases, and clauses—to account for how such stylistic effects are achieved. As one consequence, discussions of style can remain impressionistic and decontextualized, or, as Olinger (this volume) puts it, "adisciplinary, ageneric, and afunctional." A framework for examining style therefore helps to remove the mystery from writing, making visible the language-level choices writers make within contexts and that readers may be expecting and valuing. One key goal for such close attention to language is to develop students' ability to identify and account for patterns of language choices—that is, students' "metalinguistic ability" (Ray 2015, 579).

Metalinguistic ability is important for at least two related reasons. First, it enables students and instructors to move beyond impressionistic labels, to reflect explicitly on textual expressions and their functions (Swales 1990; see also Cheng 2018). Second, use of metalanguage assists students in conscious monitoring of their language choices while drafting and revising. As Brian Ray explains, students with control of stylistic terminology can better consider "the active manipulation of language with conscious attention to surface form [and] stylistic effect" (2015, 579), a claim supported in emerging research (Concha and Paratore 2011).

In this chapter we propose that the concept of stance offers a valuable focus and metalanguage for examining written style, especially in academic prose. By *stance*, we refer to writers' expressions of attitudes,

DOI: 10.7330/9781646420117.c006

epistemic commitment, and interaction with the reader, which have been examined most extensively in discourse studies in composition and applied linguistics (e.g., Vande Kopple 2002; Barton 1993; Hyland and Sancho Guinda 2012; Aull and Lancaster 2014). This research approaches stance as linguistic expressions by which writers "present themselves and convey their judgements, opinions, and commitments" (Hyland 2005, 176). In other words, stance includes not just a writer's overall viewpoint—as in, "What is your stance on climate change?"—but explicit expressions of attitudes (e.g., *fortunately, interesting, important*), certainty (e.g., *the data **clearly** show, it would **seem** that*), and interaction with readers' views (e.g., *please note that, of course, it is true that . . . but*). Writers, that is, express stance toward at least three entities as they write: toward propositions, toward evidence (or the status of knowledge), and toward readers.

Academic expectations related to stance are important, subtle, and often difficult for instructors to articulate (Lancaster 2014). Academic writers, for instance, are frequently expected to argue for a position while also displaying sustained consideration of alternative views (Wolfe, Britt, and Butler 2009). More difficult still, student writers may be expected to project an "engaged" style that is critical but not attacking or dismissive (Lancaster 2016b; Soliday 2011). How to accomplish such styles of stance-taking can be wholly unclear for student writers, especially undergraduate writers (Hood 2004; Aull and Lancaster 2014), because they are usually tacitly rather consciously valued (Soliday 2011).

Before proceeding, let us offer a brief example analysis to help illustrate our claim that stance analysis can elucidate style in academic writing. Consider the following concluding paragraph from an upper-level undergraduate student's research report written in a psychology course.[1]

(1) To conclude, this paper seeks to highlight the many concepts of immigrant psychology that surface in Marie's narrative. I have shown how she was subjected to much structural discrimination at the immigration courts due to language barriers, and also racism of a much subtler form as she was systematically measured and whitened by her supporters with their nonetheless benevolent and kind actions. She also provided us with an interesting case study of shifting multiracial identities, and proved how fluid and contextual these identities are. No narrative is complete without a discussion of gender and its effects on the immigrant. Marie's narrative highlighted important gender differences and the negotiation of cultural boundaries where culture and gender are conflated. Lastly, I concluded with her acculturation attitudes that tie up these concepts. Through all her experiences, Marie's perseverance and determination shone through and made her story a tremendous source of inspiration for all immigrants. (PSY.G0.05.1)

This passage strikes us as a fairly ordinary stretch of academic prose. Without particular panache or flare, it accomplishes the purpose of a concluding paragraph by reiterating main points and arguments made. Using impressionistic labels, we might characterize the style as "academic" and also authoritative, committed, and engaged. How are these qualities achieved? First, the writer conveys attitudinal stance when describing Marie's narrative as *interesting* and *important* and as *a tremendous source of inspiration*. Language-level choices like this convey engagement with and appreciation for the subject matter under discussion, qualities that research suggests are valued in student coursework writing (Soliday 2011). Additionally, the style is marked by high commitment, achieved through epistemic stance markers that linguists call amplifiers or boosters: *I have shown; proved; no narrative is complete; all her experiences*. Finally, in terms of interactional stance, the writer identifies herself as an involved analyst through overt self-mentions (e.g., *I have shown; I concluded*) while remaining mostly distant from the reader with the exception of one reader-inclusive pronoun (*She also provided us with . . .*). Cumulatively, these stance expressions create a writing style that can be described as academic, committed, and engaged, which seems appropriate for the conclusion to an analytical report in a psychology course.

Our discussion of the above passage and the metalanguage we use provide an example of what we mean when we assert that attention to stance offers a way to analyze specific expressions in academic writing that together contribute to particular stylistic effects. The sections below strive to define stance in more detail and to illustrate the value of attending to stance as a part of style in academic writing. We do this in two ways. First, throughout our discussion, we include examples from student writing to help illustrate how instructors and students might analyze stance as part of style. Second, we attempt to bring together two bodies of research that we see as importantly related: studies of style in composition and studies of stance in composition and applied linguistics. In so doing, we underscore that analyzing recurring stance expressions illuminates ideas about style, just as theories of style help illuminate how stance creates overall textual effects. We close with challenges and tips for teaching stance awareness in writing classrooms.

STANCE AND STYLISTIC EFFECTS

Stance is not an easy concept to pin down, as evidenced by multiple volumes devoted to explaining it (e.g., Hyland and Guinda 2012). We

Table 6.1. Dimensions of stance

Stance Dimension	Descriptor	Frequently used expressions	Example words and phrases
Attitudinal	Stance toward the subject matter	Expressions of affect and evaluations of things	*important/ importance, significant, useful, appropriate, valid*
Epistemic	Stance toward evidence and status of knowledge	Hedges; boosters; appearance-based evidentials; modal expressions, etc.	*perhaps; the evidence shows/suggests; it is clear that; it would seem that*
Interactional	Stance toward readers and others' voices	Adversatives, concessives, denial-counters, code glosses	*however; nevertheless; of course; is not that . . . rather that; in other words*

define stance according to three overlapping dimensions: attitudinal stance (or stance toward the subject matter at hand); epistemic stance (or stance toward the evidence and status of knowledge); and interactional stance (or stance toward the reader and others) (cf. Hyland 2005; Martin and White 2005). These dimensions are elucidated further in table 6.1.

Distinguishing these three dimensions is analytically and pedagogically useful. Note, for instance, that the epistemic stance expressed in example passage 2, written by a first-year university student, differs quite dramatically from that expressed in passage 3, written by a fourth-year undergraduate in an economics course.

> (2) As technology continues to develop, there is no doubt that social media will become a resource for people to collaborate on ideas and organize protests. However, it will **never** cause a revolution because . . . (first-year undergraduate directed self-placement essay)

> (3) However, this case is **not without** concerns. There is the **possibility** for abuse **if** the producer sets different maximum prices for different retailers, allowing some to reap higher profits. There is also a **possibility** that for new retailers to enter the market they would have to charge higher prices initially, in which case a maximum price **could** deter competition. It **appears**, then, that maximum price fixing does the greatest harm when set below a competitive level. (fourth-year undergraduate research paper in economics)

In 2, the epistemic stance is certain. It is expressed in a highly committed manner (*never cause a revolution*). In contrast, the stance expressions in passage 3 create a more circumspect style, or one characterized by reduced commitment achieved through frequent low-probability expressions (*could, possibility, potentially*), appearance-based evidentials (*it appears*), conditionals (*if*), and other wordings (*not without, based purely on the models*). To be sure, there are plenty of other wordings one could notice. However, a focus on epistemic stance alone in this case enables us to raise pointed questions about possible patterns of difference between first-year and upper-level undergraduate writers, as pursued in Aull and Lancaster (2014), as well as possible patterns of difference between disciplines and genres (e.g., Lancaster 2016b; Aull 2017).

At the same time, these three dimensions do overlap in important ways. For example, frequent use of hedges with self-mentions such as *it seems to me* and *in my personal view* works interactionally and epistemically. That is, such expressions help reduce the writer's commitment to claims (epistemic stance), a move that then opens up dialogic space for alternative views (interactional stance). Consider, for instance, the stylistic effect of hedged self-mentions from this graduate student's research paper written in a course on natural resources and environment:

> (4) While it may still be possible to successfully carry out a recovery plan for the Mount Graham red squirrels, **I would think** the impact of such a population decline would not leave them unaffected. More specifically, it could be helpful to conduct research regarding the remaining genetic diversity within the Mount Graham red squirrel gene pool. **I would imagine** that much of it has been lost since their population is now down to only a few hundred squirrels. This research could also be helpful in determining if there are any genetic traits that make the Mount Graham red squirrel more vulnerable to habitat destruction than other squirrels. (NRE.G1.21.1)

We would characterize this text's style as reflective and dialogically open, which is achieved at least partly through the epistemic and interactional stance expressions bolded above. Another example of overlap includes the use of hedges to cushion critical evaluations (e.g., *It appears that Socrates failed to consider*) (Lancaster 2016c). In a formulation such as this, we can discuss stance as occurring on all three dimensions. The attitudinal stance is critical (*failed to consider*). The epistemic stance is measured or uncertain (*it appears that* instead of *it is clear that*). And the interactional stance is dialogically open, inviting alternative views.

Our general point is that stance expressions do not operate in isolation; they work together across sections of a text and whole texts and contribute to overall stylistic effects. Accordingly, these dimensions of stance, the language-level expressions that accomplish them, and the metalanguage for describing them offer concrete resources for identifying and discussing style.

RESEARCH ON STYLE AND STANCE
Style in Composition Studies

Thus far, our discussion of style has made use of a metalanguage that may be unfamiliar to many readers. However, our broader points about style and stance follow from and extend existing discussions of style in composition studies. Style in composition studies has been conceived as patterned language choices that create meaning and thereby offer a set of rhetorical resources for writers. This conception is informed by rhetorical traditions as well as mid- and late-twentieth-century composition research that used linguistic theory (see Ray 2015, 108). The interdisciplinary nature of style and the fact that language choices in writing provide "explicit linguistic link[s]" to rhetorical principles (Stodola 2013, 62, 66) explain this synergistic relationship between style scholarship and linguistic approaches. Such an interdisciplinary approach enables style to illuminate genre conventions (Duncan and Vanguri 2013, xv) and pinpoint criteria for assessing style (Vanguri 2013).

The conceptualization of style in composition includes three tenets that especially resonate with our view of stance as part of style. First, style has been viewed in terms of linguistic resources, writers' choices from these resources, and resulting patterns. These resources reflect as well as shape the larger discursive contexts within which writers are working, including genres and discourse communities. Accordingly, style is not mere artifice, divorced from content, though many students and instructors, including those described by Olinger and Pace in this volume, may perceive and describe it as such. Rather, style is instrumental for making meaning and accomplishing rhetorical goals. Style is, in other words, "the use of written language expressions as habitual patterns, rhetorical options, and conscious choices at the sentence and word level" whose effects "extend to broader areas of discourse and beyond" (Butler 2008, 3; see also Connors 1997, 257).

Second, and relatedly, style in composition has been seen as a part of patterned social interactions in discourse. Writers' stylistic choices, that is to say, are driven largely by interpersonal considerations. These include the "voice" or authorial persona the writer wishes to project; the relationship with the reader the writer seeks to create; and the writer's engagement and negotiation with others' views and voices in the discourse. The critical discourse analyst Norman Fairclough, drawing from M.A.K. Halliday's theory of register (e.g., Halliday 1978), has relatedly defined "styles" of discourse as "ways of being" (Fairclough 2013, 11)— as constituting social or personal identities. James Paul Gee (2014) also associates style with social identities, contrasting between the vernacular prose style of "an everyday person" and the more distant, formal style of a disciplinary specialist. For Gee, as with Fairclough and Halliday, the style of a text is wrapped up with performances and judgments of social identities. Viewed through this lens, stylistic choices can be understood as reflecting and constituting the writer's aims vis-à-vis pertinent discourse communities. As Johnson (chapter 3) describes, style helps forge "intersubjective connection" between writer and reader. And, as Keith Rhodes writes, "To become seriously immersed in style is to become acutely aware that language is most essentially interpretive, a never-ending negotiation between vast cultural constructs" and the particular viewpoint of a writer (Rhodes 2013, 91).

Third, style has been viewed as meaning-making within existing constraints of language. Holcolmb and Killingsworth emphasize the "rule-governed, conventional, and deviant behavior" with respect to language choices to help students recognize different levels of meaning-making. Specifically, they delineate *grammar* as a rule-governed and largely stable system of meanings, whereas *style* refers to a writer's set of choices within that system (including following or deviating from them), and *convention* is "the shifting ground of linguistic restriction between grammar and style, between definite rules and clear choices" (2013, 131). They write:

> Within the textual arena, students examine how all the words on the page interact with one another to form patterns and meanings. Here students gain practice in applying different vocabularies of analysis (those from traditional grammar, linguistics, or rhetoric), and they become more accustomed to following closely the word-by-word choices of an author as they unfold in a given text. (125)

The above three considerations, all of which depict style as created by or enacted through recurring language choices, suggest that style should be seen as closely connected to writers' selections of meanings from a larger social semiotic system—especially, selections of meaning made in light of interpersonal considerations related to stance, social identities, ways of being, and so forth. Understood in this way, the style a writer creates is not just a personal, idiosyncratic way of writing that another might write differently; it is far more systematic and collective than that: the creation of style is a process whereby writers negotiate meanings and social relationships. Academic writing, too, can be examined for its complex array of stylistic considerations in light of writer-reader interaction within communities of readers. It is certainly not, as Bacon (2013) emphasizes, somehow "without style."

Finally, in terms of our argument for metalanguage, style scholarship in composition also underscores the importance of equipping students with a robust stylistic terminology or metalanguage (Butler 2008). Crystal Fodrey likewise suggests that we offer students "a rhetorical vocabulary to discuss works in progress" (2013, 241). Without a clear set of metalinguistic concepts, as William FitzGerald suggests, students cannot bring the important stylistic knowledge they already possess to the surface, because they "[lack] a vocabulary" to name what they know (2013, 48). These final points underscore the importance of supporting students' ability to recognize and articulate how language-level choices contribute to stylistic effects.

Stance Studies in Composition and Applied Linguistics

Like studies of style, stance research is deeply interested in patterned language choices that relate to how writers negotiate genre and discourse community expectations. Stance expressions have been noted in research in college composition in the past (see, e.g., Beach and Anson 1992; Booth 1963), but they have garnered particular attention in more recent linguistics-focused research in composition and English for academic purposes. For example, Ellen Barton and William Vande Kopple have explored how stance expressions index disciplinary epistemologies while also preserving cohesive textual relationships, which undergraduate students may not notice without explicit attention to language (Barton 1993; Vande Kopple 2002). More recently, corpus-based research shows that stance patterns distinguish student writing by level, with developing student writers expressing stance differently from advanced peers and published academic writers (Aull and Lancaster 2014).

In particular, comparative analysis shows that advanced student writers express epistemic and interactional stances differently from first-year students (Aull and Lancaster 2014; Lancaster 2016b; Aull, Bandarage, and Miller 2017). Upper-level students frequently express epistemic stance in ways that are more measured and narrower in scope, as seen above in examples 3 and 4 in contrast to example 2. They also tend to create more involved interactional stances as they pause to engage imagined readers. These qualities are achieved through interactional devices technically referred to as code glosses (*in other words*) and as concede-contrast markers (*Author X provides valuable insight; however, . . .*). In short, advanced writers typically show more modulation in epistemic commitment and more involvement with potential reader concerns.[2]

In addition to such developmental patterns, corpus-based research also distinguishes student writing by relative effectiveness, with high-rated papers projecting different stance qualities than lower-rated ones. Barton (1993), for instance, found that, while expert essays she analyzed adopted what she called a "contrastive" and "competitive" epistemological stance, the student essays more often assumed a stance marked "shared social agreement" (1993, 765). Importantly, the student essays that did build a more contrastive stance received higher scores. This expectation to adopt a contrastive and generalized academic stance was affirmed in Lancaster's (2016b) study of upper-level undergraduate writing in economics and political theory, as well as in Wu's (2006) analysis of first-year writing. Other qualities of stance that appear to be valued in undergraduate contexts include reflectiveness (North 2005a, 2005b; Soliday 2011) and critical distance (e.g., Lancaster 2016a).

Research on stance in academic writing highlights two specific reasons that analyzing stance expressions is valuable for students. First, research shows that stance expressions influence readers' impressions of writing quality and, in the case of student writing, of students' engagement with course material (see, e.g., Soliday 2011; Brown and Aull 2017). Second, valued ways of expressing stance are rarely taught, discussed, or otherwise made transparent to students, which means they remain largely hidden in writing assessment (Wingate 2012; see also Biber 2006; Hyland and Guinda 2012; Soliday 2011). To counter such tacit expectations, these studies highlight that tracking stance expressions with the help of stance metalanguage can help make valued qualities of academic prose more transparent.

Bringing Together Style and Stance to Help Students Develop a Metalanguage and Analyze Academic Writing

We hope we have shown how style and stance research connects in valuable ways: style research emphasizes the value of awareness of meaning-making language patterns and students' metalinguistic ability to recognize them; similarly, stance research emphasizes the value of stance awareness and a corresponding metalanguage for discussing stance. At the same time we have likewise underscored that many academic writing expectations regarding stance expressions and their stylistic effects remain tacit, operating beneath instructors' explicit awareness (e.g., see Lancaster 2014, 2016b; Soliday 2011). A good reason for this, surely, is that responding to the writer's epistemic, attitudinal, and interactional stances is not a common lens—or an explicit framework—for evaluating writing. Instructors, instead, are more accustomed to making judgments about "content" and a vague notion of style. Indeed, Star Medzerian Vanguri (2013) points out that "style" frequently appears on grading rubrics but with inconsistent and usually vague explanations.

Our own research and teaching have endeavored to connect overall stylistic effects to specific language-level stance choices, specifically in analysis of academic writing with students. We now turn to these pedagogical possibilities. First, we offer example sentences and metalanguage that we use with students as part of analyzing stance in academic writing. The table shows the three dimensions of stance we have noted above, some typical linguistic resources associated with each dimension, specific examples of stance expressions used in student papers, and the corresponding stylistic effect of those example stance expressions. In the examples the disciplinary category of respective upper-level papers is noted parenthetically (see Aull and Lancaster 2014). Ideally, by engaging in this type of analysis, students and instructors can have meaningful conversations about how certain stance selections unfold and contribute to an overall textual style; such discussions can also help highlight discursive values that may be privileged in academic discourse, including, for example, critical distance and the foregrounding of reason over emotion (cf. Lancaster 2016a; Thaiss and Zawacki 2006).

In our experience, students are often surprised to see how rich and complex stance choices are in what appear on the surface to be dry, impersonal, or "style-free" texts. But we have also found it important to guide students to focus *descriptively* on cumulative stylistic effects, including why those effects may be appropriate/effective in particular rhetorical contexts. It would be misleading, for example, for students to conclude from Barton (1993) that markers of contrast will somehow make writing "better" across contexts, or to conclude from Aull and Lancaster (2014) that hedging is always good and boosting claims is always bad. Instructors, instead, need to assist students to interpret the expression of stance in context. Why, for example, might a writer choose to use hedges to reduce epistemic commitment to a particular claim given the genre and particular argument? Along these lines, "stance awareness" is, in our view, a more reasonable pedagogical goal than mastery of particular stance expressions.

By stance awareness, we refer to the following points. First, we refer to awareness of the various ways that writers use language to take a stance toward ideas, evidence, and readers. Second, we refer to awareness that specific stance expressions frequently cluster together within texts as well as cooperate with other stance expressions to create overall stylistic effects that shape readers' impressions. Third, we refer to awareness

Table 6.2. Stance examples and stylistic effects

Dimensions	Lexico-Grammatical Resources	Example Stance Expressions	Example Stylistic Effects
Attitudinal Stance	Attitude markers, often adjectives and adverbs	Young's account of oppression provides a **useful** analysis in the case of the film *The Battle of Algiers*, demonstrating . . . (Political Theory)	Evaluative engagement with texts, ideas, and arguments
		At the end of the day, Love has written a book that is highly **affecting, disturbing**, and, most importantly, **illuminating**. . . . (History)	Affective engagement with texts, ideas, and arguments
Epistemic Stance	Hedges; boosters; appearance-based evidentials; modal expressions	Since the argument hinges on these three ideas, and Socrates **could** be wrong about each of them, **I think** it is safe to conclude that he did fail to distinguish pleasure and the good. (Philosophy)	Reducing certainty or commitment based on available evidence
		This model **shows** that the difference in market share between the firms in an oligopoly is irrelevant . . . (Economics)	Raising certainty commitment based on available evidence
Interactional Stance	Concessions; adversative connectors; negation	**While that may be true**, the circumstances pertaining to this case show clearly that, economically, it makes sense to allow the horizontal price-fixing, except with lower prices. (Economics)	Concede something your reader may think, then offer a counter
		One might argue that the correspondences between Plato and Livy noted here are simply coincidences. . . . **To this, I respond** that Livy tailored his narrative to emphasize how the kings fit the Platonic model. (Classics)	Let your reader make an objection, then rebut it

of how to examine texts in terms of stance, which we believe happens through use of a framework such as that illustrated in table 6.2.

Facilitating Stance Awareness

In our own courses we begin with guided student analysis, so that students practice recognizing stance expressions and begin to infer and articulate their stylistic effects. For instance, we might ask students to examine two different passages, such as from different genres (see examples 5 and 6 below). As students analyze and annotate, they consider what they perceive in light of how the writers do the following. Later, students consider how they approach these negotiations in their own writing and in writing across disciplines and other genres.

1. How/where writers make their presence known or else hide overt presence when making judgments
2. How/where writers express affect or attitude toward their own or others' views
3. How/where writers take a stance toward the evidence they're using, either by raising or reducing commitment toward, or certainty about, that evidence
4. How/where writers take a stance toward the anticipated reader, creating a reader-in-the-text with certain characteristics (e.g., critical, aloof, involved)
5. How you might explain differences across texts in light of audience, purpose, genre, and/or discipline

For instance, students might consider the differences in passages 5 and 6, in which we have bolded several types of stance expressions:

> (5) It is **difficult to conclude** from these two studies if the mating system of Sarasota dolphins is polygynous, promiscuous, or **possibly** something else. **Evidence is supported for both** a polygynous and a promiscuous mating system. **It might be possible** that two alternative strategies exist in this population, such as in the eastern Pacific spinner dolphins. (From upper-level student report in biology [BIO.G0.06.1])

> (6) **I argue** it is **important** to distinguish between racial stereotyping, racial prejudice, and political tolerance. Kim's theoretical schema helps **us** understand why these analytical wedges are **necessary**, and, **I claim**, **should** force **us** to reconsider how and why **we** measure racial prejudice. (From upper-level student argumentative essay in political science [POL.G3.01.1])

Even these short examples do suggest genre-based distinctions in terms of stance expressions and the style they help convey. Passage 5 contains several epistemic stance expressions that hedge or qualify the statements. Furthermore, the sentence openings (*It is difficult to conclude; Evidence is supported; It might be possible*) draw attention to epistemic observations. These recurring choices contribute to a circumspect and detached style that is common in upper-level reports (Hardy and Friginal 2016). By contrast, passage 6 conveys attitudinal stance (*important, necessary*), epistemic stance (*should*), and interactional stance (*I argue, us, I claim, we*) in stance expressions that together create a more overtly persuasive and interpersonal style that appears to be appropriate for an upper-level argumentative essay (Hardy and Friginal 2016).

After a few class sessions, students become more comfortable recognizing and categorizing stance expressions that relate to readers' concerns and writers' attitudes and evaluations. They also become more comfortable discussing and practicing using different stance expressions in their drafting and writing workshops. Students annotate course readings, peer drafts, and their own writing for stance expressions and thus repeatedly practice analyzing language-level choices that create particular stylistic effects. Along the way they learn to develop their own questions about stance expectations. For example, they might ask whether the differences between 5 and 6 are more field-specific (i.e., characteristic of writing in biology versus political science) or genre-specific (i.e., characteristic of research reports versus argumentative essays, irrespective of field) or a combination. Armed with questions like these, our students continue to conduct their own mini-investigations of stance expressions in databases of writing such as MICUSP or collections of articles they themselves gather from their other courses.

CONCLUDING REMARKS: ATTENDING TO LANGUAGE IN ACADEMIC WRITING

In this chapter we have proposed that stance awareness, facilitated by a meaningful metalanguage, is needed in writing instruction so that instructors and students can attend explicitly to important stylistic expressions that are at play in academic texts. As we have found in our own teaching, such awareness and metalanguage offer resources for asking new questions about writing, for monitoring and evaluating micro-level stance choices when writing, for reflecting on the discursive practices students already command, and for potentially recontextualizing those practices to meet the demands of other academic, disciplinary, and generic writing situations.

At the same time, the study of stance comes with challenges, particularly for composition students and instructors unaccustomed to systematic analysis of language-level choices. We close with several challenges, followed by possible ways to navigate these challenges, for incorporating attention to stance as part of an approach to style in composition.

Challenges for Teaching Stance
1. Extending consciousness-raising about stance, especially its interactional goals, requires a shift in beliefs about language and relationship to

meaning-making, as it troubles the content/style dichotomy upheld by many students and instructors.
2. Instructors need to have discussions with students about (a) descriptive versus prescriptive views of language and (b) form versus functions in language.
3. With the previous point, instructors need to assist students' writing development and capacities to make judgments about appropriate and effective stance expression in context. They need to learn, for example, how to draw students' attention to hedging without giving way to decontextualized, prescriptive linguistic ideologies (e.g., "hedging is good; be sure to hedge more").
4. More work needs to extend ours here to account for stance as part of style in non-academic texts and other academic disciplines.

Tips for Teaching Stance
1. Discuss with students what sorts of stances are valued in the field and/or genre and/or task, and consider how these are different from or similar to non-academic genres with which students are familiar. With students, consider how meaning and reader-writer relationship change when a stance marker is added or removed.
2. Identify valued stance options in assignment prompts (e.g., "play the role of concerned student").
3. Point out effective choices regarding stance expressions, and their corresponding stylistic effects, in reading material.
4. Have students "play" with stances—for example, rewriting passages, moving from one epistemic and interactional stance to another—and discuss the stylistic effects of the differences.
5. Give students opportunities to reflect on their own stance expressions, inserting metacognitive comments while writing.

With and through these challenges, attention to stance as part of style in writing classrooms moves us closer to a clear, concrete framework for illuminating style in terms of patterned uses of language.

NOTES

1. This and several other examples below are from the Michigan Corpus of Upper-level Student Papers (or MICUSP), a searchable online collection of 829 A-graded papers written by students in a variety of departments and genres. Note that examples from MICUSP are offered with their unique identifiers. These show the discipline (e.g., "PHI" for philosophy; the student's year, e.g., "G1" for first-year graduate student; and the paper number). MICUSP also notes the student's self-identified gender.

2. These patterns emerged in corpus-based research. For example, Aull and Lancaster (2014) used AntConc corpus linguistics software to compare stance expression in three groups of writers: new college students; upper-level students; and professional academic writers (in the Corpus of Contemporary American English).

REFERENCES

Aull, Laura Louise. 2020. *How Students Write: A Linguistic Analysis*. New York: Modern Language Association.

Aull, Laura Louise, Dineth Bandarage, and Meredith Richardson Miller. 2017. "Generality in Student and Expert Epistemic Stance: A Corpus Analysis of First-Year, Upper-Level, and Published Academic Writing." *Journal of English for Academic Purposes* 26: 29–41. doi: http://dx.doi.org/10.1016/j.jeap.2017.01.005.

Aull, Laura Louise, and Zak Lancaster. 2014. "Linguistic Markers of Stance in Early and Advanced Academic Writing: A Corpus-Based Comparison." *Written Communication* 1: 33.

Bacon, Nora. 2013. "Style in Academic Writing." In *Centrality of Style*, edited by Mike Duncan and Star Medzerian Vanguri, 173–190. Anderson, SC: Parlor Press.

Barton, Ellen L. 1993. "Evidentials, Argumentation, and Epistemological Stance." *College English* 55 (7): 745–769.

Beach, Richard, and Chris M. Anson. 1992. "Stance and Intertextuality in Written Discourse." *Linguistics and Education* 4 (3): 335–357.

Biber, Douglas. 2006. "Stance in Spoken and Written University Registers." *Journal of English for Academic Purposes* 5 (2): 97–116.

Booth, Wayne C. 1963. "The Rhetorical Stance." *College Composition and Communication* 14 (3): 139–145.

Brown, David, and Laura L. Aull. 2017. "Elaborated Specificity versus Emphatic Generality: A Corpus-Based Comparison of Higher- and Lower-Scoring Advanced Placement Exams in English." *Research in the Teaching of English* 51 (4): 394.

Butler, Paul. 2008. *Out of Style: Reanimating Stylistic Study in Composition and Rhetoric*. Logan: Utah State University Press.

Cheng, An. 2018. *Genre and Graduate-Level Research Writing*. Ann Arbor: University of Michigan Press.

Concha, Soledad, and Jeanne R. Paratore. 2011. "Local Coherence in Persuasive Writing: An Exploration of Chilean Students' Metalinguistic Knowledge, Writing Process, and Writing Products." *Written Communication* 28 (1): 34–69.

Connors, Robert J. 1997. *Composition-Rhetoric: Backgrounds, Theory, and Pedagogy*. Pittsburgh: University of Pittsburgh Press.

Duncan, Mike, and Star Medzerian Vanguri, ed. 2013. *Centrality of Style*. Anderson, SC: Parlor Press.

FitzGerald, William. 2013. "Stylistic Sandcastles: Rhetorical Figures as Composition's Bucket and Spade." In *Centrality of Style*, edited by Mike Duncan and Star Medzerian Vanguri, 37–56. Anderson, SC: Parlor Press.

Fodrey, Crystal. 2013. "Voice, Transformed: The Potentialities of Style Pedagogy in the Teaching of Creative Nonfiction." In *Centrality of Style*, edited by Mike Duncan and Star Medzerian Vanguri, 239–258. Anderson, SC: Parlor Press.

Gee, James Paul. 2014. *Literacy and Education*. New York: Routledge.

Halliday, Michael Alexander Kirkwood. 1978. *Language as Social Semiotic*. London: Arnold.

Hardy, Jack, and Eric Friginal. 2016. "Genre Variation in Student Writing: A Multi-Dimensional Analysis." *Journal of English for Academic Purposes* 22: 119–131.

Holcomb, Chris, and M. Jimmie Killingsworth. 2013. "Teaching Style as Cultural Performance." In *Centrality of Style*, edited by Mike Duncan and Star Medzerian Vanguri, 119–134. Anderson, SC: Parlor Press.

Hood, Susan. 2004. "Managing Attitude in Undergraduate Academic Writing: A Focus on the Introductions to Research Reports." In *Analysing Academic Writing: Contextualised Frameworks*, edited by L. Ravelli and R. Ellis, 22-44. London: Continuum.

Hyland, Ken. 2005. "Stance and Engagement: A Model of Interaction in Academic Discourse." *Discourse Studies* 7 (2): 173–192. doi: 10.1177/1461445605050365.

Hyland, Ken, and Carmen Sancho Guinda. 2012. *Stance and Voice in Written Academic Genres*. New York: Springer.

Lancaster, Zak. 2014. "Exploring Valued Patterns of Stance in Upper-Level Student Writing in the Disciplines." *Written Communication* 31 (1): 27–57. doi: 10.1177/0741088313515170.

Lancaster, Zak. 2016a. "Do Academics Really Write This Way? A Corpus Investigation of Moves and Templates in *They Say/I Say*." *College Composition and Communication* 67 (3): 437.

Lancaster, Zak. 2016b. "Expressing Stance in Undergraduate Writing: Discipline-Specific and General Qualities." *Journal of English for Academic Purposes* 23: 16–30.

Lancaster, Zak. 2016c. "Using Corpus Results to Guide the Discourse-Based Interview." *Journal of Writing Research* 1 (8):119–148.

Martin, J. R., and P. R. R. White. 2005. *The Language of Evaluation: Appraisal in English*. New York: Palgrave Macmillan.

North, Sarah. 2005b. "Disciplinary Variation in the Use of Theme in Undergraduate Essays." *Applied Linguistics* 26 (3): 431–452.

Ray, Brian. 2015. *Style: An Introduction to History, Theory, Research, and Pedagogy*. Anderson, SC: Parlor Press.

Rhodes, Keith. 2013. "Making Style Practically Cool and Theoretically Hip." In *Centrality of Style*, edited by Mike Duncan and Star Medzerian Vanguri, 81–96. Anderson, SC: Parlor Press.

Soliday, M. 2011. *Everyday Genres: Writing Assignments across the Disciplines*. Carbondale: Southern Illinois University Press.

Stodola, Denise. 2013. "Using Stylistic Imitation in Freshman Writing Classes: The Rhetorical and Meta-Rhetorical Potential of Transitions in Geoffrey of Vinsauf's Medieval Treatises." In *Centrality of Style*, edited by Mike Duncan and Star Medzerian Vanguri, 57–70. Anderson, SC: Parlor Press.

Swales, John. 1990. *Genre Analysis: English in Academic and Research Settings*. Cambridge: Cambridge University Press.

Thaiss, Chris, and Terry Myers Zawacki. 2006. "Engaged Writers Dynamic Disciplines." Engaged Writers Dynamic Disciplines. Portsmouth, NH: Boynton/Cook.

Vande Kopple, William J. 2002. "From the Dynamic Style to the Synoptic Articles in Spectroscopic Articles in the Physical Review: Beginnings and 1980." *Written Communication* 19 (2): 227–264.

Vanguri, Star Medzerian. 2013. "What Scoring Rubrics Teach Students (and Teachers) about Style." In *Centrality of Style*, edited by Mike Duncan and Star Medzerian Vanguri, 341–360. Anderson, SC: Parlor Press.

Wingate, Ursula. 2012. "'Argument!' Helping Students Understand What Essay Writing Is About." *Journal of English for Academic Purposes* 11 (2): 145–154.

Wolfe, Christopher R., M. Anne Britt, and Jodie A. Butler. 2009. "Argumentation Schema and the Myside Bias in Written Argumentation." *Written Communication* 26 (2): 183–209.

Wu Siew Mei. 2006. "Creating a Contrastive Rhetorical Stance: Investigating the Strategy of Problematization in Students' Argumentation." *RELC Journal* 37 (3): 329–353.

7

LOOKING FORWARD TO A NICE, STUPID, FUTURE STYLE. R U?

Jimmy Butts

> *"Personally, I have a great admiration for stupidity."*
> —Oscar Wilde

> *"Two things are infinite: the universe and human stupidity; and I'm not sure about the universe."*
> —Albert Einstein

> *"Stupidity comes in many forms."*
> —Noam Chomsky

Style, like stupidity (and intelligence), is multivalent.[1] But I have started looking forward to a nice, stupid, future style. If we look to the forefront of writing being done across different technological platforms, we see some stylistic forms that some may call stupid. Perhaps the easiest example of stupid style is the simple replacement of the word "you" with the letter "u." This simplifying, cutting, misspelling, stylized form gets written off, displaced by powerful structures that demand stylistic standardization, clarity, and correctness. On the other hand, stupidity has its own power too.

In a world of increasing pressure to perform, young people especially are both falling in line and continuing to find stylistic ways to rebel and resist the call to perfection. Meanwhile, they don't even realize how clever they are being when they write stupid stuff like *lol dont b so basic fam*. Within that simple phrase, there are several smart and intentional moves that undermine the King's English: the abbreviation of laughing out loud, the dropping of the apostrophe, the dropping of the letter "e," and the shortening of family to fam to refer to what isn't family at all. Each move is generally a simplification of language. Then there's the use of that word "basic"—a critique. On the one hand, writing on contemporary media platforms has become increasingly banal.

DOI: 10.7330/9781646420117.c007

Snapchat overlays of "hiiiiiii" have become the norm, not saying much, but deftly copying what may just be an embrace of what seems to be a safe or sanctioned sort of Orwellian newspeak. Meanwhile, education and literacy continue to face complex crisis after crisis. Hence, we may need to think more about how stupidity shows up for better or worse in our writing.

There is a call to pay attention to the future of style (see Butler 2008, 8), but also the future of stupidity. The opening to Vilém Flusser's *Does Writing Have a Future?* proclaims, "Writing, in the sense of placing letters and other marks one after another, appears to have little or no future" (2011, 3). In a section on "The Digital," Flusser warns that "it is practically a public danger to underestimate this new way of thinking as somehow stupid or even narrow" (146). The future of writing is inherently couched in an understanding of whatever gets labeled or underestimated as stupid. The hope is that these steps will eventually lead us toward kinder readings, openness, and considerations for lost voices.

STUPIDITY AS A TERM WITH A HISTORY

Stupidity has come to mean a lot of different things. Before we make any claims about the future, we might review stupidity to grasp what we mean by it. When I have mentioned that I am writing about stupidity, I get a chuckle. But the long history of stupidity is serious.[2] The term comes from the Latinate *stupidus*, to be benumbed, to be in a stupor. The study of stupidity goes back at least to Theophrastus from the third century BCE. We see in the work of Theophrastus, a contemporary of Plato and Aristotle, a description of "the Stupid Man," or the ἀναισθησία (similar to our term for anesthesia). There we see an explanation of how the stupid man does what is contrary to reason, lacking perception. The portrayal begins curiously: "Stupidity may be defined as mental slowness in speech and action" (2015). We see here a descriptive quality to stupidity pertaining to a specific style of language use.

Theophrastus also composed a now lost treatise, *On Style*. According to Doreen Innes, through the historical tracings of Diogenes Laertes, Theophrastus is a nickname gotten from Aristotle, signifying a godlike mastery of stylistic phrasing: compounding the roots *theo-* and *phras-* (1985, 251). From what Innes can gather and recreate, Theophrastus has four virtues of style: correctness, clarity, appropriateness, and ornamentation (1985, 256). Meanwhile, in his earlier characterization of stupidity, the stupid man is incorrect, unclear, inappropriate, and dull.

As T. R. Johnson notes, there is something musical about "what we've superficially known as 'clarity'" and sometimes a downgraded, natural (and maybe even unschooled) flow that might show up powerfully in unsanctioned forms or spaces (chapter 3).

People respond to style and stupidity strongly. Stupid is a stasis word, meaning it contains and creates tension. Stasis, we know, from rhetorical theory is the space where two confrontational sides come to a head, a standstill (see Crowley and Hawhee 2004, 53). No one wants to be stupid.[3] And no one wants to sound too smart for their own good. A stupid style opposes certain expectations, while we continue to hear groaning about the stupidity of young people's writing at least since the *Newsweek* special issue from 1975: *Why Johnny Can't Write* (Sheils 1975).

I first came across a serious study of stupidity while studying with Avital Ronell.[4] Her book *Stupidity* is one of the few serious philosophical forays into the matter. She borrows the term from Kant and shows us its rhetorical power. In Kant's *Critique of Pure Reason*, a short footnote reads: "Deficiency in judgement is properly that which is called stupidity; and for such a failing we know no remedy" (2000, 268). We do see deficiencies in judgment appear in various stylistic forms in writing. Stylistic decisions are judged as either appropriate or inappropriate depending on the rhetorical situation. Hence, stupid style can create an alienating effect—an opposition. Ronell opens her book, purporting to plumb stupidity's depths, with this: "The temptation is to wage war on stupidity as if it were a vanquishable object—as if we still knew how to wage war or circumscribe an object in a manner that would be productive of meaning or give rise to futurity" (2003, 3). On the one hand, we must endeavor. On the other, it is an impossible task without end.

Bernard Stiegler, working out a partial response to Ronell, avers, "The only thing that, at bottom, is worth being lived—in this life that must constantly be critiqued in order for it to be, in fact, worth living—is the struggle against stupidity" (2013, 132). He follows that thought up further in another book where he explores the *bêtise*, the dumb beast like a cow chewing its cud, and the *dummheit* of other philosophers, namely Heidegger, Deleuze, and Derrida (Stiegler 2015). Indeed, resisting ignorance and the capacity for thinking and reflection are worthwhile, though the judgment heaped upon a person seen as stupid can be overwhelming. Walter Pitkin's early book *A Short Introduction to the History of Stupidity* was one of the first forays into this dumb topic and exclaims, "Stupidity can easily be proved the supreme Social Evil" (1932, 6). But the too clever is a sin on the other side.

We have to find a way of balancing knowing with grace and see stupidity functioning as the scapegoat, as a way out, a potential salvation from critique. If there is no hope of defeating or eradicating stupidity and it seems that stupidity is invincible, it may be worthwhile then to see what we might do with it productively. If you can't beat it, join it.

So, what is stupidity? Ronell herself resists defining it because of its slipperiness (2003, 3). For our purposes, we might say that stupidity is a perceived misstep in thought, which typically appears through language use. Stupidity is a lack of knowledge that can even appear along the surface of writing or thought, or what is performed or perceived as stupid, what appears stupid or erroneous in form.

PROPOSING A STUPID RHETORICAL STYLE

What might a stupid rhetorical style look like? We have *The Idiot's Guide to* . . . everything. Why not *The Idiot's Guide to Idiocy*?[5] Style itself sits on the surface of language, so we are told. But stupid style and stupid thought may find intersections. But we are not ignoring style and looking only to meaning. There may be possibilities in seeing the future stylistic gestures of a strong intentional use of things like oversimplification and error.

Stupidity is rhetorical and affects ethos. Rhetorical questions are in some sense stupid questions, or too obvious. Stupid moves can make us think and feel terrible things. It's also almost impossible to argue with a stupid person. Thinking and writing about stupidity, or even thinking and writing stupidly, are justified in that we discover a counter stance. In this sense, stupidity is more than just *mere* error. It can be used, intentionally or unintentionally, for effect—both positively and negatively. Sometimes readers leap from seeing error to assuming the writer is stupid, and of course we know that this is a mistake. Stupid rhetors may be dismissed. As Eric Detweiler explains, "[I]t's not just a matter of protecting others' right to say terrible, stupid, and terribly stupid things" (2018). Some stupid things are really bad. Carlo Maria Cipolla has five fundamental laws of stupidity, and the last is "[a] stupid person is the most dangerous type of person" (1976, 73). While we might overlook stupid speakers, we might also reject unwilling listeners, as explained by Chaïm Perelman and Lucie Olbrechts-Tyteca in *The New Rhetoric*: "[O]ne can always resort to disqualifying the recalcitrant by classifying him as stupid or abnormal" (1971, 33). Writing off an audience, which here is warned against, leads to a natural elitist superiority, which functions as a kind of foil for stupidity.

The categorizations for patterns and figures known as vices have been typically looked down upon. From *battalogia* (vain repetition) to *catachresis* (misusing words) to *solecisms* (grammatical mistakes) to *amphibologia* (ambiguous mispunctuation) to *apocope* (cutting off the ends of words) to *aposiopesis* (breaking off midsentence), we have a long catalog of generatively stupid rhetorical moves. These additions and subtractions—interruptions and insertions—offer some potential in language nonetheless. One man's trash is another man's treasure. A virtue can be a vice, and a vice can be a virtue.

Eric Berne explains how one of the most significant games people act out is playing stupid (1996, 157). This game involves evading responsibility. This evokes the power involved in sloughing off having to answer by saying, "I dunno." Stupidity is a strong coping mechanism, a defensive stance. It is hard to counter ignorance. Saying "I don't know" might just be both the strongest and weakest rhetorical claim one can make. Even recent work on the use of hedging using modal qualifiers, as seen in the work of Aull and Lancaster, for example (chapter 6), shows how playing stupid gains a more stable rhetorical grounding, maybe, perhaps, sort of . . . We have traditions of representative figures, such as the holy fool, the village idiot, or the court jester—each having their own signature styles and influence. These figures are collectively written off as scapegoats. Now we obesess over correctness, doing everything we can to resist eror and misktakes.

STUPID STYLE: THE ERROR OF WRITING OFF STUPDITY AS MERE ERROR

Stupid style is low style. There are various writers, such as Judith Halberstam's search for value in low theory (2011), who offer us an outlet, a permission slip to go down. We find our beloved patron saints of stupidity in Spongebob Squarepants and Homer Simpson. We do not necessarily need to mimic Erasmus's *In Praise of Folly* here, but we can see, I think, the strongly affective nature of stupid style. Stylistic stupidity performs a not knowing, or not performing adeptly. Jonathan Swift's famous definition of style as "proper words in proper places" (1843, 201) opens the possibility for the counter, an improper, stupid style. There is a slowness, or an undeveloped, imperfect, or even abbreviated quality, to stupid style. Stupidity is not polished or grandiloquent, so it often appears silly or foolish, without wit. Stupidity might be laughed at or misunderstood or even seem to misunderstand. Stupid style is simplistic—not typically a long complex sentence with significant subordination. Stupidity might be obvious or oblivious, obtuse or nonsensical, trivial or empty, thick or unclear. There is also playing dumb or missing the point or lacking audience awareness. To pin down a stupid stylistic form is to discover what lies at the heart of grammatical and usage errors. I am proposing a sort of value in an intention to see faults, errors, slips, and missteps, or what we might also refer to as unintentional deviations from the set of stylistic conventions commonly referred to as Standard Edited English, as always already stylistic.

As a *tekne*, style offers forms, but ironically, stupidity contains its own *tekne*, approaches, styles, formal gestures. Nigerian professor Macpherson Nkem Azuike suggests that there are two essential understandings of style: one as beautifying decoration, and one as deviation (1992, 109). Stupidity too then offers a deviant approach—by not following the norm, either intentionally or unintentionally. With stupid style, we veer from fanciful decorum to the unpolished, unvarnished, unrefined styles of society writ large. Stupidity also allows us to think of inappropriate decorum and delivery.[6] That tension is what we are most interested in when we look at what might be called a stupid style.

It is crucial to note that stupidity and error are distinct from one another but share an integral relationship in style. Mina Shaughnessy's study of error (1979) opened up grace and space for learning rather than perfect performance, yet we still push toward a kind of common correctness. There are still basic, originary claims about error from now classic essays like David Bartholomae's "The Study of Error" (1980). What is an error anyway? We know that a misstep in writing either comes from one of two mistakes: not noticing (or caring to notice) or not knowing. Either a writer misspells something because of an unintentional slip (what we commonly call a typo, short for typographical error) or the writer did not know the rule they were breaking in the first place. Alternatively, the choice could be intentional. We know from quantitative research studies that the most frequent error used to be misspellings; now because of spell-checker technology, it's merely using the wrong word (see Lunsford and Lunsford 2008). Andrea Lunsford and Robert Connors's early study about how errors are perceived shows which errors are especially stigmatized—with things like the double negative topping the list (1988). Ain't no particular reason for it exactly, but the double negative is perceived as especially stupid, even though it has a long history that goes back to Old English, where it was used for emphasis (see Pîrvu 2014). We see chopped language resulting in fragmentation, but this form has been noted for having its own effectiveness by Winston Weathers, who referred to intentional fragments as crots under the framework of Grammar B in *An Alternate Style* (1980). Sturm and Turner (2014, 139) call this approach to writing erratological or embracing pluralities, which admits *humanum est errare*.

Peter Elbow confesseses in a brief piece on his book *Vernacular Eloquence* called "Maybe Academics Aren't So Stupid after All" (2013), "I want to explore the wisdom revealed by incoherence itself." In the actual book Elbow discusses how academic writing too can come off sounding stupid. He admits, "[T]he intonational wind usually goes out of our voice if we feel that others will criticize us or think we're stupid or make us feel unsafe in some other way" (2012, 244). He discusses trusting your inner voice or your ear, and then you will be mostly correct and not make "the kind of glairing mistake that gets the writer seen as stupid or grossly illiterate" (271). Meanwhile, if we think back to the politics of Elbow's vernacular, we see something else in particular. He talks about, for example, Black and Latinx students being called stupid when they make writing moves in alignment with their own cultural dialects (4). The intersectional identity politics of stupidity—particularly tied to correctness in writing—is not without some glaring (ine)qualities. We see stupidity tied to disability (even in the history of the usage of the word dumb) or tied to race, or sex, or class, or age. To this very point, Vershawn Ashanti Young famously reacts against Stanley Fish "teachin mo standard grammar and stuff," which leads to the perception that "dialects are dumb" (2010, 112). They aren't.

So, we know in composition studies that there has been an informed history of rightly overlooking lower-order concerns to pay heed to the main idea of a message. It's worth mentioning, then, how stupidity and error have been mis-conflated. Still, some see grammatical missteps as the equivalent of an embarrassing or stigmatized faux pas, like having spinach in your teeth (see Brockenbrough 2008, 5). Still, we might think about risking sounding dumb to do something spectacular. According to Brian Massumi in his study of affect, "This means you have to be prepared for failure. For with inattention comes risk of silliness or even outbreaks of stupidity. But perhaps in order to write experimentally, you have to be willing to 'affirm' even your own stupidity" (2002, 18). The potential for affect, both positive and negative, is quite expansive. We have also seen, for example, students feel jarringly stupid with harsh or critical commentary in the margins of their writing (see Taggart and Laughlin 2017, 6, 11). Meanwhile, stylistic renegade Victor Vitanza is known for embracing his typos:

I love typos. I turn off my spell-checker in Microsoft Word because I want those typos there. And then they get published, and editors usually have to tell the person who's, you know, going through the manuscript to try to fix it up, "Don't change any of those words! That's what Vitanza wants." And in fact Janice Walker, she—in the front of an article published in *Computers and Composition*, that journal—she had in all caps at the very top, "There are no typos in Victor Vitanza's article." In other words, they're there, but they're not typos. It's what I want. What is it that language wants? It's going back to that. (2014)

In some ways, from Theophrastus and Vitanza, the question of style and stupidity returns to the question of the will to control language.

EXAMPLES OF STUPID RHETORICAL STYLES

Our primary touchpoint example here is still the *u*. These forms that are stigmatized (I confess I have paused at seeing a u^7 in a student's paper) have their own agency, purpose, and effects. How do we respond to an out-of-place *u*, and when is a *u* out of place, if ever?[8] But we have seen simplification and mistakes being made in writing before. It is a stylistic signifier of young children's writing. The style is so codified that it can be performed as such:

> DERE MOM,
> I HOP U HAV A BOOTIFUL DAY TOMROE. U R SOO SPESHULL 2 ME.
> LOVE,
> UR FAVRITE KID

The innocence and linguistic ignorance that children perform in their writing embody a kind of stupidity or surface-level ignorance, even though we would not call a developing child writer stupid at all. Still, stylistically, we find these features in other places with intended or unintended effects.

More relevantly, perhaps, we can look to Twitter for a host of stylistic examples. Twitter is an interesting site for studying the development of various stylistic qualities of contemporary writing. Director Werner Herzog calls Twitter stupid. Dr. James Whittaker of Microsoft calls Twitter stupid. Actor George Clooney calls Twitter stupid. What are they talking about? Let's work through a few popular Twitter users as examples: Donald Trump, Chuck Grassley, and Cher. I might point out that each of these exemplars is over sixty, while several people of a certain age continue to decry the vices of young people's writing.

Donald Trump is often lambasted for what sounds a lot like stupid language use. But he is willing to return the name-calling, using the classic ad hominem fallacy, having referred to several victims as stupid over the years on Twitter including Barack Obama, Hillary Clinton, Bill Clinton, Bill Maher, Michelle Malkin, *New York Times*, the left, the Republican Party, a step, and the American people, among others. Trump has gained notoriety, as did George W. Bush, for sounding stupid as the president of the United States. Bush famously pronounced nuclear as *nucular*, which is a sort of *epenthesis*, or inserting a syllable.[9] Trump has been widely mocked for ending a tweet with a nonsense word, *covfefe*, or for long, untamed diatribes that are confusing to follow. Ryan Skinnell (2018), Edward Schiappa (in Goldhill 2017), and others have done thorough analyses of Trump's stupid-sounding rhetoric. But Trump himself is also obsessed with stupidity and with making sure that he doesn't appear stupid and that others do—a common rhetorical approach when trying to attack and defeat an opponent and show them that they're stupid. Of course, immediately whenever you start playing this particular game, it can backfire quickly.

Donald J. Trump
@realDonaldTrump

Following

Sorry losers and haters, but my I.Q. is one of the highest -and you all know it! Please don't feel so stupid or insecure, it's not your fault

9:37 PM - 8 May 2013

Ignoring the missing space after the comma, it is significant to note that when one protests their own non-stupidity, or even calls others stupid, one can come across as stupid-sounding themselves. Trump's doth protest too much in quips like: "I'm intelligent. Some people would say I'm very, very, very intelligent" (Useem 2000). The hyperbolic is often associated with the stupid because it is childlike and unreserved, or immature. Figures associated with these sorts of stupid-sounding gestures are *bomphiologia*, *bombast*, or *hyperbole*. Overuse of the exclamation point is often associated with stupidity, or air-headedness, and as a result is often discouraged in formal, academic writing!

Looking Forward to a Nice, Stupid, Future Style. R U? 123

Donald J. Trump ✓
@realDonaldTrump

Following

After having written many best selling books, and somewhat priding myself on my ability to write, it should be noted that the Fake News constantly likes to pore over my tweets looking for a mistake. I capitalize certain words only for emphasis, not b/c they should be capitalized!

7:13 PM - 3 Jul 2018

Of course, Trump, like so many, has misspelled a number of words along the way including the words *tap, has, unprecedented, peace, too, honored, counsel, Barack,* and *pore* (Abadi 2018; Ritschel 2018; Fernando 2018). For these blunders, Trump has caught flak from many, including notably J. K. Rowling, who gave us the Harry Potter books. Interestingly, Rowling has deployed an intentional stupid style as a mocking response.

> **J.K. Rowling** @jk_rowling
>
> A mug of tea, a black ink pen, Big Red chewing gum, a West Highland Terrier and something stupid Trump said.
>
> > hannah f. whitten @hwhittenwrites
> > What 5 items would someone put in a salt circle to summon you
> >
> > Mine are chocolate covered cashews, indie perfume samples, a historical romance book, a fall-themed candle, and a cardigan
>
> 4:10 AM - 6 Sep 2018

Rowling playfully misspells "Gratest" as a cheeky rejoinder to Trump's self-aggrandizing tweet, later corrected. The other tweet from Rowling here shares something interesting: that she seems to almost savor and revel in Trump's stupidity. Stupidity provides pleasure in the kind of humoring that comes from superiority, incongruity, and our collective social anxieties. Lastly, it is interesting to note that while stupidity is still something to be fixed, Trump continues to correct his tweets to avoid further condemnation. The will to correct is further pushed by Twitter accounts like @Trumps_Editors, which tauntingly post tweets that correct Trump.

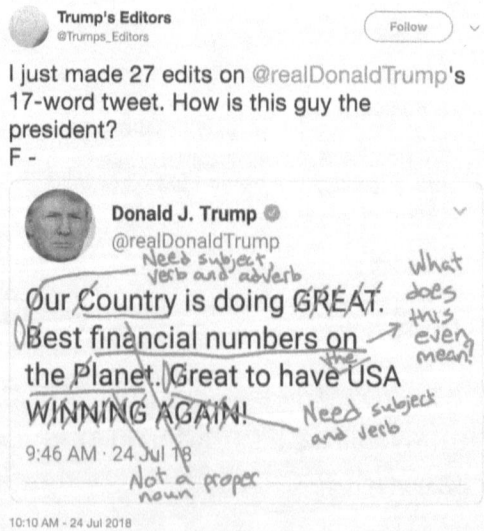

Again, this will to correct, to tease and taunt, is wrapped up in a stance against stupidity, which I certainly understand. But stupidity in the form of grammatical and spelling constructions is not the worst quality of this presidency. I tend to agree with Casey Boyle, who tweets, "Of all the BREAKING NEWS caused by this *President, his unsure grasp of spelling and grammar is not one of them. I humbly request we reroute our energies accordingly." Misspellings are easy to critique, but an *it's* for an *its* is not what troubles me most about Trump, or anyone else for that matter.

Exhibit B is Iowa senator Chuck Grassley. The senator's early tweets as examples of heavy, stupid-sounding abbreviations and modifications are par excellence with what some older fuddy-duddies are worried about in young people writing online. Grassley is not young, but he's certainly making the same moves that raise eyebrows of some conditioned, prescriptive writing sentinels of an older era.

ChuckGrassley ✓
@ChuckGrassley

Michele Obama in DsMoines to fight obesity Good Tell the Pres to bk off stupid child farm labor rules Farm children workin at home is good

9:32 AM - 9 Feb 2012

ChuckGrassley ✓
@ChuckGrassley

Constituents askd why i am not outraged at PresO attack on supreme court independence. Bcause Am ppl r not stupid as this x prof of con law

11:51 AM - 7 Apr 2012

Here, Grassley's critiques are evident, and mostly grammatically comprehensible (although I definitely have to pause to work some things out), despite not following the conventions of Standard Edited English. Dropping letters like *e* from DesMoines, the *g* from working, or even the *l* from Michelle (which is just a blatant misspelling of a proper noun), missing punctuation, a lack of some capitalization, or letters replacing words such as *r* for *are*. These would be egregious errors in a freshman composition essay but are unflinchingly at home here. Grassley, despite his style, is interested in who is stupid and takes strong rhetorical stances in these public posts. But it's easy to bash the stylistic missteps of those with whom you might disagree. The surface tension created by lower-order concerns becomes a mere distraction from really troublesome content. It is critical to look past Trump's and Grassley's stupid spelling errors to what really matters.

The most significant error in the Trump and Grassley examples is that their stupidity is not admitted or owned. They still falsely take the stance of homo sapiens, wise guys, the oh-so-smart. As such, the stupidity is inexcusable because it is present but unacknowledged. To return to Ronell's work, she suggests there is only one ethical stance: "I am stupid before the other" (2003, 60). As such, stupidity sticks with condemnation only when it is not confessed and remains at the outskirts of repression and power positioning and posturing. To be stupid is natural; to pretend not to be stupid is the only fault.

Contrarily, Cher has gained some notoriety, after the height of her singing career, for her awesomely bad use of Twitter. She owns it. In the two examples below, Cher makes similar moves to Grassley and Trump, using illogical spacing, capitalization, and abbreviations. Still, she makes two profound statements about stupidity and language use.

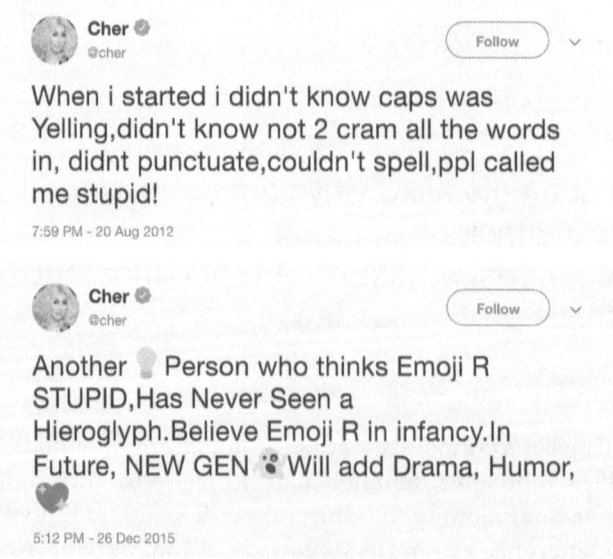

In the first tweet, Cher offers insights into conventions and why she was called stupid and then pushes three years later into an observant critique about rhetorical forms—that emoji are legitimate, and non-stupid, devices. Cher embodies here the savvy and indulgent lovable space cadet who doesn't mind flying in the face of social expectations. She is part of the NEW GEN, adding to the conversation about language expectation and what it can do if we let go.

To add one more example, Kanye West tweeted erratically in working up to his latest project with some ironic insight: "We're trying new ideas without the fear of not being perfect . . . It's just a gut feeling sometimes . . . just making stuff with your friends . . ." West's cover art for the album *Ye* contains its own brash misuse of the wrong *its* and an unnecessarily strange hyphenation of bipolar, reading "I hate being Bi-Polar its awesome" [*sic*].

Kanye has received his fair share of critique for his support of Trump, but also for his erratic style. Don Lemon, a CNN news anchor, has called Kanye West "not very bright" (Schwartz 2018), while Kanye's self-image is alternately wrapped up in being a genius and humbly attempting to let everything go. West's cleverness with language has traditionally pushed hip-hop in new directions. As Eric House extols us, hip-hop "invites an inscrutable style" (chapter 8). In the push toward difference, the off-ness of a twisted line might find something at home in new territory. The title of one track on West's album, "No Mistakes," seems to embrace the signature rejection of judgment that leans toward a very open space of compositional freedom. Is Kanye stupid? It may not even matter.

When we have millionaires and influencers making linguistic constructions that some might call stupid, it's time to pay attention. Stupidity is increasingly interwoven into our technological composing practices. We've embraced an external, virtual knowledge, accessing and processing language in memory databanks so that our heads are *in the cloud*. There is no such thing as forgetfulness, just good and bad access and recall. You can have everything and not know anything. We have the internet to hold our knowledge for us, so we've given ourselves permission to be stupid there. Instead of artificial intelligence, we need to consider the construction of artificial stupidity. Perhaps stupid memes or internet trolls playing dumb and provoking responses might be clever exemplars here. Meanwhile, simplifying gestures even happen in naming large companies, from Flickr to Tumblr, mimicking the gross simplification of digital language. The name Google is itself an intentional misspelling of the word *googol*.

Why does anyone unintentionally make public mistakes? The answer is simple: inattention, imperfect knowledge, and information overload. We're starting to glitch out as writers. We don't have the time or energy or resources to write perfectly 100 percent of the time, and it would be inefficient to try to. As Kenneth Burke suggests in his definition of humanity, we are "rotten with perfection" (1968, 16). Mistakes are still the worst thing you can make.[10] Blundering is barred. Academic writing and public discourse have shifted toward increasingly divergent models of stylistic forms, yet stupid moves remain sites of harassment and possibility.

WHY AND HOW: A VIEW TOWARD THE USES AND BENEFITS OF STUPID STYLE

Perhaps two reasons that make the future of style lean toward these perceived stupid stylistic moves are a shift in technology and a shift in attention economy. Plato thought that the technology of writing itself would make us more stupid, but now we have multiplied those technologies in texting, emailing, and tweeting. Nicholas Carr's now widely anthologized essay asks us to consider "Is Google Making Us Stupid?"

(2008). I am not advocating a reductionist technological determinism about the future of style. When people abbreviate or drop entire words, spaces, or punctuation to meet length requirements of a text or tweet, they can come across as sounding stupid. Friedhelm Hillbrand thought that 160 characters was "perfectly sufficient" when developing a length for SMS on a typewriter (Milian 2009). We negotiate our forms with the tools we use.

As we explore the stupidity that arises in and is made possible by various media platforms, we are essentially arriving at a study of *cacology*. While Ancient Greeks would have said that *kakologia* was a slanderer, a misuser of language, we can broaden the term to reflect its parts. *Cacologia* is shitty, faulty, poor, defective language. Embracing stupidity sometimes happens with punk or low forms of composition, with bands like Slightly Stoopid or Elliot Smith's raspy "Stupidity Tries."

How might we begin to think of what might be termed a stupid style productively?[11] If we embrace what might seem like error, then we are able to move past certain kinds of judgments that occur about language's imperfect deployment. Language will always be deployed imperfectly, stupidly. One day, when we finally accept this, we can be kinder to each other as more hospitable audiences of language. As such, a stupid style offers efficiencies, resistances, and sites of invention or thinking otherwise. In light of these tensions, we may feel as though we are at a standstill as we look toward the future of style. We are naturally stupid about the future, but we can begin to make some hypotheses. As such, we can reconsider another originary meaning of the term *stupid*, which is to be struck, to be overcome by feeling full of awe and amazement. Stupidity resides at this central tension of having the sense knocked into or out of an affected brain.

Let me confess my own stance. I don't think anyone is really stupid. Sometimes I feel really stupid, which doesn't feel very good. There is what is perceived as stupidity, often as it appears in language by a judging other. I want to reify whatever seems stupid—with particular attention to different rhetorical language uses—to the judgmental types. So, the call in my title, to love a *nice*, stupid future style, is about moving forward to embrace what has been discredited as deficient. We may call future style stupid from this side of history, but then we won't. Eventually, we will arrive at a world without error, not because we won't misstep, but because those erratic trifles won't matter. We may finally, one day, look past our stupidity with kindness and embrace a more perfect view of pluralities and possibility.

NOTES

1. would like to thank the Teaching and Learning Collaborative at LSU for providing writing support for faculty during the summer of 2018, during which I finished the first draft of this chapter.
2. I have come to the conclusion that I am most often at home while writing with my tongue in my cheek.
3. See Brookshire 2013, which states that most Americans believe the impossible: that they have above average intelligence.
4. I want to acknowledge that while Ronell has become enmeshed in some questions of propriety publicly *after* I had begun writing this chapter, I do still, however, find her work especially relevant here. I have decided to continue citing her in the same fashion that we continue to cite many white men who have made stupid choices.
5. *English Grammar for Dummies* is a real book.
6. See Mcfarlane 2012 for an especially strong consideration of how decorum and delivery works, with special attention to racialized identity.
7. The second person is generally considered to be the stupidest-sounding of the three points of view.
8. See FLOTUS's coat worn on June 21, 2018.
9. See Edbauer 2004, which notes the "strong rhetorical accounts of Bush's surprising popularity in the face of his public stupidity." Also, you can use the Internet Archive Wayback Machine to see Jenny Edbauer's blog, *Stupid Undergrounds*, which won the 2004 Kairos Award for Best Academic Blog.
10. See Sir Ken Robinson's discussion of this topic in his TED talk on education, "Do Schools Kill Creativity?" https://www.ted.com/talks/sir_ken_robinson_do_schools_kill_creativity?language=en.
11. See the wonderful one-page article by Martin A. Schwartz in *The Journal of Cell Science*, "The Importance of Stupidity in Scientific Research" (2008).

REFERENCES

Abadi, Mark. 2017. "Trump and His White House Have Made Some Embarrassing Spelling Mistakes—Here Are the Worst Ones." *Business Insider*. November 30, 2017. https://www.businessinsider.com/trump-typos-spelling-tweets-unpresidented-2018-4.

Azuike, Macpherson Nkem. 1992. "Style: Theories and Practical Application." *Language Sciences* 14 (1–2): 109–127.

Barthelme, Donald. 1997. "Not-Knowing." In *Not Knowing: The Essays and Interviews of Donald Barthelme*, edited by Kim Herzinger, 11–24. New York: Vintage.

Bartholomae, David. 1980. "The Study of Error." *College Composition and Communication* 31 (3): 253–269.

Berne, Eric. 1996. *Games People Play*. New York: Ballantine Books.

Brockenbrough, Martha. 2008. *Things That Make Us (Sic): The Society for the Promotion of Good Grammar Takes on Madison Avenue, Hollywood, the White House, and the World*. New York: St. Martin's Press.

Brookshire, B. R. 2013. "The Superiority Illusion: Where Everyone Is above Average." *Scientific American*. https://blogs.scientificamerican.com/scicurious-brain/the-superiority-illusion-where-everyone-is-above-average/.

Burke, Kenneth. 1968. *Language as Symbolic Action: Essays on Life, Literature and Method*. Berkeley: University of California Press.

Butler, Paul. 2008. *Out of Style: Reanimating Stylistic Study in Composition and Rhetoric*. Logan: Utah State University Press.

Carr, Nicholas. 2008. "Is Google Making Us Stupid?" *The Atlantic.* June 13, 2018. https://www.theatlantic.com/magazine/archive/2008/07/is-google-making-us-stupid/306868.

Cipolla, Carlo M. 1976. *The Basic Laws of Human Stupidity.* Bologna: The Mad Millers.

Connors, Robert J., and Andrea Lunsford. 1988. "Frequency of Formal Errors in Current College Writing, or Ma and Pa Kettle Do Research." *College Composition and Communication* 39 (4): 395–409.

Crowley, Sharon, and Debra Hawhee. 2004. *Ancient Rhetorics for Contemporary Students,* 3rd ed. New York: Pearson/Longman.

Detweiler, Eric. 2018. "The Weirdness of Rhetoric, the Rhetoric of Weirdness." *Textshop Experiments* 5. http://textshopexperiments.org/textshop05/weirdness-of-rhetoric.

Edbauer, Jenny. 2004. "Executive Overspill: Affective Bodies, Intensity, and Bush-in-Relation." *Postmodern Culture* 15 (1). doi: 10.1353/pmc.2004.0037.

Elbow, Peter. 2012. *Vernacular Eloquence.* New York: Oxford University Press.

Elbow, Peter. 2013. "Maybe Academics Aren't So Stupid after All." OUPblog. https://blog.oup.com/2013/02/academic-speech-patterns-linguistics/.

Fernando, Gavin. 2018. "Trump Mocked over Spelling Error | Morning Bulletin." The Bulletin. July 4, 2018. https://www.themorningbulletin.com.au/news/awkward-spelling-error-in-donald-trumps-tweent-abou/3458657/.

Flusser, Vilém. 2011. *Does Writing Have a Future?* Minneapolis: University of Minnesota Press.

Goldhill, Olivia. 2017. "Rhetoric Scholars Pinpoint Why Trump's Inarticulate Speaking Style Is So Persuasive." *Quartz.* April 22, 2017. https://qz.com/965004/rhetoric-scholars-pinpoint-why-trumps-inarticulate-speaking-style-is-so-persuasive.

Halberstam, Judith. 2011. *The Queer Art of Failure.* Durham, NC: Duke University Press.

Innes, Doreen. 1985. "Theophrastus and the Theory of Style." In *Theophrastus of Eresus: On His Life and Work,* ed. W. W. Forenbaugh, P. M. Huby, and A. A. Long, 251–268. New Brunswick, NJ: Rutgers University Press.

Kant, Immanuel. 2000. *The Critique of Pure Reason.* New York: Cambridge University Press.

Lunsford, Andrea A., and Karen J. Lunsford. 2008. "Mistakes Are a Fact of Life: A National Comparative Study." *College Composition and Communication* 59: 781–806.

Massumi, Brian. 2002. *Parables for the Virtual.* Durham, NC: Duke University Press.

Mcfarlane, Nicole. 2012. "The Racial Rhetoric of Cuteness as Decorative Decorum." PhD dissertation, Clemson University, Clemson, SC.

Milian, Mark. 2009. "Why Text Messages Are Limited to 160 Characters." *Los Angeles Times.* May 3, 2009. http://latimesblogs.latimes.com/technology/2009/05/invented-text-messaging.html.

Perelman, Chaïm, and Lucie Olbrechts-Tyteca. 1971. *The New Rhetoric.* South Bend, IN: University of Notre Dame Press.

Pinker, Steven. 2014. "Why Academics' Writing Stinks." *The Chronicle of Higher Education.* September 26, 2014.

Pîrvu, Paula. 2014. "Means of Expressing Negative Intensification in English." In *Language and Literature: European Landmarks of Identity,* 204–213. Selected Papers of the 11th Conference of the Faculty of Letters. Pitesti: University of Pitesti Press. http://www.diacronia.ro/ro/indexing/details/A14564/pdf.

Pitkin, Walter. 1932. *A Short Introduction to the History of Human Stupidity.* New York: Simon and Schuster.

Ritschel, Chelsea. 2018. "Chris Evans Corrects 'Moronic' Donald Trump's Spelling on Twitter." The Independent. August 22, 2018. https://www.independent.co.uk/news/world/americas/chris-evans-trump-concel-tweet-jk-rowling-twitter-counsel-spelling-a8503106.html.

Ronell, Avital. 2003. *Stupidity.* Urbana: University of Illinois Press.

Schwartz, Ian. 2018. "Don Lemon: Kanye West 'Not Very Bright.'" *Real Clear Politics*. August 30, 2018. https://www.realclearpolitics.com/video/2018/08/30/don_lemon_kanye_west_not_very_bright.html.

Schwartz, Martin A. 2008. "The Importance of Stupidity in Scientific Research." *The Journal of Cell Science* 121: 1771. doi: 10.1242/jcs.033340.

Shaughnessy, Mina P. 1979. *Errors and Expectations*. New York: Oxford University Press.

Sheils, Merill. 1975. "Why Johnny Can't Write." *Newsweek*, December 8, 1975.

Skinnell, Ryan, ed. 2018. *Faking the News: What Rhetoric Can Teach Us about Donald J. Trump*. Societas: Essays in Political and Cultural Criticism. Exeter: Imprint Academic.

Stiegler, Bernard. 2013. *What Makes Life Worth Living: On Pharmacology*. Cambridge: Polity Press.

Stiegler, Bernard. 2015. *States of Shock: Stupidity and Knowledge in the 21st Century*. Cambridge: Polity Press.

Sturm, Sean, and Stephen Francis Turner. 2014. "Erratology and the Ill-Logic of the Seismotic University." *Educational Philosphy and Theory* 46 (7): 1–11.

Swift, Jonathan. 1843. *The Works of Jonathan Swift*, vol II. London: W. Clowes and Sons.

Taggart, Amy Rupiper, and Mary Laughlin. 2017. "Affect Matters: When Writing Feedback Leads to Negative Feeling." *International Journal for the Scholarship of Teaching and Learning* 11 (2): 1–11.

Theophrastus. 2015. *The Characters*. Translated by Charles E. Bennett and William A. Hammond. Victoria: Leopold Classic Library.

Useem, Jerry. 2000. "What Does Donald Trump Really Want?" *Fortune*. April 3, 2000. http://fortune.com/2000/04/03/what-does-donald-trump-really-want/.

Vitanza, Victor. 2014 "Vitanzing." *Zeugma*. Podast audio. https://zeugma.dwrl.utexas.edu/vitanzing.html.

Weathers, Winston. 1980. *An Alternate Style: Options in Composition*. Rochelle Park, NJ: Hayden Book Co.

Young, Vershawn Ashanti. 2010. "Should Writers Use They Own English?" *International Journal of Communication Systems* 12: 110–117.

8
METAPHORICAL TRANSLINGUALISMS
The Hip-Hop Cipher as Stylistic Concept

Eric A. House

In a piece that identifies the stylistic flexibility and nuance within hip-hop nation language practices, H. Samy Alim unpacks the strategic usage of black discursive modes within hip-hop (2012). He touches on six specific modes (call and response, multilayered totalizing expression, signifying, tonal semantics, narrative sequencing, battling), dissecting each to illustrate their generative potential in language practices. Alim's investigation of hip-hop-based language practices offers stylistic inquiry insights on the roles of culture and identification in the effects and applications of style. But there must first be a discussion concerning the epistemologies that foreground hip-hop language practices if they are to realize the potential presented by Alim and impact the study of style within the contexts of composition studies. Otherwise, we run the risk of cultural erasure and appropriation by forcing hip-hop styles to be defined according to the logics of non-hip-hop discourses.

One discussion that might lead toward a critical understanding and application of hip-hop style begins with the cipher, a space that encourages stylistic difference in a pursuit of effective and engaging communication. Udelson (chapter 13) similarly argues for difference within future studies and applications of style, claiming that an emphasis on difference in style might afford occasions for meaningful engagement through a questioning of static conventions and rigid disciplinary lines.

This chapter utilizes the metaphor of the hip-hop cipher to argue for a translingual conception of style within rhetoric and composition that is informed by audience interaction and authorial improvisation. I draw from translingualism as a guiding theory for languaging within composition to investigate the hip-hop cipher as a space where style is informed through interactions among performers and observers, and as a space where style is informed through skillful and purposeful moments of improvisation. I illustrate the cultural and pedagogical potential in realizing a translingual perception and definition of style through the emphasis on the possibilities of interactivity and improvisation within the hip-hop cipher.

I contend that the hip-hop cipher offers an image of a space that invites an inscrutable style. Hip-hop ciphers are spaces of fluidity, where varieties of identities frequently come into contact with one another with the purpose of performing and existing. Difference is anticipated in hip-hop ciphers—in fact, difference is praised. Participants are not measured on their ability to satisfy a norm or perform within the expectations. Rather, participants are constantly on the search for the new wave, the new rhyme scheme or metaphor that no one has thought of before. They constantly search for the new move, the new step or break that one has not thought to make. One cannot package the same performance and take it to different ciphers, nor can they get away with blatantly copying another's style. The cipher offers style a workable metaphor of translingualism as it approaches performance from a perspective that anticipates difference without a necessity of evaluating or undifferentiating that difference.

My argument for and illustration of a translingual conception of style is situated within discourses of translingualism that describe difference as the norm in language practice (Lu and Horner 2013). Flexibility and resourcefulness are key functions in this approach in that translingualism boasts an ability to treat words as resources that help one achieve communicative and social objectives (Canagarajah 2013). I also situate my argument within a hip-hop rhetorical tradition, one that recognizes hip-hop as a valuable and generative space where discourses and language practices are continually negotiated (Petchauer 2012). Such negotiations rely on consistent interactions among audience and context and understand that these identifiers are not static and, as such, require an approach to discourse that is similarly fluid in its approach (Pennycook 2007).

Approaching style from the intersections of hip-hop and translingualism allows a few considerations to shine. For one, it ties style to aspects of identity and subjectivity and suggests that style isn't just a packaging of language but a continued performance of language. It also asks that style have an element of inscrutability to it, which would mean that we assume the various styles that students already enter with cannot always be assessed or comprehended according to institutionalized ways of knowing. As Jerry Won Lee argues, inscrutability as an epistemology might come with a certain level of uneasiness or negativity, but when perceived as an epistemology, it promotes a critical openness through a refusal to be read according to the constraints of a dominant ideology (2018). Difference can then be anticipated, and when difference is contacted, there is no rush to evaluate or undifferentiate difference (Lee 2018). An emphasis on an inscrutable style in rhetoric and composition might then teach us the nuances of difference and its impacts on the flows and movements in theories and pedagogies of writing.

SETTING UP THE CIPHER

Before breaking down and theorizing the cipher and its potential in stylistic studies, I would like to take a brief moment to provide some definitions of the cipher. Michael Newman describes ciphers as existing strictly within the realm of rapping, naming them to be an improvised round-robin session where participants spit rhymes over beats, beatboxes, or a capella (2005). H. Samy Alim similarly focuses on rap as central to the cipher, stating it to be a linguistic training field for MCs (2012). He defines it to be the space where "hip-hop cultural modes of discourse and discursive practices . . . converge into a fluid matrix of linguistic-cultural activity" (2012, 552). Both Alim and Newman recognize that there exists some form of competition within ciphers, but through that competition rests an opportunity for all participants to improve and develop their crafts.

I depart slightly from Alim's and Newman's definitions of ciphers by suggesting that ciphers are not exclusive to rap. I have both been involved in and witnessed a variety of ciphers that included the other traditional hip-hop pillars. I have seen DJs go back and forth, showcasing their ability to juggle beats, scratch, and loop sounds in manners that illustrated their creativity and individuality. I have witnessed b-girls and b-boys breaking to the beat, flipping and spinning their way through awes and applause. I have seen graffiti artists illustrate their capacity to transform a simple wooden slab into a vibrant collection of colors and tags. I have been in both formal and informal spaces where scholars and intellectuals have shared ways in which hip-hop shapes their professional lives, whether that be the classroom, the community center, or corporate America. And I would argue that each of those spaces resembled the function of the cipher named by Alim and Newman. All of those spaces required a level of improvisation, flexibility, and interactivity. All of those spaces allowed the identity of the participants to shine as they existed while being contested through the interactions and connections with others who were simultaneously existing and performing. The idea of the cipher as a linguistic training field sounds exciting, but I propose a more spacious definition to account for a multitude of methods so that other ways of knowing and being can all impact the cipher. Besides, if the cipher is perceived as a linguistic training field, then one can argue that the languages of the turntable, the spray can, and the body inform a hip-hop language to the same capacity as that of rap, making the cipher a space where all discourses that inform hip-hop might come into contact with others.

I wish to draw from this definition of the cipher as a fluid and contested discursive training field in order to contemplate ways in which an inscrutable style might be imagined. It is important to first note that this approach to style and composition should not be thought of as a trendy lesson or assignment that an instructor could implement to showcase a desire to connect with students whose language practices have been peripheralized. Similar to Lee, I am instead arguing for theoretical approaches that, when brought into the classroom, function from a place that transforms perceptions of pedagogy itself or, in other words, translanguage pedagogy itself (Lee 2018). The idea of an inscrutable style should be foundational in the class space as students and teachers all collectively enter the cipher. The instructor operates from a position in which their role is not necessarily to define and make normative the different styles that exist, nor is it their role to outline a formulaic, normative, or academic style. They enter the cipher just as vulnerable as any other participant, and at any given moment their own stylistic understanding can change when it comes into contact with the discourses that make up the space. As for the students, it isn't their job to try to mimic or conform to an imagined or idealized style, nor is it their responsibility to pander with some predetermined variety, switch, or mesh of codes. Rather, the cipher remixes style by requiring that students stay in a space of continual interaction, becoming sensitive to the moments when their performances might impact the discourse.

What, then, would be the implications of imagining the composition class space in a stylistically inscrutable manner? For one, it starts with an understanding that, while engaged in the cipher, neither the student nor the teacher operates hierarchically. I do not mean to suggest that neither the teacher nor students could magically operate outside of institutional power whenever they wished to do so. Judith Butler reminds us that such discursive politics shape us and our situations, and as such we do not take position or operate outside of them (Butler 1999). I do mean to suggest that, in terms of thinking through style in the classroom, a necessary prerequisite is that the class space functions through student-teacher interactions that prioritize the differences in perspectives and knowledges, recognizing that all interactions within the cipher will evoke movement and all contact in the cipher is generative.

To get more specific, the framing of the cipher requires that an instructor consider that styles and strategies must switch from student to student, class to class, semester to semester, year to year. It is not necessarily their job to define the specifics of and applications for a style, as much as it is their purpose to manage the interactions of the cipher. They too are participants, but teachers have a responsibility to be sensitive to the constraints of time and space that impede on any communicative act. As a metaphor, teachers might be considered DJs. They recognize constraints and they do have their own styles that add into the equation, but they also understand that the concept of style within a cipher unfolds through continual performances of those who inhabit a space. As DJs do, teachers should be paying attention to the styles that students bring to the class space, playing the type of tracks that a space needs to come alive, slowing it down if everyone needs a moment to chill, giving generative cues to performers yet similarly receiving cues to help the overall vibe. Translation: teachers need to know the manners in which students compose, consider the types of assignments and activities that might benefit students, consistently check in with students, and both give and receive feedback.

None of these practices is unique to hip-hop or translingual pedagogy. In fact, it would be more accurate to say that they come from legacies of feminist and critical pedagogies. I understand that evoking a potentially radical form of pedagogy that also demands increased labor from already overworked composition instructors might seem precarious. However, I might also add that as the exemplary culture in this chapter, hip-hop has never been described as a safe or static culture. Historically, any normalized or mainstream conception of hip-hop has always been met with extreme resistance and critique. It is from this same culture of resistance and critique that I present hip-hop to stylistic inquiry as I ask composition theorists and instructors, including myself, to stay open enough and imagine the peripheralized students who might benefit from pedagogies rooted in liberatory theories and practices.

Students are similarly purposed with vulnerability within their performances. The cipher will move and give back any energy that is given to it. If students wish to perform according to their instructors or the subjects that inhabit their disciplines, then the cipher will produce the occasion for it. If a student wishes to bring a performance of their home life, their history, or their culture, then the cipher will provide the occasion for that interaction as well. Regardless of a participant's purpose, the cipher reacts to interaction. This means that the cipher relies on the energy of its participant to function and will respond to any energy given to it. Putting forth a performance is a risky act as one cannot know the exact impact of or reaction to their performance. The cipher recognizes that risk, yet participants should not stagnate for fear of misstepping as the cipher doesn't demand perfection. It only asks that one performs according to their own identity and that one be willing to allow that performance to move and impact the energy in the cipher.

AN IMAGE OF STYLE IN THE CIPHER

I have attempted to define a frame of a pedagogy informed by the hip-hop cipher. It is one that asks all participants to subscribe to an epistemology of inscrutability, which means interactions refuse to be read according to the politics and logics of a normative discourse that has as its purpose the reading and undifferentiating of difference. It is now necessary to move the discussion to some imaginings of what specifically style looks like within the cipher, or within a pedagogical space informed by inscrutability. I offer a couple of considerations and want to state that in no way are my imaginings even close to an exhaustive list. One of my purposes with offering the hip-hop cipher as a metaphor for stylistics is that the emphasis on fluidity and inscrutability creates a critical openness that invites critique and reinvention. That purpose alone suggests that there needs to always remain more to say and more to critique. For the sake of moving the conversation, I propose a few options that are informed through hip-hop.

Style within the cipher is dependent on interactivity. A stylistically static composition, meaning one that was informed through a linear progression from invention to drafting to revision to evaluation, rarely offers an opportunity for students to revisit after an evaluation has been attached to it. As Alim (2012) suggests, the cipher is a training field of sorts, which is to say that one's composition in the cipher is never truly complete despite any form of evaluation coming into contact with it. Any evaluation within the cipher is nothing more than feedback that directly impacts the changes, shifts, and evolutions of style. And it must be noted that the evaluations within the cipher are not handed down through hierarchy. Evaluations within the cipher are communal, coming from a critical reading and analysis of the way one's composition in that moment connected to its purpose. But evaluation of a composition within the cipher is another step in the constant process of realizing style. In our current paradigms, style often stands in as an additive to the whole composition. One important consideration that hip-hop suggests is that the composition should remain open and interactive in order to give a glimpse into a fluid style.

Consider, for example, portfolio assignments that ask students to compile their work from a quarter or semester into a workable document highlighted with a reflection where students are tasked to argue the ways in which their work resembles outcomes and expectations placed on them. This type of assignment would appear to have as a purpose the opportunity for students to showcase cohesion and understanding for the overall purpose of the course through illustrating their ability to meet requirements. Stylistically speaking, this assignment assumes that students will be able to demonstrate an intimate understanding of the way to write as it was defined by their programming, in which case evaluation rests on students showing the areas where they have either failed or succeeded in defining themselves according to the outcome. Instead of measuring their style to a model, the cipher asks that style be defined through an investigation of the multiple moments of composing. The cipher isn't as much interested in students' ability to explicitly argue what they have learned at the end, especially as that learning relates to a normalized ideal. Rather, the cipher requires interactivity within each moment in order to provide opportunities to witness the ways in which styles unfold in all manners and directions. The style associated with the portfolio is then entirely dependent on marking the changes and switches across time and space, and not on an ability to argue understanding of an imagined ideal.

Tangible spaces within hip-hop exist that I think forward this specific type of interactivity. One accessible space that often functions as a digital cipher is a web space titled Genius, a forum where lyrics from numerous songs are posted and hyperlinked so that the community might annotate and discuss lyrics from their favorite tracks. Genius was originally a space where rap songs were exclusively annotated (its original name was Rap Genius), but it since has expanded to other genres and includes other features such as artist profiles and song deconstruction interviews in an attempt to become a larger music and media brand. The site itself offers plenty to consider in conversations concerning overall interactivity of texts and compositions, but I would like to focus on the core content of Genius and highlight the potential for the function of that content in reimagining style.

Genius provides a highly interactive space that organizes compositions by author or artist, and song lyrics are annotated by anyone who wishes to participate. Genius utilizes a ranking system based on past participation to differentiate levels of contributors that is slightly problematic in its desire to create hierarchies among contributors, to suggest one's comments might be more "correct" than another's simply because one contributes more. However, I think looking at the overall method utilized in Genius provides some insights worth considering.

By presenting each composition as an interaction, Genius invites a space that synthesizes stylistic analysis and evaluation. Annotations within Genius typically occur at a level of literal comprehension, with contributors tending to comment on what exactly a line in a song means, stopping the comment just before moving into a more analytical response. There are moments, however, where contributors hone in on the effects of a clever rhyme scheme or reference. It is the unpacking of these effects where the potential lies for style, as it opens up the effects for conversation. Contributors have a visible space to name what a specific move does for them, and the act of naming the effect is made available for further conversation. Style is then defined and negotiated through the interaction; all participants are invited to react and respond to the movements of the composition in a form that makes each and every word available for annotation.

Genius did not invent the technology for annotating writing. Any word processor can achieve the same function by utilizing commenting functions already embedded in the technology. Rather, Genius functions within legacies of hip-hop that appropriate technologies to achieve larger purposes, similar to the ways in which DJs tampered with the record player to keep the party going. By incorporating commenting and annotating functions with rap music, Genius is able to call attention to the ways in which styles are defined and negotiated by those who constantly interact and engage with the texts. Teachers might utilize technology similarly to invite interactivity within students' writing, focusing on the effects and movements of the writing through the conversations and reactions that the writing evokes. Style can then be evaluated by noting the ways in which readers react to the movements, which is to say that reader positionality cannot be ignored in evaluations of style. For that reason, formal stylistic evaluation might be difficult, even impossible, in an academic setting due to its subjective prerequisite. I then propose that a style dependent on interactivity exist in a place that invites assessment through reader reactions, negotiating how a specific type of person reacts to a specific type of style and stays separate from evaluative practices that place a definitive value on the composition. Stylistic success in this instance is in the fluid conversation, not the static evaluation. In the case of the portfolio assignment, student usage of style is assessed through the conversations surrounding the effects of their writing, rather than evaluated based on their abilities to match an outcome.

Style within the cipher is also dependent on improvisation. A stylistically static composition, meaning one that is predetermined based on imagined ideals of the audience and situation, cannot account for the movements and fluctuations that occur in ciphers. To account for these inevitable fluctuations, one's style must be able to read and react according to the shifts and changes in situations, meaning it must perform according to its purpose while simultaneously remaining open enough to revisit and remix.

Consider, for example, a research assignment in a composition class where students have to get familiar with the discourse that makes up a specific discipline, seeing how others go about structuring their arguments and eventually speaking their way into those arguments. This type of assignment would appear to have as one of its purposes the learning of styles and approaches to composing within a specific discourse. Students would then be expected to get familiar with the styles that make up a field, with the assumption that inhabiting a passive analyst role at first will lead to an understanding and application of a specific style. In the cipher the purpose and approach to this assignment gets shifted a little. Instead of first analyzing and eventually writing to a field or discipline, the cipher positions both students and teachers as already interior. Students are encouraged to bring anything they already know and feel about a discipline into their research as they ask questions of, provide solutions for, critique, and remix the sources that they researched. Teachers are encouraged to journey through the cipher with students, adding their own performances to the mix in order to further the movement and fluidity. The style associated with the research paper is then entirely dependent on the approach with which students maneuver into the discourse, picking and choosing the spots where they call out and critique, or where they connect and agree. The emphasis on style would then be on those maneuvers and not on the ability to match an imagined ideal. Melissa A. Goldwaithe (chapter 2) extends on the potential of audience-specific improvisations within conceptions of style, arguing that the image of the audience sets the parameters for what might be written and the manner in which it is composed.

This version of a cipher-inspired style is a little difficult to imagine playing out in the composition class space because of its ties to oral traditions that often are hard to negotiate. On one level, emphasizing a style based on improvisation is difficult in teaching composition in a formal class space because of the limits of alphanumeric text. A student can absolutely reflect on their writing afterward and be critical of the ways in which they attempted to write themselves into a discourse, but the unpredictability of the improvised encounter that evokes an occasion for a stylistic praxis is lost. The idea of the remix, however, might intervene in the (im)possibilities of improvisation within the context of the composition class space.

The concept of remix comes to mind as a method that students might wield in order to exhibit an improvisational style in the aforementioned research assignment. The remix is not a new concept, nor is it a concept whose function is unique to hip-hop; what I propose of the remix can alternatively be described as a revision. Hip-hop, however, presents the remix as a style within itself by repurposing, repackaging, and reinterpreting a text in order to shift its auras and effects (Banks 2011). Like other models utilized in composition, hip-hop performances are remixed for stylistic benefit. Typically, the overall message of the song stays the same. But a tweaked beat, a slightly shuffled hook, or a new verse extends the track in a way that promotes different effects that only could be imagined after acknowledging a prior moment of composing. The remix obtains part of its allure through an understanding of a text as a reworking of a prior composition. In this case, the improvisation of the track is found in the noticeable evolutions of the track.

Revision is then seen stylistically as a practice of anticipating and composing toward shifting contexts in order to express meaning. In the research assignment, students might take a draft of their assignment and remix their argument to fit shifting occasions and contexts, such as communicating their findings to family and friends versus a scholarly community. Evaluation could then lie in the metacognitive ability of the student as they explain the thought processes behind shifting their styles in anticipation of shifting contexts. Alternatively, they could blend improvisation with interaction, utilizing the communal approach in unpacking and analyzing both their own and classmates' remixes. Similar to what I stated about interactivity, there is nothing new about these strategies for improvisation through revision within composition. However, when approached from these hip-hop-inspired frames, we see examples of how conversations surrounding evaluation and analysis through interactivity, as well as conversations surrounding revision through improvisation, are considered stylistic through their emphasis on rhetorically expressed meaning.

CONSIDERATIONS

Of course, these two images of a hip-hop-cipher-based style would require further expansion, classification, clarification, and critique. I have implemented bits and pieces of these approaches in my own pedagogy concerning both research and portfolio work, and as a result I have experienced a general energy shift in the class in terms of working within these types of genres that often lead to stagnation. I also want to be sure in stating that a cipher-based approach to style is far from perfect, and in fact I would go as far as to say that the very epistemologies I name and attach to this approach work against naming any singular approach within the composition classroom. A translingual approach theoretically struggles against any practices of normalizing. That being the case, one cannot offer a translingual approach in a fashion that doesn't invite further critique. I offer the cipher as a potential metaphor for future pedagogical considerations of style, and in that offering I invite further conversations about both the benefits and limits.

The political realities of the classroom often dissuade instructors from inviting any epistemology that willfully requires an agreement to not know, to not be known, and to be ok with not ever really knowing. I have stated that this approach evokes a radical pedagogy, and such pedagogies are not enacted on a whim or without recognition of consequence. Yet, the realities of our institutions and of our lives demand a socially and politically cognizant pedagogy that can speak truth to the lives of all who encounter it. Something as seemingly small and simple as opening up discussions on what styles are legitimate in intellectual spaces can go quite a way in impacting our discursive capacities. Quite frankly, and for better or worse depending on whom you ask, such discussions are possibly the only reason why I find myself in this position having the audacity to write to and imagine a hip-hop-infused composition and education.

On another note, this discussion of style asks us to recognize that previous conceptions of style have never been neutral, that style—whether it is perceived as a dressing for thought, whether it is separated from function, or whether it is assumed to afford disciplinary access—has historically been situated in a field that is overly occupied with undifferentiating what is different. The hip-hop cipher teaches us strategies for existing in the difference, letting the difference exist as it is, and recognizing that, stylistically, things are only ever truly dope when they are different.

REFERENCES

Alim, H. Samy. 2012. "'Bring It to the Cypher': Hip-Hop Nation Language." In *"That's the Joint": The Hip-Hop Studies Reader*, edited by Murray Forman and Mark Anthony Neal, 530–583. New York: Routledge.

Banks, Adam J. 2011. *Digital Griots: African American Rhetoric in a Multimedia Age.* Carbondale: Southern Illinois University Press.

Butler, Judith. 1999. *Gender Trouble*, 2nd ed. New York: Routledge.

Canagarajah, Suresh. 2013. *Translingual Practice: Global Englishes and Cosmopolitan Relations.* New York: Routledge.

Lee, Jerry Won. 2018. *The Politics of Translingualism: After Englishes.* New York: Routledge.

Lu, Min-Zhan, and Bruce Horner. 2013. "Translingual Literacy, Language Difference, and Matters of Agency." *College English* 75 (6): 582–607.

Newman, Michael. 2005. "Rap as Literacy: A Genre Analysis of Hip-Hop Ciphers." *Text* 25 (3): 399–436.

Pennycook, Alastair. 2007. *Global Englishes and Transcultural Flows.* New York: Routledge.

Petchauer, Emery. 2012. *Hip-Hop Culture in College Students' Lives.* New York: Routledge.

SECTION 3

Style Forms Strategy

9

EXPECTATIONS OF EXALTATION
Formal Sublimity as a Prolegomenon to Style's Unbounded Future

Jarron Slater

If you are reading this, then you have felt the bodily demand for nourishment that insists on fulfillment. It feels like a strong urge to ingest physical sustenance, but it is also a demand and desire that cannot quite be fully expressed in language. It is, nevertheless, an impulse that is undeniably real. However, these corporal demands are not confined only to the feeling and the filling of physical appetites. In this chapter I describe generally their relationship to style. In sum, I consider stylistic demands for satisfaction and fulfilment, demands that are as formal as they are corporal. These demands, expectations, or appetites strongly influence rhetorical and stylistic acts experienced by writers and readers, speakers and listeners, and their study provides us with a glimpse of style's unbounded future.

So, within this context of somatic and stylistic desire and satisfaction, appetite and fulfilment, one might be reminded of a theory of emotional form found in both Virginia Tufte's and Richard Ohmann's work. Richard Ohmann argues that emotion enters prose in three ways—through persuasion, through self-expression, and through a doorway that is "almost beyond the power of language to describe" (Ohmann 1967, 410). This seemingly abysmal doorway, while it may be indescribable, can nevertheless be peered into when one looks at the power that the demands of completion in a sentence can have on readers. Ohmann states:

> As [a] sentence progresses, some of its demands are satisfied, others deferred, others complicated, and meanwhile new ones are created. But with the end of the sentence comes a kind of balance which results from something having been *said*. (410)

Virginia Tufte, however, states that with that description, Ohmann actually does a pretty good job of describing with language what he is trying to say (Tufte [1971] 2010, 160). Tufte then argues that emotion in prose is not entirely mysterious but is clearly based on syntax: indeed, it is the grammatical and syntactical patterns that "establish the 'demands for completion' and move us along until they are satisfied" (161). In other words, sentences and syntax, grammar and style, all have the capacity to create and fulfill desires and expectations.

This important conversation between Tufte and Ohmann happened during what Paul Butler called style's "Golden Age" (Butler 2008, 7). Butler, discussing Tufte's concept of emotional form, notes that it is a borrowing, "indirectly at least, from Kenneth Burke's concept of form as the creation and satisfying of a reader's appetite" (Butler 2010, 137). Butler invites readers to "see Burke 1968" and then states that "no one has reexamined that question recently" (2008, 144). If style is indeed undergoing a "mini-renaissance," as Tom Pace and others have shown (Pace 2013, 135; see also Duncan and Vanguri 2013; Holcomb and Killingsworth 2010; Butler 2010; Ray 2015), and if a renaissance is a way of seeing anew certain "Golden Age" texts, then it seems appropriate, even necessary, to reexamine Butler's (2008) question about Burke's concept of form.

Burke is certainly known for theories of identification and dramatism—as well as for a particularly idiosyncratic, and even mysterious, writing style—but he is not known generally for a holistic theory of style. Yet, scholars of style reference Burke as an important source for insights into the subject of style (see Fahnestock 2011; Holcomb and Killingsworth 2010; Johnson 2005). Or, to put it even more emphatically, and in the words of no less a champion of style than Richard Lanham, if one accepts Burke's theories of rhetoric, particularly dramatism, one must finally also acknowledge that "style is all there is" (Lanham 1976, 220). From that perspective, Burke, although often puzzling, will be crucial to the future of style.

But a reexamination of Butler's question about Burke's theory of form involves yet another mystifying writer. When Burke was finalizing *A Rhetoric of Motives*, he wrote in a private letter (see Beasley 2007) saying that Longinus's *On the Sublime* is a pivotal text in rhetoric studies. Yet, Longinus has historically been treated as a writer on poetics, aesthetics, and literary criticism, and the literature on him in that regard is immense (see Russell 1995 for a short bibliography). However, interest in Longinus as a rhetorical theorist—although scholars are unsure if "Longinus" is his actual name—has recently increased, particularly for scholars who see common ground between the too-oft-dichotomized realms of rhetoric and poetics (see Porter 2016; Halliwell 2011; Heath

2012; van Eck et al. 2012). Recently, other scholars have also looked to Longinus for insights into style (see Johnson 2003; Kurlinkus 2013; Fahnestock 2011). Meanwhile, Burke repeats over and over that *On the Sublime* is "the ideal text" for demonstrating the inseparability of rhetoric and poetics (Burke 1976, 63–64; 1951, 168n; see also Burke 1966, 305). For Burke, the term *poetics* is often used "as a synecdoche for aesthetic expression in general" (Clark 2015, 138). So, in this chapter I use the terms *aesthetics* and *poetics* as synonymous. In sum, a reexamination of Butler's reference to "Burke 1968" also means glancing toward Longinus and *On the Sublime*.

For the rest of this chapter, as I explore the relationship between form and the sublime, I argue for a concept of formal sublimity that creates expectations of mutual exaltation for both audience and speaker. While the notion of form involves the creating and fulfilling of expectations, desires, and appetites, the sublime simultaneously exalts audiences and speakers through their empowered, even enthymematic, cooperation with one another. Formal sublimity thus combines the theories of form and the sublime to invite speaker and audience to move toward fulfillment through participatory and emancipated cooperation. Instead of simply breaking down the all-too-common wall separating rhetoric and poetics, it instead presupposes that no wall should exist, thus providing an impetus for revealing that style's transdisciplinarity cannot be denied. Formal sublimity assumes a broad understanding of style that, far from confining style to a narrow "canon" of rhetoric, enables, by seeing the common ground between rhetoric and aesthetics, stylistic analysis from the smallest syllable to the very edges of the describable universe—and beyond.

FORM

So, let us consider Butler's invitation to "see Burke 1968" (Butler 2008, 144), a reference to a text that is the seed out of which all of Kenneth Burke's other work grew (see Wolin 2001, 6; Burke [1931] 1968, xi). That seed, first published in 1931, was named *Counter-Statement* and acts as a counter-statement, according to Jack Selzer, in three ways: first, it was a modernist reaction against esthetes who held an art-for-art's-sake mentality, who ignored rhetoric and the influence art has on society and on people, and who wrongly favored self-expression over communication; second, it countered those same moderns who rejected estheticism; third, as a text with self-contradictions, *Counter-Statement* is also a counter-statement to itself (see Selzer 1996). *Counter-Statement* is a rich source of material that will be increasingly important in the future of style, and I will hardly scratch the surface of that claim in this chapter. But I would like to provide a bit of an appetizer.

At the core of *Counter-Statement* is a highly specialized notion of form. Here, form is not merely a work's shape dichotomized from content. Rather, it emphasizes the interconnectedness between rhetoric and poetics, between art and communication, and between people and their symbolic acts. Form is a foundation for the appeal of written and spoken words. It is "an arousing and fulfillment of desires" (Burke [1931] 1968, 124). It is the creating and satisfying of appetites, the psychology of the audience (31), and "a way of experiencing" (143). Form is the making and keeping of a promise or even a covenant. Form may be likened unto a reader's dream, in which the dream's elements are controlled by the writer. Or think of a path extending forth through a shaded wood. As long as readers keep following the path, they also obey it (see Burke [1931] 1968, 142). Readers may get off the path—may stop reading—at any time. But writers meanwhile attempt to subtly show readers why they want to stay on the path. Thus, as Greig Henderson has stated, "The rhetoric of form not only has a suasive impact upon the audience; it also has a suasive impact, conscious or unconscious, upon the author. While we are using the formal, rhetorical, and ideological resources of language and literature, they are using us" (Henderson 2001, 140). So, form includes but is not limited to expectations or demands created and fulfilled by syntax or grammar. Its scope is even larger than that.

Form illustrates the inseparability between rhetoric and poetics. For symbol-using creatures, form includes the latent capacity to feel, to make sense of, and to appreciate a variety of arrangements, processes, attunements, and abstractions, including instances of contrast, alignment, repetition, balance, proximity, shape, antithesis, gradation, and so on (see Burke [1931] 1968, 46). These "innate forms of the mind" (46) are commonly given Greek and Latin names and called rhetorical figures, though they are also called rhetorical devices or formal patterns (Burke [1950] 1969). These "potentialities of appreciation" are rhetorical descriptions of aesthetic, or poetic, processes, since, as Gregory Clark recognizes, *poetics* is often used "as a synecdoche for aesthetic expression in general" (Clark 2015, 138). Formal patterns also make lines of argument (see Fahnestock 1999) in a variety of fields and disciplines, and they should be practical and not just embellishments. Another way to think about form's different but coexistent and cooperative realms of rhetoric and poetic can be found in T. R. Johnson's discussion of how "clarity" in style can be understood through the lens of rhythm (see Johnson, chapter 3).

THE SUBLIME

Many have sought to discover the sublime, and Longinus does not offer a single, straightforward definition of it. How could he, or anyone, define something that may actually be indefinable? Not only that, but an act of defining it might impose a definition onto something that otherwise resists definition. Rather, Longinus provides what perhaps amounts to a better way: he gives a plurality of statements about it and a plethora of examples that reach toward it; for it just may be that reaching toward it ourselves and helping others to discover it is often the best we can do. As James I. Porter states, Longinus did not compose *On the Sublime* to inform readers but to teach them how to produce sublimity for themselves (Porter 2016, 59). In addition, it should be noted that Longinus is not the innovator of the sublime (see Porter 2016), but his work does represent an important theoretical tradition.

The word *sublime* comes from the Latin *sublimare*, which means to place something in an elevated position. It can also refer to the act of exalting, elevating, or glorifying. The word *sublime* is used to translate a Greek term, *hupsos*, which refers to height, while an equivalent term, *megethos*, or "greatness," is frequently used as well (see Heath 2012, 12; cf. Grube [1957] 1991). Burke provides insightful commentary on this "key term," *hupsos*: while it is "usually translated 'sublime,'" it also approaches "what we mean by 'moving,'" not in the sense of "moving an audience to a decision, but as when we say of a poem, 'How moving!'" (Burke [1950] 1969, 65). Burke's commentary here on the word *hupsos* as a way of expressing marvel or wonder illustrates the idea that *On the Sublime* bridges rhetoric and poetics. In other words, a complementary perspective of *hupsos* might also refer to an expression of awe when people feel as if they have been carried away by a work of art and their aesthetic experiences with it. While *On the Sublime* is normally considered to be a work of poetic or aesthetic criticism, Burke's commentary on it, especially his use of the word "moving," brings to mind the idea that rhetoric's "basic function" is to "*move people*" (Burke [1950] 1969, 41), as well as Cicero's belief that the basic offices of rhetoric are, as we know, to teach (*docere*), to delight (*delectare*), and to move (*movere*). Argument attempts to change people's minds, but rhetorical aesthetics influences attitudes, and attitudes are incipient acts (Burke [1950] 1969, 42). The poetic/aesthetic is thus concerned not with merely getting people to do something but with a felt experience that an audience has in relation to a work. That experience will doubtless influence the audience's actions, but it is the experience that Burke emphasizes over the action here. The feelings and desires a reader has prepares that person for certain kinds and ways of acting. Rhetoric and poetic entail and imply one another.

The sublime thus involves a reaching-toward, even a quest, for the highest, the unsurpassable, the superlative, or even the best. As an attempt to arrive at the highest degree, the sublime also naturally affiliates with the divine. So, a quest for the sublime involves uses of terms that are high up, great, and exalting. Think of a hiker journeying to the top of a mountain who, upon reaching the summit, looks out across the majestic landscape and beholds a serene scene that fills the hiker with feelings of awe and respect. The sheer beauty of the marvelous outlook bestows, as it were, new life on the one who sees it. It inspires the viewer with respect, admiration, amazement, and even reverence. Thus, sublimity springs from five sources: elevated thoughts, strong emotion, certain rhetorical figures, noble diction, and a dignified organization of words, all of which inspire divinity and nobleness. Aiming at what is greatest, it surpasses humans, being a gift from the gods themselves. Sublimity is the fruit of noble passion in the right place (Longinus [1957] 1991, 11), and it is an echo of one who has a greatness of soul (see Longinus 1995, 185). It lifts people, even to the mind of God (277). People can thus be inspired "with an invincible passion for what is great and more divine" than themselves, so that "even the limits of the universe do not constrain our intellectual vision" (Heath 2012, 23). The scope of the sublime ranges from the smallest syllable to beyond the boundaries of the known universe (see Longinus 1995, 275–277, 289; Halliwell 2011). Thus, the sublime elevates writers and readers—together—to a superlative divine.

Interspersed among descriptions of the sublime one finds suggestions on how to achieve it. Sublimity is achieved by imitating authors who are themselves sublime (Longinus 1995, 211). When acting in benevolence and truth, people resemble the gods, and through distinction and excellence in expression, people gain immortality (163). Greatness is a prerequisite for sublime expression; writers who aspire for greatness do all they can to "train [their] minds into sympathy with what is noble and, as it were, impregnate them again and again with lofty thoughts" (185). Since "[s]ublimity is the echo of a noble mind," one must eschew the ignoble thoughts and nurture the enlightening. It is like the Pythian priestess who by divine power becomes impregnated by holy vapor and thereby delivers oracular prophecy (211–213). This imitation is not plagiarism (213). It is also not rote repetition of nor a blindness toward the real faults of great authors: for while all writers who attain sublimity also contain imperfections, these sublime-yet-imperfect works are infinitely better than flawless-but-mediocre works (267–269).

Better to take risks and attain sublimity than to not try anything at all for fear of failing to attain an impossible, flawless standard. This kind of imitation should not be confined to a partial selection of writers from one era or discipline, nor should it be interested only in those considered to be elitist. Longinus also directs his work against mechanical handbooks that prescribe hard-and-fast rules for writing effectively. Instead, he writes to show people how they can discover their own sublime style for themselves, which obviously goes beyond robotically following sets of rules. To prescribe a rule for discovering the sublime once and for all robs the sublime-seeker of the quest of transcendence that may itself be the very mark of excellence.

FORMAL SUBLIMITY

One of the clearest descriptions (Clark 2015, 28) of how formal patterns work also points toward the sublime. The passage is found on the well-known page 58 of *A Rhetoric of Motives*, on which Burke states that form's "'universal' appeal" creates attitudes of "collaborative expectancy" (Burke [1950] 1969, 58; see also Slater 2018). The formal patterns induce identification and cooperation because they enable readers to participate with the speaker in the formation of the speech (Burke [1950] 1969, 57). Intriguingly, Burke transitions to the passage known for discussing formal or stylistic identification by referencing Longinus, who, he says, mentions a "kind of elation wherein the audience feels as though it were not merely receiving, but were itself creatively participating in the poet's or speaker's assertion" (Burke [1950] 1969, 57–58). So formal patterns can be used in such a way that invites audiences and speakers to co-create a speech or an argument or a story. When providing that commentary, Burke probably has this passage in mind: "For the truly sublime naturally elevates us: uplifted with a sense of proud exaltation, we are filled with joy and pride, as if we had ourselves produced the very thing we heard" (Longinus 1995, 179). In other words, the sublime lifts us, and we feel as if we are co-creating or co-collaborating with speakers or writers in the creation of a work of art or an argument. Burke then asks, "Could we not say that, in such cases, the audience is exalted by the assertion because it has the feel of collaborating in the assertion?" (Burke [1950] 1969, 58).

Formal sublimity in writing or speaking ennobles audience members through their enthymematic participation with one another. The cooperation and collaboration of written and spoken acts are enthymematic in the sense described by Lloyd Bitzer: "[E]nthymemes occur only when speaker and audience jointly produce them" (Bitzer 1959, 408). In other words, speaker and audience both work together to create an argument that lifts both up to new heights. But formal sublimity is also enthymematic in a sense not described by Bitzer. Sublime-infused writing or speaking also ennobles people through their enthymematic participation in creation. Together, those involved create by reaching for something that both desire and expect. Thus, it is not just the idea, the argument, or the story that is shared, but it is also the feeling, the emotion, the desire, and the hope of creating something better together. Longinus also mentions subtle "ideas of words, thoughts, things, beauty, musical charm, all of which are born and bred in us," and all of which have the power to bring emotion into the hearts of audience members so that everyone who hears the speaker shares the same emotions (Longinus 1995, 287). So, listening with real intent to understand can empower an audience with creative abilities, while speaking with a desire to facilitate audience cooperation lifts both speakers and listeners, writers and readers, to a higher plane, right up to the sublime itself.

FORMAL SUBLIMITY AND TRANSDISCIPLINARITY

Formal sublimity's assumption that rhetoric and poetics/aesthetics are inherently intertwined, as well as its cooperative reach for mutual grandeur, provides a way of understanding style's cross-, trans-, and multi-disciplinarity. Formal appeal is universal because of its potential for application and appeal in various situations (see Burke [1950] 1969). Meanwhile, for "Bodies that Learn Language" (Burke [1935] 1984, 295), style and figuration are universal on the level of the human body (see Slater 2018; Hawhee 2009, 72–74, 100). Here, "universal" does not deny difference, nor does it imply a bland indistinguishability. "Universality" refers to the common ground, the margin of overlap, the possibilities and potentialities for identification among different entities. So, even though times and people change, art and literature continue to appeal because of these "potentialities of appreciation," which are inherent in the very seeds of human life (Burke [1931] 1968, 46). "Art [is] 'eternal' in so far as it deals with the constants of humanity," which "constants of humanity" are "the recurrent emotions, the fundamental attitudes, the typical experiences" (Burke [1931] 1968, 107). Think of a seed, which may or may not grow when planted. Not all seeds grow in all conditions, but if a seed is good, it will grow with the right environment and the right amount of water and sunlight. Just so, the seeds of formal appeal, whether those seeds grow into making an actual appeal or not, can be found universally in the bodies and minds of symbol-using creatures. Formal appeal considers the relationship between rhetorical influence and the aesthetic processes through which people, under certain conditions, can possibly experience that influence and thereby be influenced.

Formal appeal, even the "potentialities of appreciation" discussed earlier, can be found among a variety of disciplines. They enable a conversation to be carried on between one area of specialization and another. They empower specialists to speak to nonspecialists by transferring meaning from one thing to another. Since form can be found wherever symbol-making, symbol-using, symbol-misusing, and symbol-loving creatures act, and since form can potentially be experienced by anyone "under certain conditions" (Burke [1931] 1968, 149), style reveals trans-, multi-, and cross-disciplinarity. When rhetoric and poetic are freed from narrow interpretations that separate them from each other, and when style is liberated from vulgarly being understood as a narrow "canon" of rhetoric, interrelatedness of subjects and style's transdisciplinarity reveals itself. The ubiquity of formal patterns evidences the universality and transdisciplinarity of style. The story that rhetoric and poetic never were fully separate enables stylistic commentary across disciplines. Neither Burke nor Longinus felt bound to only one field; both provide insightful commentary on subjects as various as rhetoric, philosophy, poetry, literature, science, statues, ecology, epic, medicine, history, political discourse, religion, natural inquiry, the gods, psychology, drama, architecture, art, myth, music, speech, and many others. In other words, form's universal appeal and its implied logic of the interconnectedness of rhetoric and poetic, along with the prominence of the formal patterns or devices, all mesh together to provide evidence for style's transdisciplinarity.

A BRIEF EXAMPLE

When introducing the subject of style to readers of *The Writer's Style*, Paul Butler asks: "When something we read, see, or hear affects us profoundly, how do we write or speak about it effectively? If we are inspired by a certain . . . ineffable quality . . . what lexical and rhetorical choices are available to us to describe the way we think or feel?" (Butler 2018, 3). Butler's book gives an answer to those questions: style.

Throughout his book, Butler provides readers with many definitions and ways of understanding style. For example, Butler discusses style as rhythm, manner, a way of writing, contextual, rhetorical, inseparable from meaning, choice, academic discourse, diction, syntax, deviation from the norm, attention, emotion, identity, individual expression, voice, persona, lingua franca, argument, analysis, interpretation, imitation, form and structure, shape, generative and inventive, digital and visual, correctness, clarity, concision, cohesion, coherence, and emphasis. For Butler, not only can style be a particular lens for seeing in a certain way, it also can be a way of acting in a certain way: style pushes the envelope, disrupts conventional thinking, illuminates unstated associations, shows and masks a mind at work, makes the familiar new, values ironic or indirect meanings. Style also reveals true meanings, makes something more memorable and enduring, uncovers a writer's attitude or tone, exposes conflicts and unintended meanings and, of course, transcends genre and constraints. Not only that, Butler also crosses disciplinary boundaries when he seamlessly moves from subjects as wide-ranging as rhetoric, literature, politics, journalism, French art, museums, fiction, technology, disease, social media, hashtags, philosophy, pop culture, nature, and others. Butler's goal to discuss rhetoric and style enables him to easily move from one discipline to another (see Butler 2018).

Butler also shows how style enables one to point toward something beyond language even while describing something that enables knowledge to be transferred from one discipline to another. Take, for example, Butler's stylistic analysis of art historian Albert Boime's commentary on Vincent van Gogh's *Starry Night*. For Butler, style is what enables Boime to ponder and communicate the "celestial phenomena" (Boime 1984, 88) in *Starry Night* and even, in Butler's words, to "capture" some of the "ineffable qualities" in that work (Butler 2018, 5). Butler describes Boime's uses of the cumulative sentence, schemes, tropes, personification, passive and active voice, polysyndeton, antimetabole, antanaclasis, alliteration, and antithesis, saying that "Boime actually shows his affinity for van Gogh's work of art through *style*" (6). Butler does not need to be an art historian to discuss Boime's analysis. Rather, style provides Butler with the ability to explain what Boime is doing to influence readers. Butler comments on Boime's style at both a micro and a macro level, such as when Butler discusses Boime's uses of alliteration, as well as how Boime extends toward the ineffability of the artwork itself. Indeed, Boime and Butler both are trying to lift readers to a higher understanding, something that reaches, quite literally, toward a dark night sky that is infinitely deep. Meanwhile, the use of words reminding one of tasting a delicacy—"savoring" and "relish[ing]" (Butler 2018, 6–7)—bring this chapter full circle.

COLLABORATION AND EXPECTATIONS OF EXALTATION

In sum, formal sublimity points to the idea that different people can work together to create expectations of mutual exaltation among each other. By nurturing and expanding our views of one another, formal sublimity helps us to see, yes, even the *divine* potential in each person, thus creating a space in which hope for working together can be cultivated. Formal sublimity creates expectations of mutual exaltation.

Formal sublimity also elucidates style's transdisciplinarity through the potentialities of universal appeal. Since it assumes that differences can complement without contradicting, formal sublimity helps people to cooperatively transcend disciplinary boundaries. Formal sublimity attempts to lift speaker and audience to new vistas together that enable them to work together across their differences. It opens up new ways of seeing the rhetorical influence of people's aesthetic and rhetorical processes. It sees together the seemingly estranged concepts of rhetoric and poetic and, by being universal in its potential for appeal, may be found and used across, in, and throughout myriads of disciplines. Nevertheless, since it is somewhat abstract, it also reminds us, to some extent, of "peering over the edge of things into an ultimate abyss" (Burke 1966, 5).

Ultimately, formal sublimity's invitation to cooperate assumes that people are exalted together or not at all. By delivering expectations of exaltation, formal sublimity unbinds style because it shows how style is not limited to a narrow "canon" of rhetoric but instead reveals style's transdisciplinarity, one that enables style to potentially speak on any subject, from the smallest syllable to the grandest reaches of the universe, and beyond. These are some of the ways in which creating expectations of exaltation is crucial to style's unbounded future. And this is just a prolegomenon.

REFERENCES

Aristotle, Longinus, and Demetrius. *Poetics: On the Sublime/Longinus*; Translated by W.h. Fyfe. *On Style/Demetrius*; Translated by Doreen C. Innes. Cambridge: Harvard University Press, 1995. Print.

Beasley, James P. 2007. "'Extraordinary Understandings' of Composition at the University of Chicago: Frederick Champion Ward, Kenneth Burke, and Henry W. Sams." *College Composition and Communication* 59 (1): 36–52.

Bitzer, Lloyd. 1959. "Aristotle's Enthymeme Revisited." *Quarterly Journal of Speech* 45 (4): 399–408.

Boime, Albert. 1984. "Van Gogh's *Starry Night*: A History of Matter and a Matter of History." *Arts Magazine* 59 (4): 86–103.

Burke, Kenneth. 1951. "*Othello*: An Essay to Illustrate a Method." *The Hudson Review* 4 (2): 165–203.

Burke, Kenneth. 1966. *Language as Symbolic Action: Essays on Life, Literature, and Method*. Berkeley: University of California Press.

Burke, Kenneth. [1931] 1968. *Counter-Statement*, 3rd ed. Berkeley: University of California Press.
Burke, Kenneth. [1950] 1969. *A Rhetoric of Motives*. Berkeley: University of California Press.
Burke, Kenneth. 1976. "The Party Line." *Quarterly Journal of Speech* 62 (1): 62–68.
Burke, Kenneth. [1935] 1984. *Permanence and Change: An Anatomy of Purpose*, 3rd ed. Berkeley: University of California Press.
Butler, Paul. 2008. *Out of Style: Reanimating Stylistic Study in Composition and Rhetoric*. Logan: Utah State University Press.
Butler, Paul, ed. 2010. *Style in Rhetoric and Composition: A Critical Sourcebook*. Boston: Bedford/St. Martin's.
Butler, Paul. 2018. *The Writer's Style: A Rhetorical Field Guide*. Logan: Utah State University Press.
Clark, Gregory. 2015. *Civic Jazz: American Music and Kenneth Burke on the Art of Getting Along*. Chicago: University of Chicago Press.
Duncan, Mike, and Star Medzerian Vanguri, eds. 2013. *The Centrality of Style*. Anderson, SC: Parlor Press.
Fahnestock, Jeanne. 1999. *Rhetorical Figures in Science*. New York: Oxford University Press.
Fahnestock, Jeanne. 2011. *Rhetorical Style: The Uses of Language in Persuasion*. New York: Oxford University Press.
Halliwell, Stephen. 2011. *Between Ecstasy and Truth: Interpretations of Greek Poetics from Homer to Longinus*. Oxford: Oxford University Press.
Hawhee, Debra. 2009. *Moving Bodies: Kenneth Burke at the Edges of Language*. Columbia: University of South Carolina Press.
Heath, Malcolm. 2012. "Longinus and the Ancient Sublime." In *The Sublime: From Antiquity to the Present*, edited by Timothy M. Costelloe, 11–23. Cambridge: Cambridge University Press.
Henderson, Greig. 2001. "A Rhetoric of Form: The Early Burke and Reader-Response Criticism." In *Unending Conversations: New Writings by and about Kenneth Burke*, edited by Greig Henderson and David Cratis Williams, 127–142. Carbondale: Southern Illinois University Press.
Holcomb, Chris, and M. Jimmie Killingsworth. 2010. *Performing Prose: The Study and Practice of Style in Composition*. Carbondale: Southern Illinois University Press.
Johnson, T. R. 2003. *A Rhetoric of Pleasure: Prose Style and Today's Composition Classroom*. Portsmouth, NH: Boynton/Cook.
Johnson, T. R. 2005. "Writing with the Ear." In *Refiguring Prose Style: Possibilities for Writing Pedagogy*, edited by T. R. Johnson and Tom Pace, 267–285. Logan: Utah State University Press.
Kurlinkus, William C. 2013. "An Ethics of Attentions: Three Continuums of Classical and Contemporary Stylistic Manipulation for the Twenty-First-Century Composition Classroom." In *The Centrality of Style*, edited by Mike Duncan and Star Medzerian Vanguri, 9–36. Anderson, SC: Parlor Press.
Lanham, Richard A. 1976. *The Motives of Eloquence: Literary Rhetoric in the Renaissance*. New Haven, CT: Yale University Press.
Longinus. [1957] 1991. *On Great Writing (On the Sublime)*. Translated by G. M. A. Grube. Indianapolis: Hackett.
Ohmann, Richard. 1967. "Prolegomena to the Analysis of Prose Style." In *Essays on the Language of Literature*, edited by Seymour Chatman and Samuel R. Levin, 398–411. Boston: Houghton Mifflin.
Pace, Tom. 2013. "*Inventio* and *Elocutio*: Language Instruction at St. Paul's Grammar School and Today's Stylistic Classroom." In *The Centrality of Style*, edited by Mike Duncan and Star Medzerian Vanguri, 135–152. Anderson, SC: Parlor Press.
Porter, James I. 2016. *The Sublime in Antiquity*. Cambridge: Cambridge University Press.

Ray, Brian. 2015. *Style: An Introduction to History, Theory, Research, and Pedagogy.* Anderson, SC: Parlor Press.
Russell, Donald. 1995. "Introduction." In *Longinus, on the Sublime.* Translated by W. H. Fyfe, revised by Donald Russell, 145–158. In *Aristotle, Poetics; Longinus, on the Sublime; Demetrius, on Style.* Cambridge, MA: Harvard University Press.
Russell, Donald. 1995. *Longinus on the Sublime.* Translated by W. H. Fyfe, revised by Donald Russell. In *Aristotle, Poetics; Longinus, on the Sublime; Demetrius, on Style,* 159–305. Cambridge, MA: Harvard University Press.
Selzer, Jack. 1996. "Kenneth Burke among the Moderns: *Counter-Statement* as Counter Statement." *Rhetoric Society Quarterly* 26 (2): 19–49.
Slater, Jarron. 2018. "Attitudes of Collaborative Expectancy: Antithesis, Gradatio, and *A Rhetoric of Motives,* Page 58." *Rhetoric Review* 37 (3): 247–258.
Tufte, Virginia. [1971] 2010. "The Relation of Grammar to Style." In *Style in Rhetoric and Composition: A Critical Sourcebook,* edited by Paul Butler, 155–164. Boston: Bedford/St. Martin's.
van Eck, Caroline, Stijn Bussels, Maarten Delbeke, and Jürgen Pieters, eds. 2012. *Translations of the Sublime: The Early Modern Reception and Dissemination of Longinus' Peri Hupsous in Rhetoric, the Visual Arts, Architecture and the Theatre.* Leiden: Brill.
Wolin, Ross. 2001. *The Rhetorical Imagination of Kenneth Burke.* Columbia: University of South Carolina Press.

10
CIVIL STYLE
Reexamining Discourse and Rhetorical Listening in Composition

Laura L. Aull

INTRODUCTION: CIVIL DISCOURSE AND COMPOSITION

If today's calls for civil discourse are increasingly urgent, they are also increasingly focused on higher education. The Association of American Colleges and Universities called 2012 a "crucible moment" for college learning and democracy's future, which Andrea Leskes extended with a "plea" for civil discourse as a specific responsibility of higher education (Leskes 2013). By the 2016 US presidential election, over 100 college presidents signed open letters calling for civil discourse on their campuses; many other colleges issued related statements,[1] and events in the past year at Middlebury College and the University of California Berkeley show the complex challenges of fulfilling those expectations.[2] In such missives civil discourse is generally characterized as respectful exchange with verified information and open-mindedness toward multiple views, and college campuses are highlighted as sites for preserving such values.

In an editorial in *Inside Higher Education*, compositionist John Duffy highlighted first-year writing courses as long-established sites for such efforts. "For much of its history," he argued, "the first-year writing class has been an arena for teaching values and virtues like honesty, accountability . . . [and] fair-mindedness" (Duffy 2017b). Indeed, not only has composition teaching endeavored to "create for all citizens civic engagement through *access* to the language uses, spoken and written genres, discourses, vocabularies of government, law, and culture" (Bleich 2005), but composition scholarship specifically champions principles related to judicious treatment of readers and alternative perspectives. These principles, discussed in more detail in the next section, are described variously as a standard of ethics for academic writing (Harrington 1981), generosity toward readers (Stotsky 1992), and honesty and mutual respect between writer and reader (Duffy 2017b).

DOI: 10.7330/9781646420117.c010

To date, discussions like these have especially focused on describing and theorizing ethical and civil standards for writing rather than connecting those principles to patterned language use or style. In other words, they tend to identify shared values but not the ways these values are manifest in word- and sentence-level choices. In this way they are consistent with historical and theoretical developments in composition in the late twentieth century. These include, especially, the turn away from linguistics and grammar (e.g., see Connors 2000; Kolln and Hancock 2005; MacDonald 2007; Butler 2008) and the social-turn emphasis on genre context and social action rather than language.[3] Activity theory and rhetorical genre studies since the 1980s, for instance, tend to frame discourse as tangential or reflective rather than constitutive; David Russell's widely read overview of activity theory describes, "Genres are not constituted by formal features, then, but by recurring social actions that *give rise to* regularities in the discourse that mediates them" in a given activity system (1997, 226; emphasis mine). By 2009, Amy Devitt described that three decades of genre-based research had "largely . . . set aside" language or form, overwhelmingly conceptualizing genres as "acting in social and cultural contexts" (2009, 27). Methodologically, this paradigm means that genre analysis conventionally focuses on "the interactions of people with texts" via ethnographic and case study methods (Russell 1997, 226) rather than also on patterns that recur across texts (Aull 2015b).

Composition scholars of style, rhetorical grammar, and discourse studies suggest that a result of the separation between language, on one hand, and composition research on genres and student writing, on the other hand, is that the field lacks a framework for approaching rhetorical choices at multiple levels of discursive meaning (Butler 2008), including stylistic grammar (Ray 2015) and recurring lexis and grammar (Aull 2015a; Aull and Lancaster 2014). Instead, style is often conflated with mechanics only or is seen as entirely idiosyncratic, as discussed by Khan, Olinger, and others in this volume. A related result is that while we can point to shared values concerning civil exchange, we have little research on how such values are enacted in recurring discourse: we have, that is, little research on the *discourse* of civil discourse. Such research and related teaching, I propose, could be an important contribution of composition research focusing on style in academic writing. Current concerns about US public debate as polarized, divisive, and dysfunctional (Duffy 2017a, 242) make it a particularly important time to offer it.

To this end, this chapter makes a case for discourse analysis that illuminates how civil exchange is realized in patterned language choices.

To do so, it brings together research on rhetorical principles in composition and research on patterned discourse in academic writing. This synthesis helps illuminate what I am calling *diplomatic evidentiality* as a part of a civil style in academic writing. This two-part rhetorical quality underscores diplomacy, in that writers draw explicit attention to others' contributions and potential concerns, and evidentiality, in that writers draw explicit attention to evidence and how it substantiates their contribution. It is a quality, in other words, that emphasizes both "rhetorical listening"—a stance of openness in relation to other texts and views (Ratcliffe 2005)—and a writer's own convictions, in that order.

My synthesis between rhetorical principles and linguistic features has two aims. One is to highlight shared values in academic writing across disciplines that are related to civil exchange and are re/inscribed at the level of discourse. The second is to show that bringing together rhetorical and linguistic scholarship helps propel urgent discussions about civil and ethical writing practices beyond the level of rhetorical principles alone, to encompass their (often tacit) enactment in discourse.

ETHICAL AND RHETORICAL VALUES IN COMPOSITION

Compositionists have debated the role of discussions related to personal political ethics in writing classrooms for over a century. Late nineteenth-century writing curricula suggested students' writing should reflect on the ethical nature of society and "matters of moral obligation and improvement" (Jolliffe 1989, 171), while twentieth-century developments suggested students should read multicultural texts in order to gain a greater appreciation for diverse ideologies (Knoblauch and Brannon 1993) or should develop "rhetorical authority" to argue persuasively about their own viewpoint, "achieving consensus on a pluralistic grouping of ways to do academic discourse" (Bizzell 1992, 258–259). As Friend described in the 1990s, compositionists "often envision themselves as agents of social change who try to promote critique of dominant ideologies and empower students to become active participants in the larger political world" (Friend 1994, 548).

While these discussions focus on which viewpoints are presented, discussions like those noted in the introduction focus on principles for presenting any given viewpoint. Such scholarship, in other words, concerns values related to how writers engage readers and develop ideas, regardless of the topical (or propositional) content of those ideas. Duffy describes this as a focus "on the ethics of rhetorical practices," including the "fair-mindedness in considering the other side"—rather than, for instance, views explicitly addressing "economic injustice, environmental destruction, gun violence, or other topics" (2017a, 244). Put another way, first-year composition courses aim to teach students that regardless of the topic, writing must "begin with relationships of trust grounded in expectations of honest exchange" (Duffy 2017b). David Harrington suggests that such honest exchange may be new to early college writers: "Ethical writing . . . means disciplined attention to a number of processes, such as insistent inquiry to get to the heart of a problem . . . with which many beginning college students have had little previous experience" (1981, 13). For Harrington, such "insistent inquiry" seems related to being open-minded about hypotheses and main ideas: "One technique used by many of the most productive scholars," he writes, "is to formulate not just the hypothesis that one expects to prove but several alternative hypotheses covering as many plausible solutions as one can imagine" (14).

The focus on openness toward readers and alternative explanations is likewise emphasized in other areas of composition scholarship. Feminist rhetorical traditions, for instance, encourage looking and listening instead of only speaking one's own view (Ratcliffe 1999; Foss and Griffin 1995; Lunsford 1995), practices also described in Leskes's characterization of civil discourse (Leskes 2013). Years of work on the "big five" personality traits inspired the emphasis on "openness" in the *Framework for Success in Postsecondary Writing* (CWPA, NCTE, and NWP 2011; Poe, Inoue, and Elliot 2018). In research on writing across the curriculum, Thaiss and Zawacki show that two key characteristics of academic writing are that it shows that writers have been "open-minded" and have anticipated a reader who may object or disagree (2006, 5–7). Alternatively, research suggests that writers who produce "one-sided" writing, rather than writing with openness to alternative views, are less successful (Salig, Epting, and Rand 2018, 315).

These discussions point to shared values related to the need for academic writers, even as they develop their own claims to show thoughtful attention to readers, possible objections, and alternative explanations. They also imply that these values are related to written language, though they tend to focus more on the values themselves rather than on written choices that enact such values across texts.[4]

STYLE AND ETHICAL VALUES IN COMPOSITION

Composition scholarship on style shows more specific interest in connecting ethical writing practices with writing strategies. In *Out of Style*, Paul Butler reviews Aristotle's association between style and three of the four virtues (later listed by Theophrastus), clarity, appropriateness, and correctness without ornamentation. Equally illuminating in Butler's review is that Aristotle's ideas fully conflate rhetorical principles and language use: he described failure to fulfill the virtues as the fault of "bad taste in language" (2008, 35). In *Style: An Introduction*, Brian Ray offers a more recent historical perspective, tracing the prejudices of early twentieth-century composition scholarship that "equated eloquence with virtue and flatness with moral vices such as 'laziness'" (2015, 109) until more nuanced approaches to language, influenced by structural linguistics, temporarily arose in the mid-twentieth century in composition studies.

Mike Duncan and Star Vanguri's edited collection *The Centrality of Style* (2013) includes several chapters that investigate ethical writing and style. Kurlinkus notes a number of historical claims that conflate style and ethical writing habits, including "Let the virtue of style be defined as 'to be clear'" (Aristotle); "We owe readers an ethical duty to write precise and nuanced prose" (Strunk and White); and Joseph Williams's "Write in a way that draws attention to the sense and substance of writing, rather than to the mood and temper of the author" (Kurlinkus 2013, 9). These maxims, like Duffy's rhetorical virtues for composition, underscore attention to the reader and frown upon one-sided attention to the writer (a sentiment also reflected in Strunk and White's advice to place the writer in the background). For his part, Kurlinkus wants to move such discussions more pointedly to stylistic choices as manipulation of the audience, and style, thus, as something for which writers must take responsibility. Questions he poses for style along three different ethical continuums include point of attention (where do the author's stylistic devices direct the audience's attention?); apparent mediation (does the rhetor's style appear deceptive or just?); and felt agency (does the audience feel silenced or encouraged to analyze and critique the text's construction, reasoning, and so forth?) (10). Like Duffy, Kurlinkus sees ethical writing in terms of a relationship, but he sees style similarly: "I thus define ethics, like style, as an always local and contextualized process by which one negotiates an 'appropriate' relationship between rhetor and audience" (11).

In the same collection, Duncan draws attention to the overlapping nature of written strategies and ethical writing practices, which college writers are in the process of learning. He writes: "An insistence on a thesis, on a specific question of interest, on warranted evidence for claims, on supporting citations . . . all these add power. Once a student knows how these work . . . they become . . . ethical friends" (2013, 162). In his discussion, Duncan emphasizes the overlap between ideas and the writing strategies used to describe them: "Style and content are the same thing. The form of the discourse empowers its content" (162).

Also in *The Centrality of Style* and most directly addressing written stylistic features and their relationship with civil critique, Zak Lancaster applies systemic functional linguistics appraisal theory to track interpersonal style in writing. He shows, for example, how Joshua Cohen and Joel Rogers's written style makes their critique of Chomsky polite and indirect, rather than attacking: they use qualifiers like *seems* and *usually* to soften the claims; they place Chomsky's use of evidence (versus Chomsky the person) in the theme position; and they show positive evaluation prior to their critique (Lancaster 2013, 199–201). The positive evaluation (or concession) that precedes their critique is the only statement that places Chomsky (rather than his views) in the subject position (i.e., *Chomsky presents reams of evidence . . .*).

Lancaster's analysis of Cohen and Rogers's style demonstrates how recurring language-level choices make their critique less personal. The writers' use of *Chomsky's view* and *the/that claim*, for instance, provides a grammatical way to position the idea rather than the person as the point of departure for the critique. In so doing, the writers construct a "critically distanced stance" rather than a personal, attacking one (2013, 200). Their additional use of hedges *seems* and *usually* (rather than, e.g., *completely* or *frequently*) suggests their negative evaluation leaves some space for objection. Lancaster underscores that students can conduct analyses of important subgenres such as critiques in order to recognize dialogically expansive choices (e.g., *this seems to be the case*) and dialogically contractive choices (e.g., *this is definitely the case*, which uses what Williams calls "intensifiers"). In the next section I build on Lancaster's analysis to more specifically consider what recurring features seem related to a civil style.

DIPLOMATIC EVIDENTIALITY IN ACADEMIC WRITING

Lancaster's description of expansive and contrastive choices offers one way to consider how academic writers both support their own views, on one hand, and attend to others' views—potential questions, disagreements, or exceptions—on the other. Balancing expansive and contrastive choices furthermore seems to provide one a way to frame how to be diplomatic while also resisting dangerous forms of consensus (Hooks 1989). More pointedly, I see discourse patterns discussed by Lancaster and described below as contributing to *diplomatic evidentiality*, an aspect of civil style wherein written features both open and close dialogic space, leaving room for readers' reasoning and potential objections while also developing and emphasizing the writers' ideas.

Research in composition and in applied linguistics explores written lexical and grammatical features commonly referred to as "stance" markers, or "validity markers" or "evidentials." These markers help adjust knowledge claims by expressing less or more certainty or scope vis-à-vis a claim. These include the hedges *seems* and *perhaps* discussed by Lancaster, which help adjust epistemic stance to leave room for alternative perspectives. Swales describes the long-standing, widespread use of hedges as "rhetorical devices both for projecting honesty, modesty, and proper caution in self-reports, and for diplomatically creating research space in areas heavily populated by other researchers" (1990, 175). Hedges are also described as displays of indirectness or politeness that reduce the imposition on the reader (Hinkel 2006). Indeed, corpus analysis of academic phrases used to entertain possible objections shows that they tend to be indirect rather than direct (e.g., *It could be argued that* rather than *you may object that*) (Lancaster 2016, 442).

While stance markers like hedges downplay claims, stance markers like boosters and generality markers can help writers strategically emphasize the certainty or scope of their contribution. Also called "amplifiers" or "intensifiers," boosters are words such as *clearly, certainly,* and *without a doubt* (e.g., *the findings **clearly** suggest that*) that show full certainty toward claims made (Hyland 2005). Generality markers such as *every* or *all* emphasize the wide applicability of a claim (e.g., ***all** of these examples display that*) (Aull, Bandarage, and Miller 2017). Frequent use of these features is associated with spoken rather than written discourse (Hinkel 2006), but boosters can be used strategically to emphasize the contribution or evidence of the writers (Lancaster 2011). In addition, published academic writers sometimes use generalizations, especially in the beginning or end of academic essays, in order to show urgency about a topic or claim (e.g., ***everyone** agrees that the most prosperous states in the world are well-established democracies*) (Aull, Bandarage, and Miller 2017). Finally, presenting one's stance diplomatically can be aided by concede-counter moves that acknowledge or concede contributions to alternative perspectives before countering them (e.g., *Gladwell is correct that . . . however*) (Aull and Lancaster 2014; Thompson 2001).

For students, creating discursive space for concession and potential disagreement can be a new expectation of college-level writing. Research shows that published academic writing in the Contemporary Corpus of American English (COCA) academic subcorpus displays a closer balance between certainty and possibility, while early college writers err heavily on the side of certainty (Aull 2015a). In addition, new college students' frequent use of generalization markers contrasts the more circumspect stance featured in advanced student and published discipline-specific writing, suggesting that students are still learning to account for potential exceptions or alternatives in the scope of their claims (Aull, Bandarage, and Miller 2017).

Attention to written choices like hedges, boosters, generality markers, and concede-counter moves can also help highlight disciplinary and genre-based differences. For instance, in published research articles, Hyland shows that there are more stance features—both more hedges and more boosters—in philosophy research articles, as writers outline interpretive reasoning and stake their own claims. By contrast, there are fewer hedges and boosters in natural science disciplines in which the research process rather than the writers' reasoning is foregrounded (2004, 2005). At the same time, all studies noted in this section suggest that typically, academic writing, regardless of discipline, will show a kind of diplomatic evidentiality in that it tends to be indirect when introducing objections or critiques and to balance expansive and contractive choices. To return to Lancaster's example passage, diplomacy is realized in Cohen and Rogers's concession and the use of a hedge in their critique (italicized and bolded below, respectively), and evidentiality is realized in the detailed counter they subsequently offer (the *three ways* they outline after the quote below). They write, "*Chomsky presents reams of evidence for the [propaganda] model.* . . . Nonetheless, Chomsky's view of the media and the manufacture of consent **seems** overstated in three ways. First . . ." The grammatical structure of this example furthermore places *Chomsky* in the grammatical subject position in the concession, but his *view* in the subject position in the critique. These language-level choices at once show cautious diplomacy in the writers' critique as well as support and conviction in their assertions.

ATTENTION TO CIVIL STYLE IN THE WRITING CLASSROOM

Students can analyze features of this diplomatic evidentiality in both their reading and their writing. For instance, I have students annotate the subjects of critiques (or what I call the "leading actors" in a critique), as well as hedges, boosters, generality markers, and concessions regularly: in their peers' drafts before peer workshop, in their own drafts before they turn them in, in the scholarship they read for class, and in the freely available, A-graded student papers from the

Michigan Corpus of Upper-level Student Papers (MICUSP) (Römer and O'Donnell 2011). In one annotation task, students put a box around all words and phrases they see as contracting dialogic space, or closing space for exceptions or objections (e.g., words like *obviously* or *all*); and they put a circle around all words or phrases they see as opening (or expanding) discursive space by leaving room for potential questions or objections (e.g., words/phrases like *might* or *not all*). After annotating throughout a term, students become more and more adept at recognizing how writers use language-level features to create discursive space for questions and alternatives as well as develop their own contribution. By way of concise examples, I offer two passages from MICUSP that my students and I have annotated and discussed. In the passages, choices that expand discursive space appear in bold, while contractive choices are underlined.

The first passage appears in a research paper written by a second-year graduate student in natural resources, titled "Impact on Atmospheric Carbon Dioxide Levels."[5]

> <u>In my analysis, I assumed that</u> sequestration <u>is</u> equivalent to fixation (as it represents the earth's ability to sequester carbon in vegetation). **However, one could also consider** man-made carbon sequestration and storage (CCS) techniques in devising a practical, comprehensive strategy to reduce GHG concentrations (for instance, the possibility of trapping emissions from coal-fired power plants and burying them underground). <u>I also applied</u> learnings from my literature review to assess which levers **could in fact be** altered and by how much. The results of the scenario modeling show that <u>the most effective lever</u> in altering atmospheric carbon dioxide levels <u>is</u> emissions: the range in carbon dioxide concentrations that result from halving or doubling emissions is the highest, at 1,229.9 ppm in year 2200 or 2,072.5 ppm maximum.

This student's writing shows diplomatic evidentiality by (1) emphasizing the student's own assumption and later, conclusion, and by (2) noting an alternative consideration in detail. First, the student writer focuses on her analysis and then outlines an alternative approach. She then moves back to her own application, which shows an approach that was open to multiple assessments. In the final sentence, the student asserts what there is in fact a *most effective lever*, which is described thereafter. This example also illustrates how possibility modals like *could* are used in academic writing to hedge an assertion; other examples include *To this I* **would** *reply, Some* **would** *argue that,* and *It* **could** *be argued that* (Lancaster 2016, 447, 449).

The second example passage appears in a proposal written by a third-year graduate student in biology, titled "Linking Scales to Understand Diversity."[6]

If small-scale "details" matter, we need to ask how much complexity we need to incorporate into large-scale models **if we seek to** both understand and predict the dynamics of global quantities (Pascual 2005). **I would add that** these details **do not have to be** small, since **we are not always** studying global quantities. **We may also ask** whether patterns are shaped by extrinsic factors or dynamics—**perhaps it matters** that the system is open. The best hypotheses of complex systems remain parsimonious while appealing to processes occurring on other spatial, temporal, or organizational scales to describe a pattern.

This student's writing shows diplomatic evidentiality by (1) attending to existing research (by Pascual), (2) drawing the reader into the writer's reasoning (via *if*-statements and self-mentions); and (3) asserting the student's own view. The student writer offers hedged assertions *I would add that* and *do not have to be* followed by the dialogically expansive, hedged phrases *not always, we may also ask*, and *perhaps it matters* (bolded above), before she moves to the dialogically contractive outline of what is proposed as *the best hypothesis*.

CONCLUDING REMARKS

Ellen Barton describes evidentials as "the underlying perspective on knowledge represented in a text" (1993, 146), a description that emphasizes the interconnectedness of patterned language, ideas, and the reception of those ideas. In the discussion above I have outlined academic writing strategies that suggest that one shared perspective underlying academic knowledge is that it requires diplomatic evidentiality—an important aspect of a civil style that foregrounds the reader and potential objections as well as the writers' own contributions. These strategies help support a style, in other words, that leaves room for alternatives and invites readers into writer reasoning (Hyland and Tse 2004; Swales 1990) and that shows a writer's view as one among existing views and potential disagreements (Aull and Lancaster 2014). Such strategies are textual manifestations of the open-mindedness espoused by Duffy, Thais and Zawacki, and others. In this way, they help us think about how to provide textual anchors for describing why and how civil discourse is realized in academic writing at a time it is sorely needed.

NOTES

1. See *Inside Higher Education* for the statement signed by college presidents: https://www.insidehighered.com/news/2016/11/18/110-college-presidents-issue-letter-trump-urging-him-speak-out-against-harassment; see also Audrey Williams June's

article in *The Chronicle of Higher Education* http://www.chronicle.com/article/With-Postelection-Tensions/238423.

2. See a statement issued by Middlebury College students here: https://brokeninquirblog.wordpress.com/2017/03/12/broken-inquiry-on-campus-a-response-by-a-collection-of-middlebury-students/; and see coverage of Ann Coulter's cancelled speech at UC Berkeley here: https://www.nytimes.com/2017/04/26/us/ann-coulter-berkeley-speech.html.

3. Although, interestingly, Crowley suggests that the "best hope for the contribution of linguistics to composition has always lain in its potential to enrich students' mastery of style" (Crowley 1989, 487).

4. An exception from twenty-five years ago is Stotsky's effort to illustrate four umbrella principles for academic writing—respect for the purpose of academic language, for other academic writers, for integrity of the subject, and for the integrity of the reader—via a handful of scholarly passages from published academic writing. Stotsky closely analyzes the passages to show how those principles are fulfilled or violated. As Fulkerson detailed, Stotsky's impulse to provide textual examples of ethical standards of academic writing was undermined because some of the writing seemed to break the rules espoused by it; furthermore, "whether [the examples] are representative is arguable" (Fulkerson 1992, 238).

5. MICUSP paper label: NRE.G2.07.1. Note that students selected a gender when submitting papers to MICUSP, and I use the corresponding pronouns in this analysis.

6. MICUSP paper label: BIO.G3.02.1.

REFERENCES

Aull, Laura Louise. 2015a. *First-Year University Writing: A Corpus-Based Study with Implications for Pedagogy*. London: Springer.

Aull, Laura Louise. 2015b. "Linguistic Attention in Rhetorical Genre Studies and First-Year Writing." *Composition Forum*, Special Issue on Genre, 31 (Spring).

Aull, Laura Louise, Dineth Bandarage, and Meredith Richardson Miller. 2017. "Generality in Student and Expert Epistemic Stance: A Corpus Analysis of First-Year, Upper-Level, and Published Academic Writing." *Journal of English for Academic Purposes* 26: 29–41. doi: http://dx.doi.org/10.1016/j.jeap.2017.01.005.

Aull, Laura Louise, and Zak Lancaster. 2014. "Linguistic Markers of Stance in Early and Advanced Academic Writing: A Corpus-Based Comparison." *Written Communication* 31 (2): 151–183.

Barton, Ellen L. 1993. "Evidentials, Argumentation, and Epistemological Stance." *College English* 55 (7): 745–769.

Bizzell, Patricia. 1992. *Academic Discourse and Critical Consciousness*. Pittsburgh: University of Pittsburgh Press.

Bleich, David. 2005. "Rhetorical Democracy: Discursive Practices of Civic Engagement." *College Composition and Communication* 57 (1): 184–192.

Butler, Paul. 2008. *Out of Style: Reanimating Stylistic Study in Composition and Rhetoric*. Logan: Utah State University Press.

Connors, Robert J. 2000. "The Erasure of the Sentence." *College Composition and Communication* 52 (1): 96–128.

Crowley, Sharon. 1989. "Linguistics and Composition Instruction 1950–1980." *Written Communication* 6 (4): 480–505.

CWPA, NCTE, and NWP (Council of Writing Program Administrators, National Council of Teachers of English, and National Writing Project). 2011. *Framework for Success in Postsecondary* Writing. https://files.eric.ed.gov/fulltext/ED516360.pdf.

Devitt, Amy J. 2009. "Re-Fusing Form in Genre Study." In *Genres in the Internet: Issues in the Theory of Genre*, edited by Janet Giltrow and Dieter Stein, 27–47. Amsterdam: John Benjamins Publishing.

Duncan, Mike, and Star Medzerian Vanguri. 2013. *The Centrality of Style*. Fort Collins, CO: WAC Clearinghouse.

Duffy, John. 2017a. "The Good Writer: Virtue Ethics and the Teaching of Writing." *College English* 79 (3): 229.

Duffy, John. 2017b. "Post-Truth and First-Year Writing." *Chronicle of Higher Education*. May 8, 2017.

Foss, Sonja K, and Cindy L Griffin. 1995. "Beyond Persuasion: A Proposal for an Invitational Rhetoric." *Communications Monographs* 62 (1): 2–18.

Friend, Christy. 1994. "Ethics in the Writing Classroom: A Nondistributive Approach." *College English* 56 (5): 548–567.

Fulkerson, Richard. 1992. "Connecting Civic Education and Language Education: The Contemporary Challenge." *Rhetoric Review* 11 (1): 235–239.

Harrington, David V. 1981. "Teaching Ethical Writing." *Freshman English News* 10 (1): 13–16.

Hinkel, Eli. 2006. "Hedging, Inflating, and Persuading in L2 Academic Writing." *Applied Language Learning* 15 (1/2): 29.

hooks, bell. 1989. *Talking Back: Thinking Feminist, Thinking Black*. Boston: South End Press.

Hyland, Ken. 2004. *Disciplinary Discourses: Social Interactions in Academic Writing*. Ann Arbor: University of Michigan Press.

Hyland, Ken. 2005. "Stance and Engagement: A Model of Interaction in Academic Discourse." *Discourse Studies* 7 (2): 173–192.

Hyland, Ken, and Polly Tse. 2004. "Metadiscourse in Academic Writing: A Reappraisal." *Applied Linguistics* 25 (2): 156–177. doi: 10.1093/applin/25.2.156.

Jolliffe, David A. 1989. "The Moral Subject in College Composition: A Conceptual Framework and the Case of Harvard, 1865–1900." *College English* 51 (2): 163–173.

Knoblauch, C. H., and Lil Brannon. 1993. *Critical Teaching and the Idea of Literacy*. Portsmouth, NH: Boynton Cook Publishers.

Kolln, Martha, and Craig Hancock. 2005. "The Story of English Grammar in United States Schools." *English Teaching* 4 (3): 11.

Kurlinkus, William. 2013. "An Ethics of Attention." In *The Centrality of Style*, edited by Mike Duncan and Star Medzerian Vanguri, 9–36. Fort Collins, CO: WAC Clearinghouse.

Lancaster, Zak. 2011. "Interpersonal Stance in L1 and L2 Students' Argumentative Writing in Economics: Implications for Faculty Development in WAC/WID Programs." *Across the Disciplines* 4 (8).

Lancaster, Zak. 2013. "Tracking Interpersonal Style." In *The Centrality of Style*, edited by Mike Duncan and Star Medzerian Vanguri, 191–212. Fort Collins, CO: WAC Clearinghouse.

Lancaster, Zak. 2016. "Do Academics Really Write This Way? A Corpus Investigation of Moves and Templates in *They Say/I Say*." *College Composition and Communication* 67 (3): 437.

Leskes, Andrea. 2013. "A Plea for Civil Discourse: Needed, the Academy's Leadership." *Liberal Education* 99 (4): 44–51.

Lunsford, Andrea A. 1995. *Reclaiming Rhetorica: Women in the Rhetorical Tradition*. Pittsburgh: University of Pittsburgh Press.

MacDonald, Susan Peck. 2007. "The Erasure of Language." *College Composition and Communication* 58 (4): 585–625.

Poe, Mya, Asao B. Inoue, and Norbert Elliot. 2018. "Introduction: The End of Isolation." In *Writing Assessment, Social Justice, and the Advancement of Opportunity*, edited by Mya Poe, Asao B. Inoue, and Norbert Elliot, 3–38. Fort Collins: WAC Clearinghouse.

Ratcliffe, Krista. 1999. "Rhetorical Listening: A Trope for Interpretive Invention and a 'Code of Cross-Cultural Conduct.'" *College Composition and Communication* 51 (2): 195–224.

Ratcliffe, Krista. 2005. *Rhetorical Listening: Identification, Gender, Whiteness*. Carbondale: Southern Illinois University Press.

Ray, Brian. 2015. *Style: An Introduction to History, Theory, Research, and Pedagogy*. Anderson, SC: Parlor Press.

Römer, Ute, and Matthew Brook O'Donnell. 2011. "From Student Hard Drive to Web Corpus (Part 1): The Design, Compilation and Genre Classification of the Michigan Corpus of Upper-Level Student Papers (MICUSP)." *Corpora* 6 (2): 159–177.

Russell, David R. 1997. "Rethinking Genre in School and Society: An Activity Theory Analysis." *Written Communication* 14 (4): 504–554.

Salig, Lauren K., L. Kimberly Epting, and Lizabeth A. Rand. 2018. "Rarely Say Never: Essentialist Rhetorical Choices in College Students' Perceptions of Persuasive Writing." *Journal of Writing Research* 9 (3): 301–331.

Stotsky, Sandra. 1992. "Conceptualizing Writing as Moral and Civic Thinking." *College English* 54 (7): 794–808.

Swales, John. 1990. *Genre Analysis: English in Academic and Research Settings*. Cambridge: Cambridge University Press.

Thaiss, Chris, and Terry Myers Zawacki. 2006. *Engaged Writers and Dynamic Disciplines: Research on the Academic Writing Life*. Portsmouth, NH: Boynton/Cook.

Thompson, Geoff. 2001. "Interaction in Academic Writing: Learning to Argue with the Reader." *Applied Linguistics* 22 (1): 58–78.

11
APPLIED LEGAL STORYTELLING
Toward a Stylistics of Embodiment

Almas Khan

AFFLICTIONS OF LEGAL WRITING STYLE AND THE CALL FOR REFORM

> "[Y]ou could speak abstractly and enlighten lawyers, instead of concretely without, it seems to me, logical justification."
> —Supreme Court Justice Stanley Reed, in a letter to fellow Justice Felix Frankfurter (1946)[1]

Justice Reed's private message here chastising his colleague about the wording of a judicial opinion confirms the prevalent public perception of writing style in the law: legal documents are composed in a cryptic code.[2] Following this line of argument, lawyers deliberately privilege insular modes of reasoning and abstract diction over discourse that may be accessible to the broader population. Such a belief about legal prose may be responsible for the proliferation of lawyer jokes (see Galanter 1998, 816) but may more seriously contribute to the American public's general low regard for lawyers. A 2013 Pew Research Center survey found that lawyers ranked at the bottom overall for respondents who were asked which of ten professions contributed "a lot" to social well-being ("Public Esteem for Military Still High" 2013). Judges have also expressed frustration about attorneys, with a federal district court judge requiring an attorney to re-plead a prolix complaint. Quoting a federal rule of civil procedure that a complaint "shall contain . . . a short and plain statement of the claim showing that the pleader is entitled to relief," the judge recommended that the plaintiff's lawyer "study William Strunk, Jr. & E. B. White['s] *The Elements of Style*" (*Politico v. Promus Hotels, Inc.* 1999, 233–234).

Awareness of legal writing style's importance dates back centuries, with the Committee on Style for the US Constitution being one of the most momentous historical examples (see Stewart 2007, 179–180, 225,

230, 232).³ Robert Cover's axiom opening his essay "Violence and the Word" searingly captures the significance of how legal texts are worded: "Legal interpretation takes place in a field of pain and death" (Cover 1986, 1601). Recognizing the serious social ramifications attached to writing in the law, scholars have recently interviewed Supreme Court justices and prominent attorneys about their writing, published monographs on legal writing style, and composed articles offering writing tips for practitioners (LawProse n.d.; Garner 2013; Wydick 2005; Lebovits 2018). Contemporary publications have also delineated the consequences of a subpar writing style in legal documents, ranging from a needless prolonging of litigation to the loss of legal claims and disbarment (see, e.g., Fisher 2003–2004).

Canvassing this literature gives rise to a primordial question: what is "style" in the legal writing context? Stephen Armstrong and Timothy Terrell, who have over two decades of experience teaching legal writing programs for attorneys and judges, recall the surprise they have encountered when introducing the subject to practitioners: "Style, they [the program participants] assume, is something a reader encounters in literature; lawyers, on the other hand, are just hardworking, anonymous purveyors of careful legal analysis" (Armstrong and Terrell 2008, 43).⁴ According to the authors, lawyers and judges typically equate style with subjective preferences or, contrarily, more objective technicalities like grammar. While acknowledging that style in legal writing encompasses these dimensions, Armstrong and Terrell maintain that "a document's organization and overall approach to its readers" constitutes vital elements of its style as well (43). Rather than being a mere nicety, then, style is something "*embedded*" in a legal text, being integrally linked to, yet remaining discernable from, the text's substance (43).⁵

Adopting Armstrong and Terrell's capacious understanding of legal writing style, this chapter will analyze the emergence of what I term a stylistics of embodiment in contemporary legal rhetoric. Although abstract, rule-centered views of law and legal discourse have historically dominated the profession, more corporeal, human-centered perspectives have recently gained prominence.⁶ Rules are in this rendering a means to attain humanistic ends, and a new style of legal discourse is necessary for law to realize its profoundest raison d'être. The Applied Legal Storytelling (ALS) movement today most conspicuously promotes a stylistics of embodiment, and the following section will discuss critical legal theories informing ALS, identify ALS's main attributes, and describe ALS's popular resonances. Next, the chapter will conceptualize key features of a stylistics of embodiment by evaluating illustrative law review articles and court opinions. The judiciary's incorporating stylistic strategies inspired by ALS into opinions involving major legal questions suggests the continued vibrancy of the scholarly enterprise, as well as ALS's growing import for practitioners. In addition, the hybrid technical-creative writing styles in the examples indicate promising directions of inquiry for composition scholars studying innovative stylistic developments in other professional fields.[7]

TRACING THE EVOLUTION OF A STYLISTICS OF EMBODIMENT IN CRITICAL LEGAL THEORY

The first concerted call for a more embodied legal writing style in the United States arguably came from reformers associated with legal realism, which has been crowned "the major intellectual event in 20th century American legal practice and scholarship" (Leiter 2007, 1). Academics, lawyers, and judges associated with the group, which flourished from the turn of the century to World War II, advanced a pragmatic, liberal-oriented view of law. Legal realists generally de-emphasized the significance of rules in legal decision-making and correspondingly underscored the importance of "human factor[s]" in comprehending law (see Pound 1909, 464). Several legal realists sought a stylistics to reinforce this substantive aim; federal circuit court judge Jerome Frank recommended that colleagues study literature for a "needed corrective of generalizations in meeting individual human problems," referencing his experiences "teaching law students to write about legal subjects for non-lawyers" (Frank 1951, 38). The Plain English movement pioneered by David Mellinkoff's *The Language of the Law* (1963) has helped actualize Judge Frank's vision of expelling excess legalese from legal writing. Numerous government agencies are now obliged to communicate with the public in plain English (Martin 2000; Plainlanguage.gov n.d.), potentially increasing the public's knowledge of laws and diminishing the depth of social alienation from the legal system.

The Applied Legal Storytelling movement, whose manifesto may be Richard Delgado's "Storytelling for Oppositionists and Others: A Plea for Narrative" (1989), also seeks to demystify legal language. ALS scholars, however, emphasize how law's narrative qualities appeal to the human need for stories to understand experiences and to foster a normative community (Amsterdam and Bruner 2002, 11; Cover 1983, 5). Applied legal storytelling can contrast with more ostensibly logical methods and paradigms of legal analysis like reasoning by analogy and IRAC (issue-rule-application-conclusion), though it more typically supplements such approaches (Chestek 2008, 130–131). Many ALS scholars work in the fields of critical race theory and feminist jurisprudence, which seek to reveal the systemic nature of race- and gender-based oppression by applying critical theories to race and gender issues in law.[8] These scholars frequently analyze the relationships between identity and "the power of language," as Mari Matsuda asserts in her book *Where Is Your Body?* (Matsuda 1996, xii). While articulating "how the law embodies racism and bias" (Ross 1996, xv), ALS scholars often draw attention to the bodies (and minds) of those impacted by the legal system: aside from themselves (in a reflexive move), litigants, judges, lawyers, lawmakers, and swaths of the public at large.[9]

Critical race theory and feminist jurisprudence may appear to be of purely legal or academic interest, but the Black Lives Matter and #MeToo movements thriving today can be seen as their popular complements. Aside from sharing objectives to reveal the ingrained nature of white supremacy and misogyny, and to accordingly advocate for substantial legal, political, and social reforms, the grassroots and jurisprudential movements both espouse a stylistics of embodiment. Humanizing victims by (re)telling their stories is central to Black Lives Matter and #MeToo, as are protests constituting a means of collective embodiment to advocate for equal rights.[10] A stylistics of embodiment may thus be envisaged as a form of "intellectual activism" mediating between academia and popular culture in furthering justice (see Collins 2013, xi–xv).

CONCEPTUALIZING A STYLISTICS OF EMBODIMENT IN CONTEMPORARY LEGAL WRITING

The stylistics of embodiment influenced by the critical legal theories examined above, and conceptualized more formally here, implicates at least three senses of the root word "embody."[11] These include: one, "[t]o give a concrete form to (what is abstract or ideal)"; two, "[t]o put into a body, to invest or clothe (a spirit) with a body"; and three, "[t]o cause to become part of a body; to unite into one body; to incorporate (a thing) in a mass of material, (particular elements) in a system or complex unity" (*OED* 2018b). The first two definitions suggest a more palpable legal discourse to enflesh legal rules, while the third definition expresses the ideal outcome of this discursive transformation. "[T]he law, especially the constitution, has been a symbol of national unity as well as of social order," legal philosopher Morris Cohen affirmed during the Great Depression (Cohen 1931, 355), and the cardinal value of a stylistics of embodiment today may be in revitalizing this lofty perception of law's potential to counter the dehumanization and disunity often sanctioned in political and other forms of discourse.[12] A stylistics of embodiment also contrasts markedly with the euphemistic or disembodied style of legal writing characterizing some seminal Supreme Court cases.[13] The following discussion will scrutinize recent major cases involving voting rights, transgender rights, and abortion rights, as well as earlier watershed law review articles on hate speech, rape laws, and race-based jury nullification,[14] to illuminate key features of this humanist stylistic development. These ALS-inspired texts notably operationalize a stylistics of embodiment through anthrocentric framing, engagement with humanistic disciplines, moving portrayals of human actors in the legal system, and reflexivity about both the limits and potential of law as a human construction.

Opening lines of a text frame the reader's impression of what follows, and works by ALS authors often begin with personal stories or vignettes, rather than portraying law in the abstract as the primary prism through which the remainder of the discussion is to be viewed. An example of the latter is the Supreme Court's opinion in a 2018 case involving the validity of a travel ban applying largely to citizens from predominantly Muslim nations. The opinion begins: "Under the Immigration and Nationality Act, foreign nationals seeking entry into the United States undergo a vetting process to ensure that they satisfy the numerous requirements for admission" (*Trump v. Hawaii* 2018, 2403). By starting (and also ending) with the statute, the sentence emphasizes that law is the main actor, requiring "foreign nationals" (an othering legal term) to be vetted. In sharp relief with this law-focused approach is Susan Estrich's article advocating a more expansive view of what constitutes rape. The article begins with the author recounting her own experiences with sexual assault: "Eleven years ago, a man held an ice pick to my throat and said: 'Push over, shut up, or I'll kill you.' I did what he said, but I couldn't stop crying" (Estrich 1986, 1087). This intense portrayal of the author's body in peril demonstrates the human stakes of what the article later shows to be a complicated technical issue of how rape is and should be defined (1094–1184).

Equally impactful is the vignette opening Mari Matsuda's article proposing that racist speech be more amenable to prosecution than is currently permissible under the First Amendment. The vignette, based on an actual incident, describes a black family in a small-town Texas coffee shop receiving a card from a white man containing this threat: "You have just been paid a visit by the Ku Klux Klan" (Matsuda 1989, 2320). The generic nature of the vignette (omitting names) invites readers to imagine themselves as the victims, and particularly whether racist speech of this nature causes harm equivalent to that of a physical assault, thus also meriting criminal punishment. Matsuda's and Estrich's narrative framings foreground the bodies of victims who may seek legal redress while potentially causing a visceral reaction in readers. This possible response, coupled with concerns about the accuracy and persuasiveness of narratives, has elicited criticism of authors over-relying on anecdotal accounts to the detriment of more traditional legal analysis (Farber and Sherry 1993, 831–840).

Conventional analytical frameworks in law tend to be disciplinarily insular, but authors embracing ALS often turn to discourse from humanistic disciplines to enrich their arguments and to appeal to an audience beyond fellow legal professionals.[15] Although the insights of other disciplines have influenced legal academia and the judiciary,[16] there remains suspicion of the practice. During oral arguments in a 2017 gerrymandering case, Supreme Court chief justice John Roberts questioned the "sociological gobbledygook" (his phrase) being presented by redistricting opponents (Milbank 2017). Judge Damon Keith's dissent from a majority decision upholding voting rights restrictions contrastingly foregrounded interdisciplinarity, commencing with a "Historical Background" (as opposed to legal background) section situating the case in the context of previous voting suppression efforts. Relying on "publicly available historical statements," the opinion interpolated eleven pages of photos and captions of those slain during the civil rights revolution, including a young black man whose death helped instigate the passage of the statute at issue in the case (*Northeast Ohio Coalition* 2016, 32–44). The poignancy of the unusual approach prompted the majority to express "deep[] respect for the dissent's recounting of important parts of the racial history of our country," while ultimately concluding that "[t]he legal standards we must follow are set out in the cases we discuss concerning the standards *embodied* in the Fourteenth Amendment and Section 2 of the Voting Rights Act" (30; emphasis mine). Whereas law appears to be the embodied entity in the majority opinion, Judge Keith's creative use of history spectrally embodies people.

Literature is another discipline informing ALS,[17] and just as literary authors utilize a host of devices (such as point of view, tone, imagery, allusions, and diction) to enliven fictional characters, proponents of ALS do likewise to humanize real-life actors in the legal system. Judge Andre Davis's concurrence in a transgender bathroom rights case, for instance, endeavored to channel the teenage plaintiff's point of view while testifying before a school board. Rather than presenting a typical recitation of legally relevant facts with citations to the written record, Judge Davis cited a YouTube video of the teenager's "compelling statement," wording that spurs readers to click on the included link to see the embodied youth (*G. G.* 2017, 2n1). Judge Davis also sympathetically summarized the teenager's testimony, in part, as follows: "He explained that he is a person worthy of dignity and privacy . . . [and] clearly and eloquently attested that he was not a predator, but a boy, despite the fact that he did not conform to some people's idea about who is a boy" (2). The judge stressed that the case was not fundamentally about bathrooms, but rather a "recognition of their [transgender peoples'] humanity" as part of "a larger movement that is redefining and broadening the scope of civil and human rights" (3).

Judge Patricia Millett's dissent in a case involving an undocumented minor immigrant's abortion rights while in federal custody similarly used literary techniques to humanize the plaintiff, particularly since the issue of the extent to which undocumented immigrants qualify as "persons" under the Constitution shadowed the litigation. Judge Millett characterized the plaintiff as a "vulnerable person[]" who, facing "terrible physical abuse in her family, . . . fled her home country and all she has ever known, and all alone undertook a life-imperiling trek for hundreds, perhaps thousands, of miles seeking safety" (*Garza*, October 20, 2017, 2). The vivid diction here cultivates sympathy for the plaintiff's plight[18] and alludes to the historical ideal of the United States as a beacon for oppressed peoples, a connection the opinion later makes explicit in asserting that "[t]he Statue of Liberty's promise to those 'homeless' 'yearning to breathe free' is not a lie" (5). Literary devices in both opinions ultimately personalize litigants from groups arguably accorded unequal rights under the law, bolstering the case for equality.

Authors applying these stylistic techniques of embodiment often reflexively call attention to the human-constructed nature of their writings and that of law more generally. Instead of being neutral and self-executing, laws are avowed to be shaped by people; new means of conceiving laws can thus help ensure that the legal system promotes human flourishing. Mari Matsuda's article accordingly rejects the premise that storytelling is a "denouncement of structure in law," instead perceiving stories as "a means of obtaining the knowledge we need to create just legal structure" (Matsuda 1989, 2325n32). This epistemological quest is shown to be a bottom-up one in Paul Butler's article recommending that black jurors selectively engage in race-based jury nullification. Butler quotes a Malcolm X speech urging for "a new system of reason and logic devised by us who are at the bottom, if we want to get some results in this struggle that is called 'the Negro revolution'" (quoted in Butler 1995, 677).

By advancing Malcolm X's vision stylistically, the authors discussed here and their critical compatriots can be seen to have taken a decisive step in the incessant process of embodying substantive justice. Such formally audacious writings by judges, lawyers, and scholars fulfill the Applied Legal Storytelling movement's ambition to reform an inequitable legal order by challenging the rhetorical assumptions on which the system rests. The future of style in legal writing is therefore bound with the future of law itself, and insights from composition studies can be expected to contribute increasingly to the development of law. Whether public faith in legal institutions will consequently be revived remains uncertain, but the rejuvenation of legal language is a promising start.

NOTES

1. Quoted in Siegel 1999, 363.
2. This chapter was sparked by conversations with my mother-in-law (as in the discipline), Professor Robin West of Georgetown Law.
3. Since the Constitution's inception in 1789, the outcome of numerous major cases has turned on dissecting the text's style. For example, the Supreme Court's controversial 2008 decision endorsing an expansive interpretation of the Second Amendment analyzed at length the amendment's "operative clause" establishing the "right of the people to keep and bear Arms" (*District of Columbia v. Heller* 2008, 576–595).
4. Such an assumption reflects the incongruous relationship that the legal profession generally has with writing style in the United States. "Good" legal prose, unlike modernist literature, is often seen as not drawing attention to itself (Opipari 2009, 141). This vaunting of an invisible style may be attributed to the aura of impartiality surrounding rule of law principles; an individualistic writing style in a judicial opinion may suggest the partiality of legal justice. Many commentators have nonetheless praised the personal writing styles of Supreme Court justices like Oliver Wendell Holmes Jr. and Antonin Scalia, indicating that the norm against individualistic legal prose may not be that ironclad. For a sampling of current debates about the legal writing styles of Supreme Court justices, see the pieces by Michael Dorf (2015), Adam Serwer (2014), and Jeet Heer (2015).
5. A discussion of what writing style entails more broadly exceeds this chapter's scope, but many other commentators also allude to the distinction between formal and substantive elements of a text (Opipari 2009, 135–36). For an overview of several conceptualizations of style in composition studies, see Laura L. Aull and Zak Lancaster's chapter "Stance as Style: Toward a Framework for Analyzing Academic Language" (chapter 6).
6. One sign of this shift is that the Law Stories series, which vivifies cases more than most doctrinal textbooks, began in 2003 and spanned several dozen volumes by 2018 ("West Academic Store" n.d.).
7. Tom Pace's chapter "Erasmus in the Professional Writing Classroom: Workplace

Genre, Designing and Writing for the Web, and the Future of Style" relatedly questions the form(style)-content dichotomy and discusses how professional writing instructors teaching web design can undermine perceptions of style as a set of writing rules (chapter 4). In a similar vein, Jon Udelson's chapter "Point of Departures: Composition and Creative Writing Studies' Shared Stylistic Values" adopts a broad understanding of style and challenges critics who assert that an insurmountable divide exists between style in composition studies and in creative writing studies (chapter 13).

8. Kathryn Stanchi, Linda Berger, and Bridget Crawford's edited volume *Feminist Judgments: Rewritten Opinions of the Supreme Court* (2016) explains feminist jurisprudence and applies the theoretical framework to recreate Supreme Court opinions. The volume *Critical Race Judgements: Rewritten Court Opinions on Race and the Law* (forthcoming in 2020 and coedited by Bennett Capers and three other scholars) is expected to explain and apply critical race theory similarly ("Professor Bennett Convenes Critical Race Theory Legal Scholars for Book Project" 2017).

9. For more information about ALS, see J. Christopher Rideout's 2015 bibliography.

10. A thorough discussion of Black Lives Matter and #MeToo is beyond this chapter's ambit, but the coverage in Christopher Lebron's *The Making of Black Lives Matter: A Brief History of an Idea* (2017) and the *Chicago Tribune*'s "#MeToo, But Now What?" story gallery (2017–2018) informed the analogies I have made here.

11. "Embodiment" is defined in part as "the action of embodying" or "the process or state of being embodied," and the word has both literal and figurative usages (*OED* 2018a).

12. For example, during a January 2018 meeting with lawmakers, President Donald Trump complained about an influx of immigrants from "shithole countries," including Haiti, El Salvador, and African nations, implying that citizens of those countries were inferior by association and unworthy of inclusion in the United States (see Dawsey 2018).

13. For linguistic and historical evidence supporting this claim, see the articles by Elizabeth Mertz (1988) and Matthew Bewig (1994).

14. The cases are *Northeast Ohio Coalition for the Homeless v. Husted* (2016), *G. G. v. Gloucester County School Board* (2017), and *Garza v. Hargan* (2017). Opinions in the cases have garnered widespread press, and the chosen law review articles are famous among legal scholars, with two of the pieces appearing on a "most-cited law review articles of all time" list (Shapiro and Pearse 2012, 1490, 1494). The articles, which exemplify the trend of "narrative scholarship" (Abrams 1991, 971) over the past three decades, are Mari Matsuda's "Public Response to Racist Speech: Considering the Victim's Story" (1989), Susan Estrich's "Rape" (1986), and Paul Butler's "Racially Based Jury Nullification: Black Power in the Criminal Justice System" (1995).

15. Melissa A. Goldthwaite's chapter, "Here's What I Would Like for You to Know, Epistolary Style as an Invitation to Read and Write Metonymically" relatedly analyzes how metonymic writing enables an author to communicate to both insider and outsider groups. Goldthwaite also focuses on authors writing about race and gender inequalities (chapter 2).

16. Regarding the court system, the most salient example may be *Brown v. Board of Education* (1954), which relied heavily on social science research to invalidate "separate but equal" laws in public schools. As for legal academia, web searches reveal several interdisciplinary courses at most institutions, plus a significant number of institutions with interdisciplinary centers and journals.

17. The relationship between the more widely recognized law-and-literature movement and ALS is nonetheless disputed; some ALS scholars contend that lawyering

applications are not on the law-and-literature movement's agenda (see, e.g., Robbins 2008, 11).

18. Supporting this claim, during an appeal in which a larger court panel adopted Judge Millett's dissent, a colleague accused Judge Millett of presenting the case with "an undeservedly melodramatic flavor" and commented that "J.D. may be sympathetic. But even the sympathetic are bound by long-standing law" (*Garza*, October 24, 2017, 31n10).

REFERENCES

Abrams, Kathryn. 1991. "Hearing the Call of Stories." *California Law Review* 79 (4): 971–1052. doi: http://heinonline.org/HOL/P?h=hein.journals/calr79&i=985.

Amsterdam, Anthony G., and Jerome Bruner. 2002. *Minding the Law*. Cambridge, MA: Harvard University Press.

Armstrong, Stephen V., and Timothy P. Terrell. 2008. "Understanding 'Style' in Legal Writing." *Perspectives: Teaching Legal Research and Writing* 17 (1): 43–47. info.legalsolutions.thomsonreuters.com/pdf/perspec/2008-Fall/2008-Fall-9.pdf.

Bewig, Matthew S. 1994. "*Lochner v. The Journeymen Bakers of New York*: The Journeymen Bakers, Their Hours of Labor, and the Constitution." *American Journal of Legal History* 38 (4): 413–451. doi: https://heinonline.org/HOL/P?h=hein.journals/amhist38&i=423.

Brown v. Board of Education. 1954. 347 U.S. 483 (1954).

Butler, Paul. 1995. "Racially Based Jury Nullification: Black Power in the Criminal Justice System." *Yale Law Journal* 105 (3): 677–725. doi: http://heinonline.org/HOL/P?h=hein.journals/ylr105&i=711.

Chestek, Kenneth D. 2008. "The Plot Thickens: The Appellate Brief as Story." *Journal of the Legal Writing Institute* 14: 127–169. doi: http://heinonline.org/HOL/P?h=hein.journals/jlwriins14&i=179.

Cohen, Morris. 1931. "Justice Holmes and the Nature of Law." *Columbia Law Review* 31 (3): 352–367. Accessed August 4, 2018. doi: https://heinonline.org/HOL/P?h=hein.journals/clr31&i=404.

Collins, Patricia Hill. 2013. *On Intellectual Activism*. Philadelphia: Temple University Press.

Cover, Robert. 1983. "*Nomos* and Narrative." *Harvard Law Review* 97 (1): 4–68. doi: http://heinonline.org/HOL/P?h=hein.journals/hlr97&i=22.

Cover, Robert. 1986. "Violence and the Word." *Yale Law Journal* 95 (8): 1601–1629. doi: http://heinonline.org/HOL/P?h=hein.journals/ylr95&i=1652.

Dawsey, Josh. 2018. "Trump Derides Protections for Immigrants from 'Shithole' Countries." *Washington Post*. January 12, 2018. https://www.washingtonpost.com/politics/trump-attacks-protections-for-immigrants-from-shithole-countries-in-oval-office-meeting/2018/01/11/bfc0725c-f711-11e7-91af-31ac729add94_story.html?utm_term=.8828eedf617e.

Delgado, Richard. 1989. "Storytelling for Oppositionists and Others: A Plea for Narrative." *Michigan Law Review* 87 (8): 2411–2441. doi: http://heinonline.org/HOL/P?h=hein.journals/mlr87&i=2433.

District of Columbia v. Heller. 2008. 554 U.S. 570 (2008).

Dorf, Michael. 2015. "Symposium: In Defense of Justice Kennedy's Soaring Language." *SCOTUSblog*. June 27, 2015. Accessed March 15, 2018. https://www.scotusblog.com/2015/06/symposium-in-defense-of-justice-kennedys-soaring-language/.

Estrich, Susan. 1986. "Rape." *Yale Law Journal* 95 (6): 1087–1184. doi: http://heinonline.org/HOL/P?h=hein.journals/ylr95&i=1106.

Farber, Daniel A., and Suzanna Sherry. 1993. "Telling Stories Out of Law School: An Essay on Legal Narratives." *Stanford Law Review* 45 (4): 807–855. doi: http://heinonline.org/HOL/P?h=hein.journals/stflr45&i=873.

Fisher, Judith. 2003–2004. "The Role of Ethics in Legal Writing: The Forensic Embroiderer, The Minimalist Wizard, and Other Stories." *Scribes Journal of Legal Writing* 9: 77–109. doi: http://heinonline.org/HOL/P?h=hein.journals/scrib9&i=83.
Frank, Jerome. 1951. "Both Ends against the Middle." *University of Pennsylvania Law Review* 100 (1): 20–47. doi: http://heinonline.org/HOL/P?h=hein.journals/pnlr100&i=38.
Galanter, Marc. 1998. "The Faces of Mistrust: The Image of Lawyers in Public Opinion, Jokes, and Political Discourse." *University of Cincinnati Law Review* 66 (3): 804–845. doi: http://heinonline.org/HOL/P?h=hein.journals/ucinlr66&i=815.
Garner, Bryan. 2013. *The Redbook: A Manual on Legal Style*. 3rd ed. St. Paul: West Academic Publishing.
Garza v. Hargan. 2017. No. 17-5236 (D.C. Cir. October 20, 2017) (order) (Millett, J., dissenting). https://apps.washingtonpost.com/g/documents/national/garza-v-hargan-appeals-court-dissent/2604/.
Garza v. Hargan, No. 17-5236 (D.C. Cir. October 24, 2017) (order) (en banc) (Henderson, J., dissenting). Accessed May 28, 2018. https://www.cadc.uscourts.gov/internet/opinions.nsf/C81A5EDEADAE82F2852581C30068AF6E/$file/17-5236-1701167.pdf.
G. G. v. Gloucester County School Board, No. 16-1733 (4th Cir. April 7, 2017) (order) (Davis, J., concurring). Accessed May 26, 2018. https://www.ca4.uscourts.gov/Opinions/Published/161733R1.P.pdf.
Heer, Jeet. 2015. "Antonin Scalia Is the Supreme Court's Greatest Writer." *The New Republic*. June 26, 2015. Accessed March 18, 2018. https://newrepublic.com/article/122167/antonin-scalia-supreme-courts-greatest-writer.
LawProse. n.d. "Garner's Interviews." Accessed March 11, 2018. https://www.lawprose.org/bryan-garner/garners-interviews/.
Lebovits, Gerald. 2018. Social Science Research Network. Last modified March 8, 2018. https://papers.ssrn.com/sol3/cf_dev/AbsByAuth.cfm?per_id=882062.
Lebron, Christopher J. 2017. *The Making of Black Lives Matter: A Brief History of an Idea*. New York: Oxford University Press.
Leiter, Brian. 2007. *Naturalizing Jurisprudence: Essays on American Legal Realism and Naturalism in Legal Philosophy*. New York: Oxford University Press.
Martin, Douglas. 2000. "David Mellinkoff, 85, Enemy of Legalese." *New York Times*. January 16, 2000. Accessed March 20, 2018. https://www.nytimes.com/2000/01/16/us/david-mellinkoff-85-enemy-of-legalese.html.
Matsuda, Mari J. 1989. "Public Response to Racist Speech: Considering the Victim's Story." *Michigan Law Review* 87 (8): 2320–2381. doi: http://heinonline.org/HOL/P?h=hein.journals/mlr87&i=1252.
Matsuda, Mari J. 1996. *Where Is Your Body? and Other Essays on Race, Gender, and the Law*. Boston: Beacon Press.
Mellinkoff, David. 1963. *The Language of the Law*. Boston: Little, Brown.
Mertz, Elizabeth. 1988. "Consensus and Dissent in U.S. Legal Opinions: Narrative Structure and Social Voices." *Anthropological Linguistics* 30 (3/4): 369–394. http://www.jstor.org.proxy.library.georgetown.edu/stable/30028132.
"#MeToo, But Now What?" 2017–2018. *Chicago Tribune*. October 16, 2017–July 18, 2018. Accessed August 4, 2018. http://www.chicagotribune.com/lifestyles/ct-me-too-20171030-storygallery.html?page=1.
Milbank, Dana. 2017. "Fake News Comes to the Supreme Court." *Washington Post*. October 3, 2017. Accessed August 5, 2018. https://www.washingtonpost.com/opinions/fake-news-comes-to-the-supreme-court/2017/10/03/3a17f86c-a87b-11e7-92d158c702d2d975_story.html?utm_term=.ea24e743923e.
Northeast Ohio Coalition for the Homeless v. Husted, No. 16-3603/3691 (6th Cir. September 3, 2016). Accessed May 26, 2018. http://www.opn.ca6.uscourts.gov/opinions.pdf/16a0231p-06.pdf.

Opipari, Benjamin R. 2009. "What Attorneys Can Learn from Children's Literature, and Other Lessons in Style." *Perspectives: Teaching Legal Research and Writing* 17 (2): 135–141. https://info.legalsolutions.thomsonreuters.com/pdf/perspec/2009-winter/2009-winter-8.pdf.

Oxford English Dictionary Online, 2018a. "Embodiment | Imbodiment, n." Accessed August 5, 2018. http://www.oed.com.proxy.library.georgetown.edu/view/Entry/60906?redirectedFrom=embodiment.

Oxford English Dictionary Online, 2018b, "Embody | Imbody, v." Accessed August 4, 2018. http://www.oed.com.proxy.library.georgetown.edu/view/Entry/60907?redirectedFrom=embody.

Plainlanguage.gov. n.d. Plain Language Action and Information Network. "History and Timeline." Accessed March 12, 2018. https://www.plainlanguage.gov/about/history/.

Politico v. Promus Hotels, Inc., 184 F.R.D. 232 (E.D.N.Y. 1999).

Pound, Roscoe. 1909. "Liberty of Contract." *Yale Law Journal* 18 (7): 454–487. doi: http://heinonline.org/HOL/P?h=hein.journals/ylr18&i=464.

"Professor Bennett Convenes Critical Race Theory Legal Scholars for Book Project." 2017. *Brooklyn Law School.* May 30, 2017. Accessed August 4, 2018. https://www.brooklaw.edu/newsandevents/news/2017/05-30-2017a?cat=.

"Public Esteem for Military Still High." 2013. *Pew Research Center.* July 11, 2013. Accessed March 25, 2018. www.pewforum.org/2013/07/11/public-esteem-for-military-still-high/.

Rideout, J. Christopher. 2015. "Applied Legal Storytelling: A Bibliography." *Legal Communication & Rhetoric: Journal of the Association of Legal Writing Directors* 12: 247–264. doi: http://heinonline.org/HOL/P?h=hein.journals/jalwd12&i=247.

Robbins, Ruth Anne. 2008. "An Introduction to the Volume and to Applied Legal Storytelling." *Journal of the Legal Writing Institute* 14: 3–14. doi: http://heinonline.org/HOL/P?h=hein.journals/jlwriins14&i=24.

Ross, Thomas. 1996. *Just Stories: How the Law Embodies Racism and Bias.* Boston: Beacon Press.

Serwer, Adam. 2014. "Conservatives Attack Sotomayor over Affirmative Action Dissent." *MSNBC.* April 23, 2014. Accessed March 18, 2018. https://www.msnbc.com/msnbc/conservatives-attack-sotomayor-affirmative-action-dissent.

Shapiro, Fred R., and Michelle Pearse. 2012. "The Most-Cited Law Review Articles of All Time." *Michigan Law Review* 110 (8): 1483–1520. doi: http://heinonline.org/HOL/P?h=hein.journals/mlr110&i=1536.

Siegel, David M. 1999. "Felix Frankfurter, Charles Hamilton Houston and the 'N-Word': A Case Study in the Evolution of Judicial Attitudes Toward Race." *Southern California Interdisciplinary Law Journal* 7 (2): 317–373. doi: http://heinonline.org/HOL/P?h=hein.journals/scid7&i=323.

Stanchi, Kathryn M., Linda L. Berger, and Bridget J. Crawford, eds. 2016. *Feminist Judgments: Rewritten Opinions of the Supreme Court.* New York: Cambridge University Press.

Stewart, David O. 2007. *The Summer of 1787.* New York: Simon & Schuster.

Strunk, William, Jr., and E. B. White. 1999. *The Elements of Style.* 4th ed. London: Pearson.

Trump v. Hawaii, 138 S. Ct. 2392 (2018).

"West Academic Store." n.d. *West Academic.* Accessed August 4, 2018. http://store.westacademic.com/Store/?search=stories+series.

Wydick, Richard C. 2005. *Plain English for Lawyers.* 5th ed. Durham, NC: Carolina Academic Press.

12
WHAT STYLE CAN ADD TO GENRE
Suggestions for Applying Stylistics to Disciplinary Writing

Anthony Box

Composition's relationship with disciplinary writing is most apparent in the development of Writing Across the Curriculum (WAC) and Writing in the Discipline (WID) programs. WAC research focuses on a "write to learn" approach, which prioritizes the use of expressive and reflective writing as a way to enhance student learning (Bazerman et al. 2005, 57). WID developed later as a response to more specific language concerns within different disciplines. WID helps researchers "understand how different disciplines construct knowledge through different textual forms, and the kinds of challenges students must meet when learning to write within their chosen fields" (66). In order to address the "different textual forms" students must deal with, WID relies on genre theory. Mentions of style are often lacking.

Some WAC and WID researchers have argued that genre is enough to address issues of form. Charles Bazerman, one of the driving forces in the WAC movement, explicitly states this in his response to an Anthony Fleury article that approached the issue through style:

> I am particularly pleased that Fleury here identifies his entryway into disciplinary difference through the concept of style, even though I have found the concepts of genre and activity system to be ultimately more powerful tools to understand those differences. (2005, 89)

Other researchers have also focused on genre to explain issues of form. David R. Russell, for example, in "Contradictions Regarding Teaching and Writing (or Writing to Learn) in the Disciplines: What We Have Learned in the USA" explores the issue of form/content dualism. He explains that "the link between form and content is genre, but genre conceived not as textual forms subject to taxonomic classification, but 'genre as social action'" (Russell 2013, 165). Here, Russell draws on Carolyn Miller's work, which argues for the importance of including context to traditional definitions of genre based on form and substance. "Genre in this way," she writes, "becomes more than a formal entity; it becomes pragmatic, fully rhetorical, a point of connection between intention and effect, an aspect of social action" (Miller 1984, 153).

Genre is one way to approach this dualism, but it is not the only way. The idea of the form/content dualism vs monism is an important aspect of stylistic study. Louis Milic, for example, explored the link between form and content in "Theories of Style and Their Implications for the Teaching of Composition." Milic offers three theories of style: "the theory of ornate form, or rhetorical dualism," which implies that "ideas exist wordlessly and can be dressed in a variety of outfits, depending on the need for the occasion" (1965, 67); "the individualist or psychological monism" theory, which argues that "style is the man" (67); and the "most modern theory of style, Crocean aesthetic monism . . . which denies the possibility of any separation between content and form" (67).

Much of Richard Lanham's work also focuses on the tension between form and content. Lanham conceives of style as extending far beyond written texts, but his ideas stem from *oscillatio*, a rhetorical figure of his own design. *Oscillatio* explains how our minds perceive and pay attention to things. According to Lanham, our minds must oscillate between focusing on form and content. He explains that "we alternatively participate in the world and step back and reflect on how we attend to it. We first write, absorbed in what we have to say, and then revise, look at how we have written it" (Lanham 2006, xiii).

While style and genre are closely related, and often focus on similar aspects of writing, it can be helpful to mark the distinctions between them. In "Tracking Interpersonal Style: The Use of Functional Language Analysis in College Writing Instruction" Zac Lancaster explains that composition studies has "de-centered" language because of "the social turn," explaining that "the increasing use of social constructionist theories to examine texts . . . had the effect of shifting attention away from the texts themselves to their larger social contexts" (2013, 194). He argues that "the social turn" goes too far in redirecting composition's focus away from linguistic concerns, so that "the field's theoretical understanding of language and how it functions as a meaning-making resource has been under-explored" (194). Brian Ray clearly summarizes Lancaster's approach to genre and style, explaining that the choices authors make "contribute to a sense of the writer's style and, over time, they accumulate across authors and texts to shape a genre's stylistic expectations" (2015, 138).

Paul Butler also attempts to mark the boundary between genre and style. He likens style's history in composition to a "diaspora" and argues that style has "migrated" or "dispersed" into genre (2008, 89–90). Butler then takes Anis Bawarshi's genre analysis of syllabus writing and extends the analysis through stylistics, arguing that "by using direct tools of stylistic analysis, [Bawarshi] would have had access to additional resources to understand the rhetorical and generic forces at work in syllabus construction" (91).

Both Lancaster and Butler argue that style can add to an analysis of genre. Throughout the rest of this chapter, I will attempt to show one way this sort of addition can take shape. I then hope to suggest other ways that style can be useful to genre analysis and disciplinary writing. To do this, I will examine some examples of academic writing from two different disciplines: counseling psychology and composition.

I will begin with an example from *The Counseling Psychologist*. The following paragraph is an excerpt from "Character Strengths and First-Year College Students' Academic Persistence Attitudes: An Integrative Model," taken from the most recent edition of *The Counseling Psychologist* (at the time of writing, of course).

> Specifically, our integrated model suggests that character strengths are directly related to academic integration, and academic integration, in turn, is related to institutional commitment.
>
> Additionally, research and theory suggest that the quality of existing familial and peer relationships are confounded with hope (Fruiht, 2015), gratitude (Kong, Ding, & Zhao, 2015), and academic persistence variables (Dennis, Phinney, & Chuateco, 2005). Therefore, controlling for the unique contributions of perceived social support in the present model should provide a more precise picture of how character strengths uniquely predict student persistence attitudes. Likewise, given that college students are a diverse group of individuals representing many different cultural perspectives, preliminary race and/or ethnicity and gender explorations of the present model are necessary. Indeed, although researchers have not found any notable differences in positive psychology scores between men and women, at least one study suggested that the positive benefits of hope may not always occur in samples of Black college students (Banks, Singleton, & Kohn-Wood, 2008). (Browning et al. 2018, 613)

What sorts of observations can be made about the above writing? One could make the same observation that Aull and Lancaster make about their example in chapter 6 (this volume): "This passage strikes us as a fairly ordinary stretch of academic prose." Absent of any "panache or flare," both paragraphs accomplish their given purpose. Like Aull and Lancaster's example, the above passage's use of metalanguage helps explain why we consider it to be "academic." But, where Aull and Lancaster focus on the purpose the metalanguage is used for, my analysis is more concerned with how particular instances of metalanguage are integrated into the text structurally.

Notice how each of the four sentences in the example begins. Every sentence begins with a single word of metalanguage, followed by a comma. Only then can the sentence proceed. In this example we have the words "specifically," "additionally," "therefore," "likewise," and "indeed." Each of these words communicates something to the audience. If we use Aull and Lancaster's definitions, we see that these words all take an "interactional stance," meaning they work to make connections within the writing. Each of the four words in our example seeks to forge a different type of connection between what came before and what comes next. The words the writers chose do serve a purpose, but the choice to begin every sentence in the paragraph with the same kind of structure may have a negative effect on the reader.

The issue here, then, is with cohesion and coherence. Joseph Williams and Joseph Bizup, in *Style: Lessons in Clarity and Grace*, use the related terms "cohesion" and "coherence" as a way to explain how writers produce clarity and "flow." The authors explain that "we judge a sequence of sentences to be *cohesive* based on how each sentence ends and the next begins. We judge a whole passage to be *coherent* based on how all the sentences in it cumulatively begin" (Williams and Bizup 2017, 65).

What Williams and Bizup are referring to is the "given-new contract" developed by Herbert H. Clark and Susan E. Haviland. They explain:

> The given-new contract is concerned with a distinction the speaker is obliged to make between given information and new information. In all languages, probably (Chafe, 1970), declarative sentences convey two kinds of information: (1) information the speaker considers given—information he believes the listener already knows and accepts as true; and (2) information the speaker considers new—information he believes the listener does not yet know. (Clark and Haviland 1977, 3)

When this contract, or convention, is broken, communication can break down or become inefficient.

Consider again the passage from *The Counseling Psychologist*. What information is new? What is given? And, remembering Williams and Bizup's explanation of cohesion, where in each sentence does the new information occur in relation to the given information? Look at the first sentence: "Specifically, our integrated model suggests that character strengths are directly related to academic integration, and academic integration, in turn, is related to institutional commitment." This sentence serves to show the relationship between three main concepts:

What Style Can Add to Genre   189

"character strengths" (which serve as one of the main focuses of the article), "academic integration," and "institutional commitment." Using the given-new contract, as well as Williams and Bizup's definition of cohesion, one would expect the following sentence to begin with one of these terms. Instead, the authors choose to lead with "the quality of existing familial and peer relationships" and end the sentence with "hope, gratitude, and academic persistence variables." (I should mention that at this point in the article, the authors can be reasonably certain that the reader will know that the "character strengths" they are interested in are "hope" and "gratitude.") So if the authors were to follow the "given-new contract," they would want to connect "character strength" at the end of one sentence to "hope and gratitude" at the beginning of the next. Instead, they have saved "hope and gratitude" for the end of that sentence, moving from new to given.

This decision becomes even more confusing when we look at the next sentence: "Therefore, controlling for the unique contributions of perceived social support in the present model should provide a more precise picture of how character strengths uniquely predict student persistence attitudes." Again, if cohesion is achieved by relating the end of one sentence to the beginning of the next, then logically we would expect "existing familial and peer relationships" to occur at the end of the preceding sentence, so it would align with "the unique contributions of perceived social support." To simplify this argument, look at how the flow of ideas works if we display it visually.

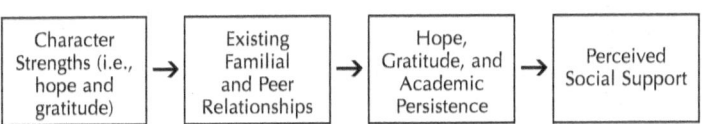

Logically, the flow of ideas does not make sense. Simply flipping the middle boxes will help the sentence achieve cohesion:

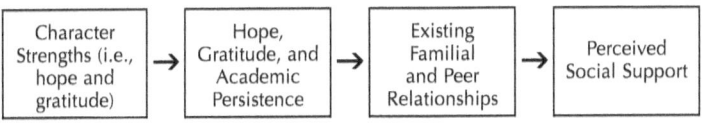

Now the flow of ideas seems more logical. Readers can track how each idea relates to the next and are not given information out of order. The given-new contract is honored. Communication is clear.

If the authors were to revise accordingly, the sentences might look something like this:

> Specifically, our integrated model suggests that character strengths are directly related to academic integration, and academic integration, in turn, is related to institutional commitment.
>
> Additionally, research and theory suggest that hope, gratitude, and academic persistence variables are confounded with the quality of existing familial and peer relationships. Therefore, controlling for the unique contributions of perceived social support in the present model should provide a more precise picture of how character strengths uniquely predict student persistence attitudes.

It's not perfect. Flipping around the middle sentence as I have might not create the relationship the authors intended, and the terms used in these sentences could be altered to draw stronger connections among sentences. For example, the connection between "character strengths" and "hope and gratitude" is implied contextually but could be made more explicit. Still, even though more revisions are needed, the "flow" of this passage has been improved by attending to cohesion.

Though we have addressed cohesion, establishing coherence is equally important in helping readers make sense of a piece of writing. Williams and Bizup explain that coherence is created when the beginnings of sentences relate to one another in an extended piece of writing. They suggest using related topics in the subject position of sentences as a way to "focus our attention" (2017, 71).

What topics hold the subject position in the example passage? "Our integrated model" is the subject of the first. "Research and theory" is the subject of the first sentence of the second paragraph. The next sentence begins with a gerund, which makes the subject "controlling for the unique contributions of perceived social support." The next sentence uses "college students" as a subject, and the final sentence uses "researchers." This is a diverse set of topics that does not have much in common. Instead of beginning each sentence so differently, the authors may try to organize their thoughts around the main idea of the paragraph. In this case the paragraph seems to be about the variables they want to control in the study they are conducting. Organizing each of the sentences to begin with a variation of that idea would be one way to create coherence throughout the paragraph.

Instead of actual coherence, the authors seem to be using what Williams and Bizup call "faked coherence." Faked coherence happens when writers "[lace] their prose with conjunctions like *thus, therefore, however*, and so on, regardless of whether they signal real logical connections" (2017, 75). Notice how every sentence in the example starts in this way. In order to mask the lack of cohesion or coherence within the passage, the authors rely on metalanguage to connect their sentences.

They force the metalanguage to do work that should be done structurally, forcing and faking coherence.

Coherence is attempted with varying degrees of success throughout the article, but the use of "interactional metalanguage" in this way is constant. Over and over again the authors rely on this structure of beginning their sentences with metalanguage. The result is a barrage of *therefores*, *thuses* and *moreovers* that can feel a bit overwhelming. Williams and Bizup advocate using these kinds of words no more than "a few times a page," because "your readers don't need them when your sentences are cohesive and the passage they make up is coherent" (2017, 75).

The authors of the counseling psychology article use these words much more than "a few times a page." Over the course of the article (which has about seventeen pages of text), eight sentences begin with "Thus," five begin with "However," five begin with "Moreover," five begin with "Specifically," four begin with "Indeed," and three begin with "Therefore." Add to this a list of words that are only used once or twice, like "additionally," "accordingly," or "together," and numbered words that use the same construction, like "first," "next," "second," or "lastly." These examples are not distributed evenly throughout the paper, causing some pages or paragraphs to be oversaturated with this sentence construction. This in turn heightens the overwhelming feeling readers may experience. Whether or not coherence is logically created, the over-reliance on metalanguage in this way suggests an artificial attempt to create flow. The writing doesn't so much as lead the reader through logical arguments as it grabs them by the hand and drags them along.

This trend doesn't seem to be unique to this first article. Another article in the same issue of *The Counseling Psychologist* titled "Discursive Psychology: Implications for Counseling Psychology" is characterized by the same use of metalanguage. Below is a fairly typical stretch of prose:

> Here, Speaker 1's talk is heard as "doing" an invitation, which is made evident with Speaker 2's response, "Okay, I'll go with you." In this instance, no direct invitation is given, such as "Would you come along?" Rather, Speaker 1 formulates an implicit invitation. Whether one is giving an invitation, blaming, seeking advice, complaining, negotiating, making a case, etc., such social activities often occur through language, and these very social activities are the subject of study when conducting a discourse analysis. That is, language "performs" or "does" social life. It is not simply a neutral reflection of social life; rather, it is through language that things (like invitations, excuses, or even racial identity) are accomplished. Notably, this notion provides an interesting contrast to research on the positive social effects of engaging in the expression of language through writing. (Lester 2018, 578)

Notice again how the sentences tend to begin. The authors rely on the same sentence construction as the previous article in that they frequently begin with metalanguage followed by a comma. In this paragraph we have "here," "in this instance," "rather," "that is," and "notably." This is not an isolated example. The article (which spans about twenty-three pages of actual writing, not counting notes or graphs) constantly uses this structure. Fourteen sentences begin with "thus," eleven begin with "for example," eight begin with "for instance," six begin with "notably," four begin with "indeed," four with "further," and three with "instead." This article also uses numbered metalanguage much more frequently than the previous article. "First" is used to begin nine sentences, while "second" and "third" are used about as frequently.

It is worth mentioning here that this article does a much better job of constructing actual coherence, as opposed to fake coherence. Notice in the above paragraph how certain topic words, like "invitation," "language," and "social life," as well as the character of "Speaker 1," run through multiple sentences, and notice also where these topic words are placed within sentences. Actual, strong connections are built here. The metalanguage in this case only serves to emphasize these already strong connections. Williams and Bizup might argue that they are unnecessary. Although coherence and cohesion are created structurally, the overuse of this sentence structure could negatively affect flow in other ways. When nearly every sentence begins the same way (a word or short phrase followed by a pause), a monotonous rhythm is created. Readers may find this off-putting.

At this point in this analysis, it may be helpful to speculate why the use of this sentence construction is so prevalent in the two articles, which appear side by side in the same edition of *The Counseling Psychologist.* If we were to analyze more articles and find that this trend persists, we may be able to argue that it is significant to the genre or discipline of writing. Two articles are not enough to make that claim, but they do suggest an avenue for future research. Instead, we may speculate on the authors and why they choose to use that particular form so frequently.

One possibility is that their use of the form is unconscious, or unintentional. If the overuse of metalanguage really is a staple of that publication or that genre of writing, they may be copying a form that they are familiar with without questioning why they use it. Again, the evidence needed to make that claim about the genre, discipline, or article is lacking, but the possibility is worth mentioning.

A second possibility is that the readers of this particular journal (or discipline) appreciate the excessive use of metalanguage. The authors aren't writing to compositionists after all, so we shouldn't assume that they have the same values about writing as we do. Perhaps since this is a science journal, the readers do not read the same way we do. Scientific writing carries with it a history of impartiality, derived from the theory of style as ornamentation that Milic described. As Ray explains, "[S]cientific writing needed to be as devoid of artifice as possible, while endeavoring to cement the relationship between words and ideas" (2015, 72). Facts, information—that's what matters; not how they are expressed. Substance, not style. In this case the readers of the two articles we looked at might consider the metalanguage to work as some sort of road map, guiding them to the facts and knowledge they seek faster. This is possible, yet doubtful.

To explain why this second possibility doesn't seem sound, I will try and examine the reasons authors (specifically authors in psychology) write. Hartley, Sotto, and Pennebaker explore this issue in "Style and Substance in Psychology: Are Influential Articles More Readable than Less Influential Ones?" They explain that

> academics write for many reasons but we consider that two (overlapping) reasons are especially important. One is "to make the grade." The other is to make a useful contribution to society. In trying to achieve the former, we think that writers are more likely to write to a formula and to produce respectable academic prose. However, in trying to achieve the latter, we think that writers are more likely to strive to communicate as clearly as they can. (Hartley 2002, 322)

If we agree with this premise, then the authors we have been examining must balance their desire to affect "academic" prose with the desire that their ideas contribute to society. Their desire to "make the grade" could have influenced their decision to rely more heavily on the formulaic use of metalanguage we have discussed thus far.

To these desires I would add a third: the desire to have your work noticed. Yes, academics should strive to produce knowledge for knowledge's sake, but they also have to eat. Jobs, tenure, and funding can be determined by the scholarship you produce. When writing and publishing articles, academics are surely inspired by the two reasons Hartley and colleagues describe, but we should not rule out the desire for attention and reward.

The style guidelines for submitting to *The Counseling Psychologist* (which is housed in Sage Publications) are expectedly sparse. Concerns of style are reduced to matters of grammar, formatting, and citations. However, the submission form does link to a page that devotes a great deal of attention to the use of keywords. These keywords appear after the abstract and are meant to help the article appear more often in search results. The page refers to this as "discoverability." Authors and publishers alike want their work to be "discoverable," and the publishers have devoted time to help their authors game the search-engine system. They want it to be read and studied and cited. Keywords might help make an article be discoverable, but *style* is what helps make it memorable.

Richard Lanham makes this point in *The Economics of Attention*. He explains that because the internet has revolutionized how we discover and process information, and because information is increasingly valuable, our economy is undergoing significant change. Some have suggested naming this new economy an "information economy." Lanham challenges this name, explaining that economics studies the allocation of scarce resources.

> In an information economy, what is the scarce resource? Information, obviously. But information doesn't seem in short supply. Precisely the opposite. We're drowning in it. There is too much information around to make sense of it all. . . . What then is the new scarcity economics seeks to describe? It can only be the human attention needed to make sense of information. (Lanham 2007, 6–7)

This description sounds very relevant to the issue of discoverability. The publishers, on some level, recognize the need for human attention. So much academic information is readily available, thanks to online publishing and databases, that discoverability is a real concern. Their solution is the use of keywords to manipulate search traffic.

Again, I must stress that discoverability is only half of the issue, memorability being the second. As Lanham explains, "the devices that regulate attention are stylistic devices. Attracting attention is what style is all about" (2007, xi). If authors and publishers truly want to attract a larger audience, they might benefit from the use of stylistic devices. In attempting to use keywords to make articles more discoverable, publishers and authors are manipulating language to gain the attention of search engines, but they often ignore the need to cater to human attention after those articles have been discovered.

With this in mind, I offer a third possibility to explain the overbearing and formulaic use of metalanguage in the counseling psychology articles we have analyzed thus far: the authors have a lack of stylistic awareness, or a lack of stylistic familiarity. I find this possibility to be the most likely.

A lack of stylistic awareness (or familiarity) does not mean that the writing we have analyzed is necessarily bad. The first article certainly "makes the grade" of academic writing, as Hartley and colleagues would say. And the second article was actually very well-written and did many interesting things with language aside from its formulaic use of metalanguage. Stylistic awareness simply refers to how authors use language to create meaning. W. Ross Winterowd helps to explain why the relationship between style and substance is so important. He writes:

> The first job of pedagogy in rhetoric is to help the student learn to manipulate the physical elements of the system of language. Structures obviously carry meaning; it is my argument that they also force meaning. Thus, in a very real sense manner forces matter. (1970, 163)

He goes on to explain that "when the student has internalized a grammatical device, he has also acquired a 'mechanism' that can generate an original thought. Style is the manner of the matter" (167). In the case of the counseling psychologists, lack of stylistic awareness simply means that they might not have internalized a variety of stylistic devices. They might fall back on this one set stylistic device out of habit or necessity. Had they internalized more of these stylistic devices, they might have been able to construct their sentences with more variety, leading to more and different connections between their ideas and more original thoughts.

Miller's definition of "genre as social action" is worth further consideration here. Miller and others make sure to define genre as typified rhetorical actions or forms that are momentarily stabilized. Genre conventions then are useful, and so they are reused. But they are not rules or set in stone. The conventions are instead tied heavily to context. Students and established authors alike are encouraged to help define and redefine the genre they are writing in as they write in it (Russell 2013). It is this point that I believe makes the strongest case for teaching stylistic awareness alongside genre awareness. As Winterowd showed, writers internalize stylistic devices, which are then used to create new and original thoughts and form a wider variety of connections among ideas. If we expect writers (student and professional alike) to question, interact with, and redefine the genres they participate in, they will need these internalized stylistic devices, this stylistic awareness.

Stylistic awareness and genre awareness must go hand in hand. In addition to affording writers more choices as they write, stylistic awareness can also allow writers and readers more nuance and control as they interact with language (Lancaster 2013, 194). When allowed to move beyond the confines of prose writing, stylistic awareness can offer writers and publishers more ways to manipulate human attention, which can influence how often their work is read (Lanham 2007).

REFERENCES

Bazerman, Charles. 2005. "A Response to Anthony Fleury's 'Liberal Education and Communication against the Disciplines': A View from the World of Writing." *Communication Education* 54 (1): 86–91.

Bazerman, Charles, Joseph Little, Lisa Bethel, Teri Chavkin, Danielle Fouquette, and Janet Garfus. 2005. *Reference Guide to Writing across the Curriculum*. West Lafayette, IN: Parlor Press.

Browning, Brandon R., Ryon C. McDermott, Marjorie E. Scaffa, Nathan R. Booth, and Nicole T. Carr. 2018. "Character Strengths and First-Year College Students' Academic Persistence Attitudes: An Integrative Model." *The Counseling Psychologist* 46 (5): 608–631.

Butler, Paul. 2008. *Out of Style: Reanimating Stylistic Study in Composition and Rhetoric*. Logan: Utah State University Press.

Clark, Herbert H., and Susan E. Haviland. 1977. "Comprehension and the Given-New Contract." In *Discourse Production and Comprehension*, edited by Roy O. Freedle, 1–40. Norwood, NJ: Ablex Publishing Corporation.

Hartley, Clark, Eric Sotto, and James Pennebaker. 2002. "Style and Substance in Psychology: Are Influential Articles More Readable than Less Influential Ones?" *Social Studies of Science* 32 (2): 321–334.

"Help Readers Find Your Article." N.d. Sage Publishing. https://us.sagepub.com/en-us/nam/help-readers-find-your-article. Accessed October 28, 2018.

Lancaster, Zak. 2013 "Tracking Interpersonal Style: The Use of Functional Language Analysis in College Writing Instruction." In *The Centrality of Style*, edited by Mike Duncan and Star Medzerian Vanguri, 191–212. Fort Collins, CO: WAC Clearinghouse.

Lanham, Richard A. 2007. *The Economics of Attention: Style and Substance in the Age of Information*. Chicago: University of Chicago Press.

Lester, Jessica Nina, Y. Joel Wong, Michelle O'Reilly, and Nikki Kiyimba. 2018. "Discursive Psychology: Implications for Counseling Psychology." *The Counseling Psychologist* 46 (5): 576–607.

Milic, Louis. 1965. "Theories of Style and Their Implications for the Teaching of Composition." *College Composition and Communication* 16 (2): 66–69, 126.

Miller, Carolyn R. 1984. "Genre as Social Action." *Quarterly Journal of Speech* 70: 151–167.

Ray, Brian. 2015. *Style: An Introduction to History, Theory, Research, and Pedagogy*. Anderson, SC: Parlor Press.

Russell, David R. 2013. "Contradictions Regarding Teaching and Writing (or Writing to Learn) in the Disciplines: What We Have Learned in the USA." *Revista de Docencia Universitaria* 11 (1): 161–181.

Williams, Joseph M., and Joseph Bizup. 2017. *Style: Lessons in Clarity and Grace*, 12th ed. Boston: Pearson.

Winterowd, W. Ross. 1970. "Style: A Matter of Manner." *Quarterly Journal of Speech* 56: 161–167.

SECTION 4

Style Creates and Transcends Boundaries

13
POINT OF DEPARTURES
Composition and Creative Writing Studies' Shared Stylistic Values

Jon Udelson

Considering the role style may play in helping those of us in composition studies think through questions of disciplinarity entails considering the ways so-called disciplinary divides implicate writers, material practices of writing, and writing-centric fields of study. Despite scholarship seeking to find consonance between the two, one such disciplinary divide is often still thought to remain between creative writing and composition. A discourse around style, however, can help bridge this divide by helping us deliberate on, first, how and in what ways these disciplines take up a particular, shared conception of style as a form of writing knowledge and, second, how this shared conception may trouble the very existence of this divide. To not delay the point, what I'll be arguing in this chapter is that the writing values held by creative writing and composition find that consonance when understood through the techne of writing that treats style as a production of difference. Acknowledging that theories of production in creative writing and composition share a common take-off point can help us see that the two disciplines are not as epistemologically incompatible as some would argue.

In fact, by going this route we may quickly see instead that questions of disciplinary difference are often questions about individuals or groups of individuals and their statuses as professionals ensconced within institutions and iterations of program types: the ways they/we create and recognize knowledge, how they/we guard knowledge, and how they/we use knowledge to perpetuate their statuses as disciplinary autonomous professionals (see also Olinger, chapter 1). Put another way, the creative writing–composition (hence, CW-Comp) divide is better informed by what we say about the disciplines' stances toward stylistic knowledge than about any specific methodological approaches to the production of writing in or for those disciplines.

FRAMING THE DIVIDE

Since I started all this pretty nebulously, let me offer a quote from D. W. Fenza—poet, critic, scholar in the field of creative writing studies,[1] and former executive director of the Association of Writers and Writing Programs (AWP)—in order to help contextualize the issue to which I allude. In "The Centre Has Not Held: Creative Writing and Pluralism" (2011), published in *New Writing: The International Journal for the Practice and Theory of Creative Writing*, Fenza speaks of the potential appropriation of creative writing by composition. He writes:

> The composition theory-mongers can especially be relied upon for broadsides that seek to force writing programs to surrender their childish pirate flags; creative writing, they argue, needs to codify its pedagogy into something reasonable, systematic, and unified; the theory-mongers offer systems for doing this, of course, even though few of them themselves have published a wonderful book of fiction or poetry. In the academic professionalization of creative writing, there is always the danger that these academic scolds will supplant the poets, novelists, and short story writers. (212)

It should be known that Fenza has long championed the view that knowledge in and from the field of creative writing is nearly inscrutable from outside it. He has often spoken in defense of the continued isolated autonomy of creative writing programs, its practitioners and pedagogues, and the link between publication and field competence. As Mayers (2018) points out, Fenza here relies on a series of "unquestioned assumptions that seem to animate his argument." However, a "careful reading of the passage above can tease out a sort of submerged moral position: an implied belief that things *ought to be* a particular way" (58).

This assumptive, moral positioning affords Fenza the latitude to situate compositionists in a multitude of disparaging ways vis-à-vis creative writing at the programmatic level. These "theory-mongers," in their misguided practices of "codifying" creative writing's pedagogy "into something reasonable" are, in the language of assault and submission, "forc[ing] writing programs," and thus their administrators, "to surrender." And of course the "danger" Fenza sees with compositionists meddling in creative writing pedagogy and programmatics is the corruption of an institutional product: the teaching of creative writing in a particular way, determined by a particular set of disciplinary professionals who hold influence over large-scale pedagogical conventions, and executed by a particular type of professional whose highest qualification is their[2] ability to publish something codified as "wonderful" (i.e., an expression of elite writing, of "great" literature) in the world of literary consumption.

However, as just one example among many, a year *prior* to Fenza's piece, Doug Hesse (2010) wrote of composition's need to consider the affordances of the aesthetic. Hesse concedes in this discussion that creative writing offers students in vast amounts what composition for several decades had offered little of: "the rhetorical force of image and identification, metaphor and symbol, of narrative arc and character as actor and acted upon, of Burkean ratios enacted in possibility rather than constrained by given formations." In acknowledging creative writing's ability to "shape what readers think and do," and that much of it is "grounded in experience, memory, imagination, image and sound, reality shaped into texts, to represent, yes, but also to ponder and render" (48), Hesse sees creative writing in composition as doing something other than the lifeless, ineffectual, and appropriative work Fenza believes compositionists would have it do. Contrary to Fenza's fears, Hesse's call to put creative writing to work in order to aid composition students' "pondering" and "rendering" suggests composition's ability to acknowledge the quite literally "wonderful" affordances of creative writing. Hesse even goes so far as to bemoan that in composition's mid-1980s landscape, which influenced much thereafter, there existed a "perception that developing 'a style'" founded in the aesthetic or "creative" "was wrongheaded," "incommensurate with prevailing theories of textuality," and linked to the propagation of troubling structures of power (40).

Notably, then, the biggest problem with Fenza's argument is that there's just not much proof of it in the literature. While creative writing and composition do not share a particularly robust, *recent* history[3] of collaboration and partnership, a fair amount of both contemporary and not-terribly-dated scholarship in composition and other English studies fields identifies the affordances each discipline can lend the other without one necessarily dominating the other (see, e.g., Bishop 1990; Lardner 1999; Mayers 2005; Hesse 2010; Berg and May 2015; Koehler 2017). Further, a significant number of those with backgrounds in creative writing are entering into rhetoric and composition, bringing with them their accrued knowledge of the field of fine arts in order to reshape the new disciplinary territory of which they are a part. Beyond that, the field of creative writing studies continues to swell with theorists who operate across the two disciplines, and scholarship in composition (including in style studies) continues to consider the relationship between them (see, e.g., Butler 2008; Ellis 2013; Fodrey 2013; Sullivan 2015).

Now some questions: whence the origin of grievances like the ones Fenza makes? What is the nature of the continued scholarship on the incompatibility of creative writing and composition? And when can I stop having barroom conversations with my poet and fiction-writing friends who scoff at the idea of creative writing being discussed in academic contexts at all?

In what follows, I attempt to address these questions by elaborating on the ways traditional notions of disciplinarity obfuscate some of the connections between institutional creative writing and composition. I then present a labor-based perspective on style-as-difference and discuss how this perspective links the stylistic goals of programmatic creative writing and programmatic composition. Finally, I end by offering a short critique based in these linkages of a case example of creative writing studies scholarship that argues in favor of viewing creative writing and composition as epistemologically different endeavors.

DISCIPLINARY OBFUSCATION AND STYLE AS MATERIAL PRACTICE

The CW-Comp divide, I would argue, has more to do with what traditional notions of disciplinarity would have us believe about the fixedness of disciplinary boundaries than it does about anything essential to the acts of writing creatively, composing more broadly, and studying each. Thaiss and Zawacki (2006) point out that disciplines in general possess two major salient features. The first is a shared understanding of what counts as evidence and knowledge, and the second is the collection of shared methods and methodologies by which knowledge is created. Both these features are nonessential, however, and are the result of social actions within social systems. They, in other words, entail the activities of a group or several groups of people who, in the seminal words of Toulmin (1972) from whom Thaiss and Zawacki draw, share a "commitment to a sufficiently agreed set of ideals [that] leads to the development of an isolable and self-defining repertory of procedures" (359). It follows that if one does not agree with, share in, or abide by those ideals, one would have a tendency to become distanced from the larger social systems and systems of institutional power and activity that perpetuate these "repertory of procedures"—and thus the knowledge produced as an outcome of those procedures, which, in turn, reinforces the primacy of the repertory. Such a distancing does not *objectively* invalidate this outsider repertory but rather professionally casts that repertory as invisible, insufficient, or unsatisfactory.

A common misconstrual of disciplines, then, is that they are discrete, bound, and non-porous territories of knowledge production whose members are somehow autonomous to that discipline and hermetically sealed into it.[4] This view of discipline-as-bubble makes it difficult for those outside it to comment on the goings-on within. Outsiders are often made to feel they lack the proper idiom of communication needed to knowledgeably engage in debate, or else they comment on the outside discipline from inside their own bubble and so misconstrue the work of its theorists and practitioners. In this way the ability to style one's writing by the common conventions of a particular discipline—"creative writing," for example, not so much an elite form of literary production as it is a form of writing generally designated "creative" and reinforced by the continued production in creative writing programs of poetry, fiction, drama, and the like—aids in marking a writer as part of the discipline and the believed epistemological terrain it governs. From a disciplinary perspective, treading that terrain otherwise constitutes an act of trespassing. Composition cannot speak of creative writing because composition is still all too often thought of as the domain of "general writing skills instruction" (Petraglia 1995), while creative writing exists in a domain beyond mere "skill."

A discourse around style can trouble this apparent CW-Comp divide by challenging both the scholarship and "institutional-conventional wisdom" (Mayers 2005) that reinforce it. Style helps us call attention to the pedagogical goals creative writing and composition share: to consider writing as remarkable, to agitate the form/content divide, and to impact readers both intellectually and emotionally. I locate the common point of departure in these shared pedagogical goals not in overarching discussions of the relationships among epistemology, ontology, and disciplinarity but rather as embedded in discussions of labor, that is, in professional practices that come to define knowledge and method within a discipline. Keeping with a discussion of style from this angle may help scholars across the divide recognize creative writing and composition as part of the same metaphorical economy of attention (see Lanham 2006), even though their currencies may appear quite different at times.

In order to broker this conversation, I want to think about style in its capacity to attract attention through a process of differentiation. Horner (2018) notes that creative writing's primary commodity can best be described as a method to produce "difference in language, as well as in communicative practice more generally" (113). In function, this primary commodity is programmatically tasked with separating elite language from the humdrum, innovative forms from the worn.[5] A student of creative writing is often taught to find inspiration in the deeply personal and idiosyncratic, to synthesize new combinations of sound and word to create meaning beyond the denotative, and, perhaps still most commonly, to find their distinct "voice."[6] Horner notes, however, that this goal of signaling difference is not "a deviation from the norm but, rather, is the norm itself" (113). And what is style if not a way to draw attention through difference, to be memorable, and to provide a gambit for creating knowledge?

A focus on the techne of writing, in its capacity to emphasize the production rather than the reception of the written, provides a potential in-road linking creative writing with composition through a practice in style. Techne in the realm of creative writing finds purchase most prominently with the idea of craft and craft's connotations with the physical, the concrete, the laborious (see Mayers 2005; Pender 2011). For example, Alsup (2005), in her discussion of style and "literary sensitivity" in the composition classroom, writes that the process of crafting "calls to mind a fine cabinetmaker whose work is distinguished by precision: measuring, trimming, planing, sanding, polishing." Likening her approach toward producing fiction with those of numerous other creative writers with whom she has come in contact throughout her career, Alsup notes that their "word by word" and "sentence by sentence" attention "follows the same metaphor" of craftspersonship and that "what emerges from such diligent efforts is really our style" (94). For Alsup, style achieved through craftspersonship represents a "distinction" (94), one she holds for herself apart from other producers of literary work and that informs not only an aspect of her work produced but also her professional-disciplinary identity. Style, then, in this production-oriented frame, not only serves as a process of differentiation but also suggests a labor-oriented relationship among difference, memorability, and inimitability (i.e., the "distinguish[ment] by precision").

This conception of style pairs nicely with a description Butler (2010b) provides in his introduction to *Style in Rhetoric and Composition*. Therein, Butler conceives of style's perhaps most salient characteristic: "a key way to separate what is memorable from forgettable in history" (5). Butler suggests here the affordance of manipulating language (at, among other sites, the sentence level when considered within the context of alphanumeric texts) in order to call attention to a particular languaging act and argue for the notability of that act. Such a frame implicates both consciously made writerly choices designed to anticipate and impact one's receivers and, of course, the product of the array of choices themselves. Considered within the frame of techne, we may discuss style not as a vehicle for transmitting content but as content itself. And as content, we may note the way style may, in this sense, function competitively—not to *determine* what is memorable in history through some sort of objective or ahistorical process of evaluation, but rather to *make* that which will be historically memorable such. In this way, effective style is never set but is always situational and goals-driven.

Work by Lanham (2006) continues to help inform this perspective by arguing along similar lines when discussing style through the metaphor of filtration:

> The only way to make [information] useful is to filter it. Filtering thus becomes central. And here is where style comes in. We keep striving for "pure information," but the more information we have, the more we need filters, and one of the most powerful filters we have is the filtration of style. So another paradox: the utopia of perfect information brings with it the return of stylistic filtration, of, as it has traditionally been called in the west, rhetoric. (19)

It is in the rhetorical processes, in the art of persuading, which Lanham renames the "economics of attention," that lies the method for separating that which is memorable from that which is not. "Information," Lanham argues in this preface to his *Economics of Attention*, "is not in short supply in the new information economy." What is in short supply, however, is the "human attention to make sense of it all" (xi). Given the abundance of information thrust upon us each day by a variety of media outlets all calling for our attention (read: time, life itself), implicit in any of these sets of "information" is an embedded goal that style, understood through the more material underpinnings of techne, attempts to achieve. As a persuasion, it argues: *I would have you see me, I would have you remember me.*

A SHARED POINT OF DEPARTURE

I frame style in this way to articulate its function as an element of metaphorical exchange shared across creative writing and composition, one that helps question the style-based pedagogies that inform the teaching of either. Simply put, both creative writing and composition *deal* in attention. Despite programmatic goals to the contrary, they both, in other words, mindfully attend to that which makes writing capable of drawing attention and either be worth remembering or effecting a response worth remembering. If not worth remembering in the "greater" historical sense, however—that is, in the way we might remember speeches from presidents and tyrants (not necessarily mutually exclusive)—then worth remembering in the more local sense as a deviation from the norm. The project of this attention, however, is often framed in contrasting ways within the two disciplines. With regard to composition, students and teachers alike are commonly engaged in the project of mediating difference in writing (see Horner 2016, 2018). The same holds true for teachers and students of creative writing. However, while that difference in creative writing is commonly thought of in a positive light—the commodity of one's unique "voice" or sound on the page—that same difference in composition is traditionally thought of in the negative, as a nonstarter, that is, difference-as-incorrectness.[7]

As Eric House points out in this very collection, however, discourses around translingualism can help us identity "difference as the norm in language practice" (chapter 8). Within the context of this chapter's discussion, they can help us to think more broadly about the ways both the composition and creative writing course attend to difference's ability to signal based in the wide-ranging (though incorrect) understanding of an ahistorical standard of writing that is the product of language ideologies (see, e.g., Lu 1994; Canagarajah 2006, 2013; Lu and Horner 2013). As a stylistic convention, Gertrude Stein forgoes commas, and it is both a marvel and righteous rebellion; the composition student omits one before an independent clause and there's hell to pay. In both cases these actions only reference difference if we compare that difference against a standard that commonly links writing with current-traditional rhetorical pedagogies and style to "correctness" (see Lauer 2004, 45). Many of the goals of the contemporary composition course, as recent scholarship advocates, could be achieved by starting from an interrogation of how difference is stylistically produced and categorized, and then moving to challenge the "difference-as-incorrectness" paradigm. Creative writing, with its emphasis on the production of difference, has been doing something *ostensibly* similar. While creative writing's framing of difference as a programmatic norm is not without its own set of problematics,[8] its students are usually taught to respect such things as the power of Stein's dismissal of punctuation more so than they are a Strunk and White–era "rule" governing the construction of an independent clause. To wit: creative writing historically and composition, when it is taught in mind of the relationship between power and language difference, are engaged in the practice of reinventing what difference (from a perceived stylistic norm) means and why such reinvention matters.

STYLE AS DISCIPLINARY ARBITER

So far I've been arguing that style represents a way to mediate the alleged dissimilarity in the ways creative writing and composition treat difference. Far from attending to difference in writing in holistically distinctive ways, creative writing and composition find common ground in attending to difference based in a preconceived and ahistorical standard in writing. Their oft-taught genres of writing—poetry, fiction, drama, and so forth on the one end; argumentative, research, and so forth on the other—may be seen as material manifestations of style ideologies that signal their writer's participation in the discipline. A focus on producing stylistic difference from a socially constructed norm signals membership in one, while a focus on either eradicating difference or else reframing the foundations of difference signals membership in the other.

This commonality suggests that creative writing offers us yet another site at which we can employ composition's various methods to further explore dimensions of rhetoricity in texts, pedagogies, and practices. This task, however, becomes more difficult when extant scholarship still suggests that composition's methods of investigating and theorizing creative writing are off base. Such claims continue to suggest the disciplines possess irreconcilable "epistemological and ontological differences" and that "what one values as the basis for making knowledge differs from what the other values" (Bailey and Bizzaro 2017, 80). Closely examining some of this scholarship in light of my above discussion of style suggests to me that this claim is unjustifiable.

Given space limitations, I cannot draw from a large archive of scholarship that suggests the "epistemological and ontological" irreconcilability between the two disciplines. So as an extended example with which I'll wrap this chapter, I turn to Patrick Bizzaro's "Workshop: An Ontological Study" from the 2010 collection *Does the Writing Workshop Still Work?*, which I believe is representative of many of these arguments. In this essay, Bizzaro advocates for viewing creative writing as a field autonomous from both literature and rhetoric and composition, one "with a right to its own history, epistemology, and classroom activities." He evidences this claim through an examination of creative writing's signature pedagogy, the workshop, which, he posits, will help us perceive of the "disciplinary nature of creative writing" (37). While I concur that one generative way of viewing creative writing is as an autonomous field, the ways Bizzaro argues his point only reinforce the relationship between disciplinarity and disciplinary style discussed above. Citing "writer's self-reports" and "what writers do" as evidence of epistemological difference that necessitates disciplinary distinction, Bizzaro argues less for a discrete "disciplinary nature" of creative writing and more for the disciplinary construction of creative writing through shared stylistic practices and values.

Toward the end of his discussion, Bizzaro launches into a conversation about structural and stylistic choices meant to exemplify the incongruity between creative writing and composition. He discusses the difference between how he teaches a poem—which Bizzaro describes, drawing from Wordsworth, as a memorable "overflow of powerful feeling . . . recollected in tranquility" that is "worthy" of being recorded as a poem (2010, 41)—and how he teaches an argumentative essay. He writes:

> [U]nlike the teaching I do in my composition classes, my teaching in my creative writing classes often leads me to ask my students to avoid introductions and conclusions in their poems, thesis statements with clear claims, and conclusions with summaries. By contrast I spend a great deal of time helping students figure out how to introduce and conclude essays for my composition classes. (47)

Of "analyses of audience and purpose," Bizzaro writes that "these rhetorical elements are of very little consequence in a poetry writing class. Indeed, other than conversations about magazines that might publish individual poems, we seldom deal with audience" (47). And from an email correspondence, Bizzaro quotes in acquiescence a colleague and fellow poet who wrote, "I do whine about sentence fragments in first-year composition and then insist upon them in my creative writing" (47).

The issue I take with all the above examples is the way Bizzaro frames characteristics of creative writing as essential when, in reality, they are disciplinarily conventional or emblematic of a disciplinary style or approach to composing. And like all stylistic conventions presented as unimpeachable, close scrutiny impeaches them. Doesn't the *Odyssey* start with a very clear introduction to Ulysses and the unique way he thinks? Are the literacy narratives composition students are often tasked to write required to have clear, argumentative theses? How is conceiving of a flesh-and-blood receiver of a poem *not* an analysis of audience and purpose? And who is stopping any of us from appreciating a sentence fragment in an argumentative work? (So far, this chapter has had a number of them; Gertrude Stein's essays have more.) Citing these differences between creative writing and composition as evidence of epistemological difference ends up only serving as evidence of the way Bizzaro has relied on the traditional views of disciplinary boundaries as fixed. The conventions he cites, with regard to both creative writing and composition, are less processes of stylistic filtration than they are particular grammars of poetry and composition. In effect, they risk neither drawing distinction/attention nor interrogating the ideological foundations of difference-as-incorrectness.

Bizzaro sums up his examples by stating that they represent

> the very point I hope to make concerning the kinds of bedfellows creative writing and composition studies seem to be. The epistemology that gives rise to creative writing is based upon the primacy of the teacher's experience as a writer or, at the very least, the primacy of other writer's experiences as writers. Composition studies long ago forsook the research direction that would enable scholars to discover the decision-making processes of experienced writers when they write. (2010, 47–48)

More accurately, however, we might say Bizzaro is actively engaged in a process of reinforcing prescribed theories of writing in order to justify a difference between his own teaching of stylistic conventions in composition and creative writing. When he writes that "some techniques taught in composition violate certain premises of instruction based upon what writers actually do, violating then the very basis for knowing valued in creative writing" (45), he only deepens the divides he claims are axiomatic conclusions based on the "disciplinary nature" of creative writing and composition. But nature isn't responsible for the formation of writing-centric disciplines; writing is. And individuals looking to effect disciplinary-specific objectives are responsible for that which is written, how, and for what purpose.

IN CLOSING

That there exists a growing interest in the intersections between creative writing and composition is irrefutable. In order to engage in fruitful conversations across the divide, writers and scholars in each discipline must be willing to find common ground in questions about what counts as writing knowledge and who has say over that knowledge. I have been arguing through this chapter that style, understood through the techne of writing as a pathway to distinction, is the pivot on which that turn depends. While I can't provide a specific plan of action for winning over those on either side of the divide intent on treating the two disciplines altogether separately, I offer a few thoughts for moving that conversation along.

As compositionists and creative writers alike, we need to identify not only the place of creative writing in composition studies, as Hesse (2010) suggests, but the place of creative *writers* in the larger discourse surrounding composition. This shouldn't be too difficult, since, as I've argued, both composition and creative writing are committed to the same type of writing work engaging difference, albeit viewed from two polar ends. A project like this involves acknowledging that creative writing and composition take part in the same project of stylistic filtration, that is, the same economy of drawing, distributing, and paying attention. Doing so opens the gates to the shared pedagogical goals between the two disciplines: interfacing with communities of learning and in forms of writing that challenge static conventions and what those conventions obtain.

By reorienting ourselves to a view of style that is less about the practice and deployment of static conventions and more about an approach toward identifying and navigating disciplinary divides, we have already found a future for style in composition studies. And by remembering style's role in the techne of writing to find common ground, to be awestruck by difference, and to effect material change, we can look forward to building larger communities with which to share that future.

NOTES

1. Creative writing studies is, arguably, a still-emerging field. For those unfamiliar, it may be thought of as a field that investigates creative writing's pedagogy, history, social impact, and methodological underpinnings (see Mayers 2009; Donnelly 2012).
2. Note: I use the singular "they" throughout.
3. For discussions of the intermingled histories of creative writing and composition, see, among others, Myers (1996), Goggins (1999), and Dawson (2005).
4. Prior (1998; see also Bazerman 1994) points out: "[W]riting and disciplinarity are laminated, not autonomous . . . every moment implicates multiple activities, weaves together multiple histories, and exists within the chronotopic networks of lifeworlds where boundaries of time and space are highly permeable" (277). Thus, the bound knowledge we commonly associate with a discipline is, in reality, diffused across a number of sites, contexts, and timescales.
5. Whether creative writing does this is another argument altogether, and one with which Horner disagrees. Suffice to say, these are often the programmatic goals of creative writing programs.
6. Though this latter objective, as Johnson (2003) would remind us, is largely linked to composing decisions more informing a writer's greater "authorial style" than any romantic idea of inborn exceptionality.
7. Additionally, as Alexis and Leake (chapter 5) have pointed out elsewhere in this collection, popular culture often "valorizes the 'creative writer'" in a way it does not other forms of writer. Thus, while there is a deal of cultural cachet in touting a creative writer identity, it is often difficult for "academics, ghost writers, and workplace writers"—not to mention students in composition classes—to be seen as possessing any sort of writer identity at all.
8. See my discussion above of Horner (2018)—namely, that the "difference" offered by creative writing is really an allusion to difference. As well, consider the fact that creative writing programs are still often marred by romantic notions of artistic production (Teichmann and Radavich 1994) and workshops coded in both whiteness and the patriarchal (Kearns 2009). Further consider then how these issues are embedded within an enterprise we still often view as linking its signature forms of generic production to elitism.

REFERENCES

Alsup, Allison. 2005. "Persuasion, More than Argument: Moving toward a Literary Sensitivity in the Classroom." In *Refiguring Prose Style: Possibilities for Writing Pedagogy*, edited by T. R. Johnson and Tom Pace, 93–106. Logan: Utah State University Press.

Bailey, Christine, and Patrick Bizzaro. 2017. "Research in Creative Writing: Theory into Practice." *Research in the Teaching of English* 52: 77–97.

Bazerman, Charles. 1994. "Systems of Genres and the Enactment of Social Intentions." In *Genre and the New Rhetoric*, edited by Aviva Freedman and Peter Medway, 79–101. London: Taylor & Francis.

Berg, Danita, and Lori A. May. 2016. *Creative Composition: Inspiration and Techniques for Writing Instruction*. Bristol: Multilingual Matters.

Bishop, Wendy. 1990. *Released into Language: Options for Teaching Creative Writing*. Urbana: NCTE.

Bizzaro, Patrick. 2010. "Workshop: On Ontological Study." In *Does the Writing Workshop Still Work?*, edited by Dianne Donnelly, 36–51. London: Multilingual Matters.

Butler, Paul. 2008. *Out of Style: Reanimating Stylistic Study in Composition and Rhetoric*. Logan: Utah State University Press.

Butler, Paul, ed. 2010a. *Style in Rhetoric and Composition: A Critical Sourcebook*. Boston: Bedford/St. Martin's.

Butler, Paul. 2010b. "The Stylistic (Re)Turn in Rhetoric and Composition." In *Style in Rhetoric and Composition: A Critical Sourcebook*, edited by Paul Butler, 1–10. Boston: Bedford/St. Martin's.

Canagarajah, Suresh. 2006. "The Place of World Englishes in Composition: Pluralization Continued." *College Composition and Communication* 57 (4): 586–619.

Canagarajah, Suresh. 2013. *Translingual Practice: Global Englishes and Cosmopolitan Relations*. New York: Routledge.

Dawson, Paul. 2005. *Creative Writing and the New Humanities*. London: Routledge.

Donnelly, Dianne, ed. 2010. *Does the Writing Workshop Still Work?* London: Multilingual Matters.

Donnelly, Dianne. 2012. *Establishing Creative Writing Studies as an Academic Discipline*. Bristol: Multilingual Matters.

Ellis, Erik. 2013. "Toward a Pedagogy of Psychic Distance." In *The Centrality of Style*, edited by Mike Duncan and Star Medzerian Vanguri, 309–339. Fort Collins, CO, and Anderson, SC: WAC Clearinghouse and Parlor Press.

Fenza, D. W. 2011. "The Centre Has Not Held: Creative Writing and Pluralism." *New Writing: The International Journal for the Practice and Theory of Creative Writing* 8 (3): 206–214.

Fodrey, Crystal. 2013. "Voice Transformed: The Potentialities of Style Pedagogy in the Teaching of Creative Nonfiction." In *The Centrality of Style*, edited by Mike Duncan and Star Medzerian Vanguri, 239–258. Fort Collins, CO, and Anderson, SC: WAC Clearinghouse and Parlor Press.

Goggin, Maureen Daly. 1999. "The Tangled Roots of Literature, Speech Communication, Linguistics, Rhetoric/Composition, and Creative Writing: Selected Bibliography on the History of English Studies." *Rhetoric Society Quarterly* 29: 63–88.

Hesse, Douglas. 2010. "The Place of Creative Writing in Composition Studies." *College Composition and Communication* 62 (1): 31–52.

Horner, Bruce. 2016. *Rewriting Composition: Terms of Exchange*. Carbondale: Southern Illinois University Press.

Horner, Bruce. 2018. "Rewriting Creative Writing." In *Changing Creative Writing in America: Strengths, Weaknesses, Possibilities*, edited by Graeme Harper, 112–131. Bristol: Multilingual Matters.

Johnson, T. R. 2003. *A Rhetoric of Pleasure: Prose Style and Today's Composition Classroom*. Portsmouth, NH: Boynton/Cook.

Kearns, Rosalie Morales. 2009. "Voice of Authority: Theorizing Creative Writing Pedagogy." *College Composition and Communication* 60 (4): 790–807.
Koehler, Adam. 2017. *Composition, Creative Writing Studies, and the Digital Humanities*. London: Bloomsbury Academic.
Lanham, Richard. 2006. *The Economics of Attention: Style and Substance in the Age of Information*. Chicago: University of Chicago Press.
Lardner, Ted. 1999. "Locating the Boundaries of Composition and Creative Writing." *College Composition and Communication* 51 (1): 72–77.
Lauer, Janice M. 2004. *Invention in Rhetoric and Composition*. West Lafayette, IN: Parlor Press.
Lu, Min-Zhan. 1994. "Professing Multiculturalism: The Politics of Style in the Contact Zone." *College Composition and Communication* 45 (4): 442–458.
Lu, Min-Zhan, and Bruce Horner. 2013. "Translingual Literacy, Language Difference, and Matters of Agency." *College English* 75 (6): 582–607.
Mayers, Tim. 2005. *(Re)writing Craft: Composition, Creative Writing, and the Future of English Studies*. Pittsburgh: University of Pittsburgh Press.
Mayers, Tim. 2009. "One Simple Word: From Creative Writing to Creative Writing Studies." *College English* 71 (3): 217–228.
Mayers, Tim. 2018. "We Serve Writing Here." In *Changing Creative Writing in America: Strengths, Weaknesses, Possibilities*, edited by Graeme Harper, 52–68. Bristol: Multilingual Matters.
Myers, D. G. 1996. *The Elephants Teach: Creative Writing since 1880*. New York: Prentice Hall.
Pender, Kelly. 2011. *Techne, from Neoclassism to Postmodernism: Understanding Writing as a Useful, Teachable Art*. Anderson, SC: Parlor Press.
Petraglia, Joseph, ed. 1995. *Reconceiving Writing, Rethinking Writing Instruction*. Mahwah, NJ: Lawrence Erlbaum.
Prior, Paul A. 1998. *Writing/Disciplinarity: A Sociohistoric Account of Literate Activity in the Academy*. Mahwah, NJ: Lawrence Erlbaum.
Sullivan, Patrick. 2015. "The UnEssay: Making Room for Creativity in the Composition Classroom." *College Composition and Communication* 67 (1): 6–34.
Strunk, William, and E. B White. 1979. *The Elements of Style*, 3rd ed. New York: Macmillan.
Teichmann, Sandra Gail, and David Radavich. 1994. "Two Comments on 'An Apologia for Creative Writing.'" *College English* 56 (2): 217–220.
Thaiss, Chris, and Terry Myers Zawacki. 2006. *Engaged Writers, Dynamic Disciplines: Research on the Academic Writing Life*. Portsmouth, NH: Boynton/Cook Heinemann.
Toulmin, Stephen. 1972. *Human Understanding*. Princeton, NJ: Princeton University Press.

14
THE DANGER OF USING STYLE TO DETERMINE AUTHORSHIP
The Case of Luke and Acts

Mike Duncan

INTRODUCTION

Given this collection's focus, I wish to demonstrate the inherent difficulties of using style to determine ancient authorship when basic rhetorical training in the ancient world stressed stylistic imitation. Furthermore, recognizing the reversible nature of the evidence typically used to support authorship cases calls into question the authorial identification of any manuscript—ancient or modern—on stylistic grounds. Stylometric analysis has real limits, as a skilled and creative forger can trick the most critical reader; narrative inconsistencies and content analysis are far more promising for determining authorship. As style asserts itself as a relevant subdiscipline within composition studies, awareness of its limitations in identifying authorship is particularly important when considering the ever-evolving discussion of where plagiarism begins and ends in differing contexts according to different players (Butler 2005; Howard 2008; Anson 2011; Marzluf 2012; Chien 2014) and how more modern authors can equally use style to manipulate their audience's perception of authorship (Kohlrausch 2018).

My central example is the long-standing argument that the same author wrote both the Gospel of Luke and Acts of the Apostles in the New Testament (NT). The evidence, aside from Acts claiming it is a sequel, has been chiefly on style grounds, encompassing Greek diction and grammar, as well as theology. This is one of the two most important and widely held conclusions in New Testament studies, taught to seminary and biblical studies students as gospel—second only to Mark being the oldest canonical gospel.

This particular conclusion, however, is flawed. The first writers to solidify the connection (notably Cadbury in 1927) knew their Greek but assumed a similar style meant the same author. Given the prevalence of forgeries in early Christian writings, like the spurious epistles attributed to Paul, such an assumption is risky. Similar style could easily mean the opposite—a "school" of forgers writing in that style, borrowing the ethos of the original. Accordingly, I argue that a stylistic imitator (or, as a colleague once suggested, someone wearing a "Luke hat") wrote Acts—and that the evidence arrayed in support of common authorship can be reversed to support two different authors. This is a cautionary tale.

IMITATION AND FORGERY IN EARLY CHRISTIANITY

In the fourth century CE, the bishop Eusebius oversaw a Christian library in Caesarea, off the coast of present-day Israel. Eusebius's history of Christianity describes a prized holding there: a letter exchange (in Syriac) between King Abgar of Edessa and Jesus, where Abgar asks to be healed, and Jesus says he will send a disciple after he is "taken up to the One who sent me" (Eusebius 1989, 30–34). The letters are derivative of passages in the Gospel of John, with its advanced theology written in the late first century CE at earliest, well after the death of the historical Jesus. The purpose of the forged letters seems to be a convenient foundational origin story for the Christian community in Edessa around the third century CE (Ehrman 2013, 455–458).

Why did Eusebius not catch on? The "Pauline" epistles were long thought to be written by Paul until Ferdinand Baur claimed in 1845 that only four of the thirteen epistles were authentically Paul's (the modern consensus is that seven are), with the others "Pauline" by a stylistic "school" that borrowed his ethos to advance other theological agendas. Until Baur, few thought to question them closely because of the innumerable cultural and theological barriers built up over centuries against questioning the holy nature of the canonized NT. But the answer for Eusebius is more subtle. Eusebius did not conceive of history as a secular scholar might, but as pious propaganda; he may have disbelieved the letters but recognized their value as props.

In antiquity, documents were viewed as authored by whomever the text claimed, unless evidence existed to the contrary. Leeway existed if the real author was not the content author, for example, if a student wrote on his teacher's philosophy and attributed the writing to the master, and the content was accurate: "Everywhere an authorial attribution was regarded as correct and undeceptive if either the wording or the content of a particular text could be traced back to the author whose name it carried" (Baum 2017, 402). With this practice in mind, an industry of pious Christian forgeries and fabrications flourished, some working their way into the canon. The first confirmed case of a forgery in Christian writing was reported by Tertullian in his homily on baptism around 200 CE:

> But if certain Acts of Paul, which are falsely so named, claim the example of Thecla for allowing women to teach and to baptize, let men know that in Asia the presbyter who compiled that document, thinking to add of his own to Paul's reputation, was found out, and though he professed he had done it for love of Paul, was deposed from his position. How could we believe that Paul should give a female power to teach and to baptize, when he did not allow a woman even to learn by her own right? (Tertullian 1964, 37)

Tertullian's incredulity implies the method of detection—not style, but the text's doctrine concerning women was inconsistent with 1 Corinthians and 1 Timothy. Content—not style—enabled the unmasking.

Eusebius and the "Acts of Paul" are open-and-shut cases; subtler problems with authenticity lie in the gospels. The attributed names—Mark, Matthew, Luke, and John—do not appear in manuscripts before 200 CE. Justin Martyr, writing around 150 CE, paraphrases some material but refers to them instead as "Memoirs of the Apostles" in his "First Apology" (Martyr 2012, 66). As such, they circulated individually, perhaps over a hundred years, without names attached. They acquired traditional names around the time Tertullian noted the "Acts of Paul" forgery. They are not "forgeries"—rather, their authors are unknown—but they are literarily dependent on each other (Matthew and Luke copy many lengthy passages in Greek from Mark verbatim).

COMMON AUTHORSHIP BETWEEN THE GOSPEL OF LUKE AND ACTS

While common Luke and Acts authorship is generally a given (Parsons 1987, 125), a prominent dissenter is Patricia Walters, whose 2009 book reevaluated the stylistic evidence, with some recent support (Mealand 2016, 498–499). Walters examines past attempts to challenge the status quo, noting that there are two grounds by which to challenge common authorship: theological and stylistic (2009, 24). The theological is employed by Baur (1845, 12–13) and Scholten (1873, 95–99)—the dates testify to their passing from favor. The classic stylistic challenges are also old: Clark, noting peculiar linguistic characteristics in Acts (1933, 394), and Argyle, who focused on synonym usage (1974, 441–445).

Walters assaults common authorship from the latter direction, identifying her method as "stylometry"—the "science of measuring literary style" (2009, 38). This is a critical mistake; she cedes authority for measuring authorship to style, playing the same game as Parsons and Gorman, status quo defenders, who in their review commend her methods but deem her argument a "failure, though a splendid one" (2012, 149). Neither side questions the validity of stylometry to determine authorship. Parsons and Gorman do mention that genre and dating could factor in future examinations, but ultimately, the grounds for a decision is style.

This weight on style analysis ignores that differences or similarities in style establish little. If Walters is right, and there are significant differences, is that evidence of two different authors, or could it be evolution or adaptation of a single author's style, given a different context/genre between compositions? Alternatively, if the consensus is right that there are no significant stylistic discrepancies, is that evidence for a single author, or could it be taken that a stylistic imitator, banking on the reputation of Luke, wrote Acts in that style? That the stylistic "evidence" they have analyzed for minute differences in usage and diction is not only useless but worse as it provides the illusion of evidence is not considered.

If stylometry is qualified in that it cannot definitively claim authorship between two texts but offers probability and possible links between works, then it is useful. The tentative explorations of computational linguistics in this area are more defensible, if excessively optimistic (Raminal, Panchoo, and Pudaruth 2016), and recognize a large corpus is needed for any accuracy (Ding et al. 2019, 119). But when taken as grounds to dismiss complications, then stylometry fails. Lutosławski, who coined "stylometrics" (1890) at the height of a data-driven linguistic explosion, assumed that language could be reduced to data and yet, contradictorily, that all authors were unique. I have commented on this era before in regards to prose rhythm being crammed into musical notation (Duncan 2011, 587); interestingly, the Luke-Acts conclusion solidified during this period.

THE REVERSIBLE ARGUMENT OF STYLE

Reversible arguments are a common topic out of Aristotelian or Ciceronian rhetoric. A classic example in the NT is "old is better than new," most developed, ironically, in the Gospel of Luke:[1]

> No one puts a piece from a new garment on an old one; otherwise the new makes a tear, and also the piece that was taken out of the new does not match the old. And no one puts new wine into old wineskins; or else the new wine will burst the wineskins and be spilled, and the wineskins will

be ruined. But new wine must be put into new wineskins, and both are preserved. And no one, having drunk old wine, immediately desires new; for he says, "The old is better." (Luke 5:36–39)

The author is cognizant that age is reversible evidence. Such claims are then evidence-free; as such, stylistic analysis is useless to determine authorship. Duplicating any given style is trivial with moderate skill; indeed, there is a word for this phenomenon—genre.

The phenomenon of "fan fiction," where amateur authors write fiction in the universes of favored authors, may illustrate. As a young undergraduate, I wrote a novel in the style of a late science fiction author. While a trained eye would have become quickly suspicious, it made the basic stylistic maneuvers. Indeed, if Parsons, Gorman, and Walters had used the same stylometrics on my fan fiction that they used on Acts and Luke, they might conclude that they had stumbled upon a lost (and bad) novel by the author.

Walters divides the stylometric arguments for common authorship into word studies (vocabulary and phrasing) and redaction, where Luke's "editing" habits from Mark are compared to maneuvers in Acts (2009, 11–21). Of these, the first kind is more accessible. Hawkins's *Horae Synopticae*, for example, notes that some common Greek words and phrases occur in Luke-Acts much more often than in Mark and Matthew combined (1968, 27). These include ἅγιος (holy), ἄγω (take or lead), ἱκανός (able, skilled), ὁ plus a noun with some words between, and οὐ (not). Such examples would seem to support common authorship, but as any forger would strive to emulate the vocabulary and phrasing of the intended author, they are ultimately useless.

Consider ἅγιος (holy), which occurs in 27 forms 233 times in the New Testament. The three most popular forms and the totals for the texts are listed in table 14.1. A p-value here is superfluous. But does this support that Luke and Acts were written by the same person who maintained (and perhaps intensified) their vocabulary? Or is this the case of a savvy imitator, guilty of "holy" overkill? Or are these numbers inherently ambiguous, even if buttressed by other many examples?

Instruction in imitation is alive today, thriving in all writing genres—journal monographs, Harlequin romances, instructional manuals, newspaper articles, and postmodern novels, to name a few. Implicit in the development of writing is mastery of genre, and the leading method remains mimicking examples to create a competence veneer, the depth limited by experience. We associate style with uniqueness, but convincing forgeries undercut that view. A classic example of a

Table 14.1. New Testament appearances of ἅγιος (holy)

	New Testament	Matthew	Mark	Luke	Acts
ἅγιον	44	1	0	8	20
ἁγίου	42	3	0	5	21
ἁγίων	38	1	1	2	2
Totals of all 27 forms	233	9	7	19	52

related and largely successful hoax (fooling many scholars for decades) is Morton Smith's "Secret Gospel of Mark." While style analysis was ambiguous about whether his "discovery" of a nineteenth-century copy of an alternate Greek section to the Gospel of Mark was a tongue-in-cheek fake, the evidence that demonstrated the verdict was material and contextual (Carlson 2005, xviii). One solid blow included Watson noting that Smith took the basic idea from a sensational novel published in 1940 (2010, 163) and Henige observing that the entire "lost manuscript" concept is an often-used trope by forgers (2009, 40–41). Similarly, Donald Foster's famous attempt to attribute the poem "A Funeral Elegy" to Shakespeare through style analysis was ultimately debunked, but not until many years after he used the same techniques to identify his anonymous book proposal reviewer at Oxford University Press (Kahan 2015, 829). The exception proves the rule; it is one thing to identify an anonymous reader when you can confirm it with the living author, but Foster could not with Shakespeare, and thus defended a flawed conclusion for decades.

In composition and literary studies, authorial malfeasance resides in two concepts. The first is "plagiarism"—the attempt to convince the reader that one wrote the text through substitution of another author's work. The second is "forgery"—the attempt to convince the reader that someone else other than the real author wrote the text through stylistic and content manipulation (Robillard and Fortune 2007, 186–187). While both depictions aim to give the author some persuasive advantage, successful forgery is more difficult, but less dangerous, given that if the forgery is detected, the real author is not necessarily revealed. However, consistent across these two variations is the possibility of an alternative: as Carlson's investigation of Smith shows, content and context are more promising avenues to catch a fake than style. Furthermore, as I hold that content and style are mutually embedded concepts, stylometrics cannot alone make the case that its practitioners often sell. But there is another way.

THE ASCENSION IN LUKE AND ACTS

I propose an alternative method to establish authorship through content analysis of a narrative episode that only Luke and Acts depict—Jesus's ascension. The two versions, Acts 1:1–11 and Luke 24:1–53, contradict each other repeatedly. The consensus, however, is that common Luke-Acts authorship remains safe. Even Walters considers the differences trivial. I do not.

First, in Luke, one day passes from Jesus's resurrection to his ascension. On the same morning of his resurrection, Jesus appears to two apostles on the road, anonymously. When the two apostles realize who he is, they rush back to Jerusalem to tell the others, where he has appeared to Peter. Jesus then appears to the group, before leading them to Bethany and ascending in the night. Time elapsed is a day at most. In Acts 1:2, this same interval is forty days, with no reconciliation of the discrepancy.

A second problem rests in the dialogue of Jesus just before the ascension in Luke 24:44–49. This dialogue is paralleled by Acts 1:4 but extended by more dialogue in Acts 1:4–8 concerning baptism and the timing of the coming of the kingdom of God, and this content is substantially different from Luke, and there is again no explanation.

Third, in Luke, Jesus ascends (ἀνεφέρετο) to heaven with no accompaniment. In Acts 1:9, however, he is "taken up" (ἐπήρθη) and a cloud (νεφέλη) accompanies him. Then, two men in white robes appear by the apostles and chastise them in Acts 1:10–11, hinting to Jesus's return later. The absence of the two men in Luke is unexplained.

These three issues present a different problem than Jesus's baptism, the empty tomb narratives, or the arrest of Jesus, among many other examples; the accounts differ wildly on many matters, but most can be chalked up to rhetorical disagreements between the authors and variant traditions that drifted away from original tales. Here, though, the disagreement is more fundamental; the assumed common author of Luke-Acts disagrees with himself—and does so three times in succession. It may seem I am veering away from style here, but it is vitally important to show the incredible leaps of illogic by which common authorship is fiercely retained.

Explanation 1: The Common Author Blundered

Could the author have forgotten the details of the earlier ascension and written new ones? Given the skill that the author consistently displays elsewhere (and claims, in Luke 1:1–4), this scenario is nonsensical. It is possible the earlier gospel was not on hand while writing and thus the author misremembered the episode, but this raises another question: why rewrite a scene from scratch? Inexact recapitulation happens in sonatas and television soap operas, but these are neither.

Explanation 2: Scribal Interpolation

Interpolation (where a scribe altered the manuscript while copying) has been proposed (Parsons 1987, 125). All or part of Acts 1:3–11 could be interpolated, but there is no evidence in the manuscripts, and Acts 13:31 needs Acts 1.3 as much as Acts 11:16–19 appears to need Acts 1:4–5. Likewise, Luke 24:50–53 must reckon with Luke 9:51. Ehrman suggests Luke 24:51 could be an interpolation "to emphasize Jesus' bodily ascension against docetic Christologies that denied it," but fails to address Luke 9:51 (2011, 267). Further, if the differences are from separation of Acts from Luke for the purposes of canonization, there is no evidence that Luke and Acts ever circulated together separate from the New Testament.

Explanation 3: "There Is No Conflict."

Darth Vader's defense is widespread and reflexive. Of the commentaries on Luke, Bovon states: "As an experienced author . . . [the author] also knows how to keep these transitions from being unwieldy and repetitious. He likes to vary the presentations of the same truths or the same events. . . . As we can see, Luke knows how to vary things" (2012, 405). Pervo simply notes there is difficulty (2009, 34); Conzelmann observes a difference, but does not comment (1987, 5–6). Fitzmyer notes only, "Why Luke has dated the ascension of Jesus in these two different ways no one will ever know" (1985, 1588). In his Acts commentary, "forty days" may be symbolic (1997, 202).

Most disparagingly, Haenchen remarks, "Luke does not set as much store as we upon consistency in the story. . . . [T]he variance of the two versions . . . has been taken only by those scholars who hold the writer to account for each stroke of the pen and are not satisfied until each tiny stone exactly fits its neighbours" (1971, 146). This is again special pleading, disregarding Luke 1:1–4, where the author claims he has "investigated everything from the beginning"—if so, how did he miss the length of Jesus's return, even if only estimated?

Mussies marries these variations to "Hellenistic literary tradition" evidenced by poets who wrote different epigrams concerning the same story and a larger pattern of lexical variation in Luke and Acts, most prominently the three versions of Paul's conversion (1991, 176). This seemingly nuanced argument is problematic. One, these are not epigrams. Two, he equates variation in narrative only to lexical variation. Third, the multiple versions of Paul's conversion, which Mussies presents as a parallel, differ due to different fixed audiences; the two ascensions lack this excuse. Fourth, Mussies does not account for Luke 1:1–4, where the author emphasizes accuracy (ἀκριβῶς) and order (καθεξῆς). Parsons, too, posits "redundancy" and "variation" as governing narrative principles for Luke and Acts: "[W]hat is appropriate or necessary for a narrative ending is not always appropriate or necessary for a narrative beginning" (1987, 191–197). However, Parsons does not transplant Acts 3–11 into Luke to show how it cannot function well as a "narrative ending." None of these arguments reasonably explains why the supposed common author is disagreeing with himself over a key event that no other gospel records, save for the derived Markan appendix.

Explanation 4: Rhetorical Change by a Common Author

The multiple changes might suggest that a common author decided the earlier version was inadequate. With the gospel in circulation, the common author decided to write an altered version in Acts with error correction. The most nuanced case for a common author is made here—on rhetorical purpose, not style.

Here, the reason for the inclusion of the ascension, beyond the influence of older Greco-Roman and Jewish traditions of legendary figures ascending to the sky, is the closing-off of the post-resurrection appearances (Funk 1998, 494). Any "appearances" like Paul's conversion in Acts 9 are of a lesser category. If so, the first version in Luke is brutal; no appearances happen after a day. Anyone claiming to have seen Jesus after is not to be trusted.

The Gospel of John portrays two such "later" stories. Lengthening the period in Acts to forty days may subtly allow such narratives to coexist; the forty days is then a compromise. But why do this if the ascension was intended to close off appearances? Enslin once proposed that Luke had discovered a forty-day tradition between the writing of the gospel and Acts (1928, 64). No evidence exists, but the two extra stories from John suggest stories of intermediate timing (i.e., happening after a day but before forty) existed. Indeed, John 21:25 hints that more post-resurrection stories circulated.

The new dialogue could be theological clarifications to the common author's community. Acts 1:4–5 details the nature of the coming power (δύναμιν) in Luke 24:49, with an allusion to the baptism of John (Acts 18:25). Then, Acts 1:6–8 postpones the question of the coming kingdom for those who expected an immediate restoration. In both cases the words are Jesus's, more authoritative than from apostles or angels. Additionally, Acts 1:8 makes clear the physical extent of witnessing.

The angels are apocalyptic window dressing, but they have two other possible functions. The first is to motivate the apostles along to their next destination, as they do in Luke 24:6–7. Secondly, they offer a glimpse of a future Jesus, which answers two pressing questions—will Jesus return and how? We cannot assume the common author's community had any texts outside of Luke and Acts, though Mark or Marcion's heretical gospel are possible. Therefore, any questions needed to be answerable within Luke and Acts only.

The existence of the Acts ascension may suggest that Luke's was not enough. The rhetorical brilliance, then, is in the minor adjustments. Jesus still ascends as he did in Luke, but the picture is now sharper, and the author has solved several theological problems. The existence of a community with such questions is hazy, though, along with assuming desire in the author to answer.

Even if we allow community questions, though, how can we confirm that a common author of Luke and Acts would self-contradict? When performing criticism on ancient texts, we must work backward to establish rhetorical situations, because we lack knowledge of the original audience: we must guess based on the content, a functional analysis, a risky reconstruction of intent, and similar texts of roughly the same time and culture. What do two different ascensions suggest about the original readers, and what is most likely—blundering on the author's part to a passive audience, a portrait at odds with the majority of Luke and Acts, or is this deliberate change based on something that happened with the audience between the composition of Luke and Acts?

Explanation 5: Two Authors

Explanation 4 was a trap that I will now spring, by reversing the evidence and arguing that it is just another acrobatic attempt to save common authorship. The Gordian knot of the discrepancies can be resolved as Alexander did (a story that also has two versions, one in which Alexander pulls out the lynchpin holding the knot together). Here, though, I will use the sword.

What if the author of Acts is a different writer with a different agenda who wants to enjoy the authority commanded by the earlier gospel? The method would be trivial: declare in the first lines that the manuscript was the second addressed to "Theophilus" (Acts 1:1–2). With a minute's composition, the forger secures authorship for millennia. After that unimpeachable deception, with no way to prove otherwise in antiquity, they could write whatever early church history they desired.

The smoking gun is that imitation (μίμησις) was a prominent and essential skill in the rhetoric curriculum, or προγυμνάσματα, prevalent in the educated classes in the first few centuries CE in the Greek-literate world. The first assignment was typically to rewrite a fable in the same style; the second assignment was to rewrite narrative, imitating the same style (Kennedy 2003, xiii). Even if a scribe flunked the rest of the curriculum, they would have learned the necessary skills for pious forgery from the first two exercises. As such, scribes educated thusly would possess the skill to write Acts in the "style" of the gospel of Luke. The two forgeries mentioned by Eusebius and Tertullian are prima facie evidence that forgery existed early on in Christian writings. Why should Acts be treated differently?

CONCLUSIONS

Ultimately, the Luke-Acts "common author" conceit on style reigns because it is convenient. Acts as a stylistic derivative has never gained traction because few biblical scholars, theologians, or seminarians from Tertullian on down would be eager to risk their reputation and employment on claiming that the largest book in the New Testament was a forgery, and thus, the oldest account of the history of the early church would need reconsidering. Accordingly, works debate the "unity" of Luke-Acts (Bird 2007; Porter 2016, 111) without questioning authorship, and even maintain that they constitute a single genre (Smith and Kostopoulos 2017, 410). Oddly, the "Pauline" letters do not get this kind of constant preemptive defense, even though it is widely accepted that Paul employed an amanuensis, a scribe that took dictation—for example, a "Tertius" identifies himself at the end of Romans as the physical writer.

Alexis and Leake mention the claim that half of modern published writing is not written alone as presented but uses the services of ghostwriter or editor; the "real" identity of the writer(s) is typically left "out of reach" (chapter 5). Even today, making assertions about whether Author X wrote Text Y is difficult, even if the author or editors are still alive. With ancient texts, we must be even more careful and diligent about our claims.

As a rhetorician, I have no dog in this fight (though the "no conflict" argument is a clear case of a dog that will not hunt). Rather, I am concerned about overextending stylistic analysis beyond its capabilities. Invaluable for examining and understanding style within texts, even the data-driven, "scientific" might of stylometrics cannot establish authorship reliably. Taking critical factual inconsistencies seriously, however, is much more promising.

Most composition teachers deal with authorship issues only on the plagiarism side, but while we might suspect plagiarism initially through style considerations, to prove copying took place, either documentation (a copy of the pilfered text) or content analysis (examining the level of ideas) is required. Ultimately, the initial sensing of "something's off" may happen at the style level, and that gut instinct is invaluable for probing further, but defensible proof requires close reading of content and context if we wish to police authorship or, better yet, teach awareness of the distinctions that stylistic analysis cannot conclusively illuminate.

NOTE

1. References to the New Testament in English are from the New Revised Standard Version, and in the Greek are from the USB 4th edition.

REFERENCES

Anson, Chris. 2011. "Fraudulent Practices: Academic Misrepresentations of Plagiarism in the Name of Good Pedagogy." *Composition Studies* 39 (2): 29–43.

Argyle, A. W. 1974. "The Greek of Luke and Acts." *New Testament Studies* 20: 441–445.

Baum, Armin. 2017. "Content and Form: Authorship Attribution and Pseudonymity in Ancient Speeches, Letters, Lectures, and Translations—A Rejoinder to Bart Ehrman." *Journal of Biblical Literature* 136 (2): 381–403.

Baur, Ferdinand. 1876. *Paul the Apostle of Jesus Christ: His Life and Works, His Epistles and Teachings (1845).* Translated by Eduard Zeller. London: Williams and Norgate.

Bird, Michael. 2007. "The Unity of Luke–Acts in Recent Discussion." *JSNT* 29 (4): 425–448.

Bovon, Francois. 2012. *Luke 3: A commentary on the Gospel of Luke 19:28–24:53.* Translated by James Crouch. Minneapolis: Fortress Press.

Butler, Paul. 2005. "Copyright, Plagiarism, and the Law." In *Authorship in Composition Studies,* edited by Tracy H. Carrick and Rebecca M. Howard, 13–26. London: Thomson Wadsworth.

Cadbury, Henry. [1927] 1999. *The Making of Luke-Acts (1927).* Peabody, MA: Hendrickson Publishers.

Carlson, Stephen C. 2005. *The Gospel Hoax: Morton Smith's Invention of Secret Mark.* Waco, TX: Baylor University Press.

Chien, Shih-Chieh. 2014. "Cultural Constructions of Plagiarism in Student Writing: Teachers' Perceptions and Responses." *Research in the Teaching of English* 49 (2): 120–140.

Clark, Albert. 1933. *The Acts of the Apostles: A Critical Edition with Introduction and Notes on Selected Passages.* Oxford: Clarendon Press.

Conzelmann, Hans. 1987. *Acts of the Apostles: A Commentary on the Acts of the Apostles.* Translated by James Limberg, A. Thomas Kraabel, and Donald H. Juel. Edited by Eldon J. Epp and Christopher R. Matthews. Philadelphia: Fortress Press.

Ding, Steven H. H., Benjamin C. M. Fung, Farkhund Iqbal, and William K. Cheung. 2019. "Learning Stylometric Representations for Authorship Analysis." *IEEE Transactions on Cybernetics* 49 (1): 107–121.

Duncan, Mike. 2011. "Questioning the Auditory Sublime: A Multisensory-Organic Approach to Prose Rhythm." *JAC* 31 (3/4): 579–608.

Ehrman, Bart. 2011. *The Orthodox Corruption of Scripture.* Oxford: Oxford University Press.

Ehrman, Bart. 2013. *Forgery and Counterforgery: The Use of Literary Deceit in Early Christian Polemics.* Oxford: Oxford University Press.

Enslin, Morton. 1928. "The Ascension Story." *Journal of Biblical Literature* 47 (2): 64.

Eusebius. 1989. *The History of the Church.* Translated by G. A. Williamson. London: Penguin.

Fitzmyer, Joseph. 1985. *The Gospel According to Luke X–XXIV.* Garden City, NJ: Doubleday and Company.

Fitzmyer, Joseph. 1997. *The Acts of the Apostles.* New Haven, CT: Yale University Press.

Funk, Robert, and the Jesus Seminar. 1998. *The Acts of Jesus.* New York: Polebridge Press.

Haenchen, Ernst. 1971. *The Acts of the Apostles: A Commentary.* Oxford: Blackwell.

Hawkins, John C. (1909) 1968. *Horae Synopticae: Contributions to the Study of the Synoptic Problem,* 2nd ed. Oxford: Clarendon Press.

Henige, David. 2009. "Authorship Renounced: The 'Found' Source in the Historical Record." *Journal of Scholarly Publishing* 41 (1): 31–55.

Howard, Rebecca M. 2008. "The Binaries of Authorship." In *Authorship in Composition Studies,* edited by Tracy H. Carrick and Rebecca M. Howard, 1–12. London: Thomson Wadsworth.

Kahan, Jeffrey. 2015. "'I Tell You What Mine Author Says': A Brief History of Stylometrics." *ELH* 82 (3): 815–844.

Kennedy, George, ed. 2003. *Progymnasmata: Greek Textbooks of Prose Composition and Rhetoric.* Atlanta: Society of Biblical Literature.

Kohlrausch, Laura. 2018. "'I Have Chosen to Write Notes on Imaginary Books': On the Forgery of Textual Sources." In *Faking, Forging, Counterfeiting: Discredited Practices at the Margins of Mimesis,* edited by Daniel Becker, Analisa Fischer, and Yola Schimitz, 153–166. Bielefeld: Transcript Verlag.

Lutosławski, Wincenty. 1890. "Principes de stylométrie." *Revue des études grecques* 41: 61–81.

Martyr, Justin. 2012. *The Apologies of Justin Martyr.* Greenland: Suzeteo Enterprises.

Marzluf, Phillip. 2012. "Examining Teachers' and Students' Attitudes toward Plagiarism." In *Critical Conversations about Plagiarism,* edited by Michael Donnelly, Rebecca Ingalls, Tracy A. Morse, Joanna C. Post, and Ann M. Stockdell-Giesler, 7–21. Anderson, SC: Parlor Press.

Mealand, David. 2016. "The Seams and Summaries of Luke and Acts." *JSNT* 38 (4): 482–502.

Mussies, Gerhard. 1991. "Variation in the Book of Acts." *Filologia Neotestamentaria* 4: 176.

Parsons, Mikeal. 1987. *The Departure of Jesus in Luke-Acts: The Ascension Narratives in Context.* Sheffield: Sheffield AP.

Parsons, Mikeal, and Heather Gorman. 2012. "The Assumed Authorial Unity of Luke and Acts: A Review Essay." *Neotestamentica* 46 (1): 139–152.

Pervo, Richard. 2009. *Acts: A Commentary,* edited by Harold W. Attridge. Minneapolis: Fortress Press.

Porter, Stanley. 2016. "The Unity of Luke-Acts and the Ascension Narratives." In *Ascent into Heaven in Luke-Acts: New Explorations of Luke's Narrative Hinge,* edited by David Bryan and David Pao, 111–136. Minneapolis: Augsburg Fortress.

Raminal, Hoshiladevi, Shrieen Panchoo, and Sameerchand Pudaruth. 2016. "Authorship Attribution Using Stylometry and Machine Learning Techniques." *Intelligent Systems Technologies and Applications* 384: 113–125.

Robillard, A. E., and Ron Fortune. 2007. "Toward a New Content for Writing Courses: Literary Forgery, Plagiarism, and the Production of Belief." *JAC* 27 (1/2): 185–210.

Scholten, J. H. 1973. *Is de derde evangelist de schrijver van het boek der Handelingen? Critischonderzoek.* Leiden: Academische Boekhandel van P. Engels.

Smith, Daniel, and Zachary Kostopoulos. 2017. "Biography, History and the Genre of Luke-Acts." *New Testament Studies* 63 (3): 390–410.

Tertullian. 1964. *Tertullian's Homily on Baptism*, edited by Ernest Evans. London: SPCK.

Walters, Patricia. 2009. *The Assumed Authorial Unity of Luke and Acts: A Reassessment of the Evidence.* Cambridge: Cambridge University Press.

Watson, Francis. 2010. "Beyond Suspicion: On the Authorship of the Mar Saba Letter and the Secret Gospel of Mark." *The Journal of Theological Studies* 61 (1): 128–170.

15
WORDS, WORDS, WORDS, OR LEVERAGING LEXIS FOR A PEDAGOGY OF STYLE

William T. FitzGerald

I'll say it. I want my students to write with style *and* substance, to care about what they say *and* how they say it. I want attention to craft, evidenced by the well-turned phrase and *le mot juste*. I want, as Jonathan Swift famously put it, "proper words in proper places" (1907, 161). I want these things as a reader, but I also want them as a teacher who wishes the best for his students.

In saying this I risk perpetuating a false binary between style and invention, as if language is merely the dress of thought. What, then, am I really saying? That in writing pedagogy we have long ignored the resources of style, leaving the play of language for later and never quite getting around to it. I am guilty of this myself, and I hear from others that there isn't enough time to teach style and to practice style as a deliberate dimension of our pedagogy. We don't mean to neglect style, but we do. Style is quite literally an *after*thought.

I have observed that students struggle with language as a medium. Rather, they often do not struggle enough, given a lack of resources by which to do so. In saying this, I do not join in the lament that our students cannot write. They can, though we can always help them to do better, especially when we approach writing as a craft. Like all crafts, writing is rooted in the use of tools. Able writers see language as a tool, not the impediment struggling writers do. In this essay I thus turn to writing as a craft, with a focus on the basic tools of language, or in other words, *words*. Classical rhetoric assigned invention and style to distinct canons, but in reality they are deeply connected and complementary. For style is actually a second source of invention. Encounters with any formal medium occasion the generation of content. On a macro level, we can say that invention takes precedence—literally, comes before—style. But on a micro level, discourse unfolds in time, through the medium of words, the domain of style.

DOI: 10.7330/9781646420117.c015

My question, then, is how can we help students better access and leverage their stock of verbal resources? I submit that today words are an undervalued stylistic resource. And if we wish to reclaim the resources of style as no mere afterthought, we should invest again in *lexical* pedagogy. That is, we should be more attentive to words in our teaching. Admittedly, I'm old-fashioned here—*really* old-fashioned, all the way back to Aristotle as a foundation for moving forward.

WHY WORDS? TOWARD A LEXICAL PEDAGOGY OF STYLE

In ongoing efforts to "reanimate" style in composition, words suffer from comparative neglect for reasons I take up momentarily (Butler 2008). These efforts are part of a broad project since the mid-twentieth century to reclaim the rhetorical tradition, including style, for pedagogy and scholarship (Corbett and Connors 1998; Crowley and Hawhee 2011). Throughout this period, composition, where style is concerned, has focused on the sentence, not on words as constituent elements of sentences. This makes sense, because words make sense only *in* sentences. But stop to consider that sentences are only as good as the words from which they are made, and we see that to reclaim style we must attend to words as raw material for the verbal arts. With characteristic wit Mark Twain observed, "The difference between the almost right word and the right word is really a large matter—'tis the difference between the lightning-bug and the lightning" (Bainton 1890). Practicing what he preached, Twain reveals the power of style at the level of the word. Similarly, we must recognize the inventive resources of language—lexis together with syntax—at the level of the sentence and beyond.

In this line of inquiry, I locate style *as invention* insofar as language gives rise to thought. A well-furnished stock, or *invent*ory, of words, phrases, and syntactic structures enables one not only to express but also to discover arguments. Style may thus be understood as the capacity to strategically deploy language. Colloquially, style is a way with words. This characterization is consistent with Aristotle's enduring definition of rhetoric as the art of discovering in a given case the available means of persuasion (1954). Developing writers benefit from understanding words as *rhetorical*, and not simply inert forms representing ideas. Especially, students benefit from robust means of retrieval from the bank of words that is their individual vocabulary. They benefit not only from access to that bank, but from diversified verbal funds, the absence of which is as an impoverished style.

A focus on words acknowledges the available means of persuasion inherent in language choice. But this effort goes beyond prescriptive approaches to *word* choice under a heading of diction, even as it touches on abiding concerns about *clear, correct,* and *appropriate* language, qualities which, with *ornament*, comprise the classical virtues of style. I propose we re-engage with *lexis*, Greek for "style" (in Latin, *elocutio*). Here, I lean on the root of *lexis* as the domain of words, the part of formal language distinct from syntax, not its later use as an encompassing term for style. (From *lexis* is derived *lexicon*, or the full set of words available to a speaker or writer.) This focus is a return to style's earliest articulation in Book III of Aristotle's *Rhetoric*, a set of *de*scriptive and *pre*scriptive observations on what generally works by way of expression.

To begin, we must ask what happened to words in college composition. Once, composition pedagogies explicitly progressed from the word, the smallest unit of discourse, to increasingly larger units: phrase, clause, sentence, paragraph, and, finally, whole discourse. Presumably, one must master elemental units (i.e., words) before moving on. Such procedural rhetorics owe their existence, in part, to prescriptive pedagogies of Alexander Bain, who in the late-nineteenth century focused on the paragraph as the major unit of discourse. In the mid-twentieth century, New Critical paradigms in literary criticism introduced methods of close reading centered on the word as the basic unit of discourse whose scope of reference must be interrogated. A shift from a focus on words in themselves or in relation to larger units of discourse is a break from both current-traditional models of writing and belletristic models of reading in favor of more holistic approaches to texts as situated discourse.

In addition, process models of composition dominant since the 1960s privileged stages of invention, drafting, and revision. These models draw attention from lexical features insofar as texts in development are rarely stable at the level of the word. Indeed, pedagogy too focused on words risks sapping the flow of a text as it comes into being. And practices of revision too concentrated on diction can contribute to superficial changes to a text rather than substantive revision. Consider how students often employ a thesaurus to amplify their prose to poor effect.

Finally, a focus on words in composition can easily devolve into prescriptive approaches to diction. These include prohibitions on words (e.g., "avoid personal pronouns and slang terms"), zealous attention to grammatical correctness, and promotion of norms of elite speech. Diction is low-hanging fruit when intervening in service to standards of clarity, correctness, and propriety. The more progressive the approach to teaching writing, the less likely it will center on words at the expense of other levels of text. At the least, words come later, as we see in models for revising, by contrast with generating, prose (Lanham and Stodel 1992; Williams and Bizup 2010).

If a shift from the word to other levels of text is largely sound, we can still ask what is lost when, avoiding pitfalls of current-traditionalism, we lose sight of words. For apart from moves away from formalist paradigms of writing instruction, a turn from words is part of the structure of *college* composition. Our current system of literacy instruction in American higher education perpetuates in crucial ways a division in the classical era between the teacher of grammar (*grammaticus*) and, coming later in the course of study, the rhetorician who trains students in the arts of civic oratory. By and large, the study of words, including the parts of speech, belongs to primary (grammar) and secondary (high) school. In higher education, students are presumed to be finished with grammar, now fluent in reading and writing.

Here is the tell: our system of literacy instruction centers on vocabulary building for success on standardized tests like the SAT-Verbal. These assessments purport to measure readiness for college by levels of attainment based largely on *lexis*. What words do we know, by way of recall, in acts of reading? What norms of diction have we internalized? Fluency of this sort comes from long exposure to imaginative literature and expository prose. And efforts to prep students for standardized tests reveal insufficiencies in a reading-based curriculum. Hence a push to build vocabularies artificially, as distinct from the slower, but surer, processes of reading and writing in their dynamic relations.

As a result, many students arrive at college poorly resourced in terms of lexis, and style in general. What words they "know" are often highly decontextualized and unavailable for use in writing. The abandonment of grammar in composition studies (more on that below) after the 1970s resulted in a corresponding lack of attention to diction as a component of grammar. Indeed, focus on diction may be seen as symptomatic of outdated pedagogies. In a figurative handoff between the teacher of grammar and the teacher of rhetoric, then, what often gets dropped is words.

Yet I do not argue that college composition should somehow complete the unfinished work of the K–12 language arts classroom. Instead, I propose we keep on task in teaching rhetorical approaches to language. For the rhetorical agency of *lexis* is not realized in amassing a bank of knowledge about words, but in performance—with words put to use. There's an opportunity here for style pedagogy to take aim at facility with words in their vitality and variety.

AFTER SENTENCE-BASED RHETORICS, A DEEPER DIVE INTO THE POOL OF WORDS

In some ways we have been here before in linking rhetorical pedagogy with formal elements of language. In "Erasure of the Sentence" (2000), Robert Connors charts the wax and wane of mid-twentieth-century efforts to teach style through *sentence*-based pedagogies. These include groundbreaking work on generative rhetoric (Christensen 1963); exercises in imitation inspired by classical pedagogy (Corbett 1971); and regimes of sentence-combining to increase syntactic fluency and maturity (Daiker, Kerek, and Morenberg 1978). Each approach had its heyday; however, by the 1990s all of them faded from active use in the classroom and in scholarship. Connors attributes this "erasure" to a confluence of factors: anti-formalism, anti-behaviorism, and anti-empiricism (2000). Combined, these three movements, consistent with the growth of composition studies into a recognized academic discipline, led away from a default stance that the sentence was a central object of study and practice and to the neglect of syntax as a major site of effort and expertise.

The loss of the sentence was a loss for style as a whole. It came despite calls for "ReMembering the Sentence" (Myers 2003) and, relatedly, "Making the Case for Rhetorical Grammar" (Micciche 2004), as well as more direct intervention in multiple textbooks on style at the sentence level (Bacon 2012; Kolln and Gray 2012; Holcomb and Killingsworth 2010). These teaching texts by scholars in composition studies find space on the shelf beside works addressed to a more popular audience (Tufte 2006; Fish 2012; Pinker 2014).

Most of these contemporary approaches to style depart from the course I advocate here in touching only lightly on *lexical* resources, typically with respect to functional dimensions of word classes and forms (e.g., pronouns, active vs. passive voice, nominalizations). Of course, prescriptive accounts treat words in terms of usage and diction—not inspiring stuff. Despite a rich tradition of semantics in rhetorical criticism (Ogden and Richards 1923; Burke 1938; Richards 1943) and of engagement with lexical elements in the allied fields of literary stylistics (Leech and Short 2007) and applied linguistics (Carter 1998), composition studies has not turned its attention to words with a similar energy that it turned, for a time, to the sentence. (It's literary studies, especially poetics, that relishes the rhetorical effects of *le mot juste*.)

We can understand this reluctance given the drawbacks of overly prescriptive approaches to clarity, correctness, and propriety in forms of current-traditional rhetoric. Along with a fourth in *ornatus*, or ornament, these classical virtues of style find their earliest articulation in Aristotle's *Rhetoric*. A brief tour of Book III of Aristotle's *Rhetoric*, focused on style, can help us see the generative potential of a (re)turn to words, to style as lexis.

Book III rounds out Aristotle's account of rhetoric's situations and techniques of invention with rudimentary, yet exceedingly rich, observations on style and delivery. Though they do not cohere into a full, formal treatise, these observations establish lines of thought whose influence can hardly be overstated. Above all, Aristotle is concerned with the characteristics of effective *prose* as distinct from *poetry*. His observations on prose follow with similar treatment of language in the *Poetics*: "In regard to style, one of its chief merits may be defined as perspicuity. This is shown by the fact that the speech, if it does not make the meaning clear, will not perform its proper function; neither must it be mean, nor above the dignity of the subject, but appropriate to it" (Rhet III.2.1). In this seminal passage on diction, Aristotle goes on to say that, in service to the goal of "perspicuity," or clarity, rhetors must find that characteristic (for Aristotle) middle way between speech that is frigid or excessive in order to seem natural, not artificial. A poetic license does not extend to prose. From here, we can trace the entire lineage in rhetorical tradition on the principle of clarity as the essence of effective style. And likewise of *prepon* or appropriateness.

In a passage worth quoting in full, Aristotle points to "nouns and verbs" (meaning the parts of speech broadly) as the means by which we may produce a style neither flat nor inflated:

> Nouns and verbs being the components of speech, and nouns being of the different kinds which have been considered in the *Poetics*, of these we should use strange, compound, or coined words only rarely and in few places. We will state later in what places they should be used; the reason for this has already been mentioned, namely, that it involves too great a departure from suitable language. Proper and appropriate words and metaphors are alone to be employed in the style of prose; this is shown by the fact that no one employs anything but these. For all use metaphors in conversation, as well as proper and appropriate words; wherefore it is clear that, if a speaker manages well, there will be some thing "foreign" about his speech, while possibly the art may not be detected, and his meaning will be clear. And this, as we have said, is the chief merit of rhetorical language. (1954, III.2.5–7)

Here Aristotle accounts for two fundamental features of prose: first, it is *written* language, if perhaps composed for oral delivery; second, it *resembles* extemporaneous language, but with a measure of control in using unusual or unexpected language, thus lending distinction to one's prose. We can say Aristotle echoes (though actually initiates) that age-old advice to write as we speak, *but only up to a point.*

Rarely observed in responding to Aristotle on style is that he speaks specifically of words. We may zero in on clarity and propriety or on Aristotle's foundational role in the study of metaphor yet miss the centrality of lexis to his account of style. Indeed, it is instructive to compare Aristotle on lexis and syntax, for only a small portion of Book III, chapters 8 and 9, is concerned with prose rhythm and sentence structure, his famous discussion of periodic and running styles. The remainder of his account is a fertile discussion of rhetorical aspects of prose diction.

Aristotle speaks to the nature of words as our common inheritance as users of language. In my experience, his insights open doors for students. They, like everyone, react viscerally to language. More than note virtues and vices, Aristotle makes the familiar accessible by giving presence to speech phenomena. What students lack, above all, is permission to own their deep knowledge of how language works. For they value variety, normativity, and novelty in word choice, take delight in borrowed words and new coinages, and employ strategies of generality and specificity, bluntness and circumlocution. What students don't know, often, are the rules of the road that apply to language used in new situations and genres. And, most importantly, many lack a deep pool of words and the dexterity to manipulate the words they do know. What they need for that is training.

A LEXICAL PROGYMNASMATA

We cannot expect students will read Aristotle or other classical rhetoricians, nor do we need that. What we can do is put classical pedagogy in modern dress, with a renewed focus on lexical maturity and fluency. The objective is that students write at the upper end of their lexical range, choosing words carefully and deliberately. I thus propose a lexical *progymnasmata*, exercises that train students in the art of words. For models, I look to classical approaches to rhetorical education, in particular on amplification, by Quintilian, and on copia, by Erasmus. For inspiration, I turn to a recent compendium on *Rhetorical Style* by Jeanne Fahnestock (2011). And as a warrant in support of my claim that classical precursors are relevant to present concerns, I cite emerging paradigms of craft and code meshing in composition studies.

In essence, this is a call to develop strategies that foster a facility with vocabulary as a resource for an effective style. Brian Ray argues that classical-era *progymnasmata* can be repurposed to support "pedagogies of language difference" (Ray 2013, 191). I would further observe that some degree of translingualism is foundational for *all* prose composition insofar as writing is a second language in relation to speech. In this language, as in others, writers must develop *facilitas*, the flexibility advocated by Quintilian (X.i.1) that allows rhetors to improvise in new situations. This verbal flexibility, including maximizing options for choice, is necessary to wield words with skill. But how do we develop this flexibility, particularly with respect to lexis?

In broad strokes, I suggest re-engagement with classical models of style pedagogy that form a counterpart to organized systems of invention that likewise flourished in the rhetorical tradition. These are active modes of composing that grapple with possibilities in thought and expression. Here it might prove useful to reflect on where we are now by highlighting a contrast between past and present in the pedagogy of both style and invention. When we talk about invention in contemporary writing pedagogy, the default is a type of passive inspiration in which ideas and sometimes words suggest themselves in a process of *brainstorming*. Generate quickly and as much as one can, individually or with others, without stopping to censor or evaluate. A variation on this active model for composing is "freewriting," letting words and ideas flow, as popularized by Peter Elbow (1998).

These and other modes of invention have their place in a composing repertoire, yet there is room for much-neglected formal heuristics. These include inventional topoi such as the common topics of cause and effect, definition, and comparison, among other "places" to discover arguments. But style is also a site of invention, even a primary site; for we often speak before knowing what to say and write ourselves into arguments and stances. We can thus look to words as sites of invention, not just allowing them to come unbidden, but coaxing them and wrestling with them on the page.

The most potent sources still in rhetorical tradition for the inventional capacities of language are Quintilian on amplification and Erasmus on copia.

Amplification

In Book VIII of his *Institutes*, Quintilian offers strategies of *amplification* to heighten discourse and corresponding strategies for attenuation. Not all strategies are strictly lexical, but many are. They involve, for example, deliberate choice of a stronger word over a weaker to characterize a situation. Quintilian offers an example from Cicero: "I have brought before you, judges, not a thief, but a plunderer; not an adulterer, but a ravisher; not a mere committer of sacrilege, but the enemy of all religious observance and all holy things" (1921, 265). In addition, Quintilian presents the construction of comparisons and of rising or falling series in which the primary rhetorical effect is achieved in the arrangement of words. Finally, as we see from the example above, amplification may simply be a matter of accumulation, piling on, finding multiple ways to say much the same thing.

Of amplification, Robert Harris observes in *A Handbook of Rhetorical Devices* that "it involves repeating a word or expression while adding more detail to it, in order to emphasize what might otherwise be passed over. . . . [A]mplification allows you to call attention to, emphasize, and expand a word or idea to make sure the reader realizes its importance" (2012, 26). It is fair to say that as a rhetorical strategy, amplification runs counter to current composing practices, and certainly in educational contexts. Richard Lanham characterizes the dominant values of prose style in our era as "Clarity, Brevity, and Sincerity, the C-B-S theory" (2003, 1).

To challenge expectations of brevity and invite students to experiment with expanding on their thoughts, but especially their words, we can assign *exercises* in amplification, exploring how far an idea may be extended, heightened, yet still yield results rhetorically. In many cases it will become clear that amplification is not always an effective strategy. But the discoveries that arise from unwinding a spool of words may nonetheless prove useful. The idea here is not that students should necessarily incorporate amplified prose in particular texts but that drafts and stand-alone exercises provide opportunities for expansion as a resource.

Copia

Amplification finds its most significant elaboration as pedagogy 1,400 years after Quintilian. It comes from the hand of Desiderius Erasmus in his textbook *On Copia of Words and Ideas* (1963). First published in 1512, with numerous reprintings through the sixteenth century, this is the most influential treatise on style in the post-classical era. To teach Latin to English schoolboys, *On Copia* accepts the virtue of stylistic flexibility:

> [I] am not prescribing how one should write and speak, but am pointing out what to do for training, where, as everyone knows, all things ought to be exaggerated. Then I am instructing youth, in whom extravagance of

speech does not seem wrong to Quintilian, because with judgment, superfluities are easily restrained, certain of them even, age itself wears away, while on the other hand, you cannot by any method cure meagerness and poverty. (1963, 14)

In voicing this insight, and echoing Quintilian, Erasmus challenges the presumption of brevity as developmentally inappropriate for students, especially. They need *more* words, not fewer. Over time, youthful excess will take care of itself.

Among the sharp insights Erasmus offers is a concern with the deficiency of lexical resources: "It not infrequently happens that we have to say the same thing several times, in which case, if destitute of copia we will either be at a loss, or, like the cuckoo, croak out the same words repeatedly, and be unable to give different shape or form to the thought" (1963, 16). This is where many students today, writing not in Latin or Greek but in the secondary language of standard written English, find themselves—literally at a loss for words.

Having thus framed the problem, Erasmus offers a remedy through a systematic account of how to vary one's speech. These include the use of metaphors and other tropes, strategies of amplification outlined by Quintilian, and multiple techniques by way of synonymy, modification, and shifts in word classes. Erasmus famously illustrates these methods with his celebrated tour de force of 195 variations in Latin on the phrase "Your letter pleased me greatly." Here, the challenge of invention, finding more things to say, finds its complement in the affordances of style, finding more ways to say it.

In a contemporary *progymnasmata* centered on lexis, one can take this composing challenge straight from Erasmus's playbook and, as an exercise in copia, ask students to generate 50, 100, or even 200 variations on a single sentence. Indeed, this practice seems as relevant today as ever before. It's a wonder it has not been more widely adopted, in the same way that doing scales contributes to musical development. Such verbal gymnastics would intervene in the many factors that contribute to a frigid style. These include a naïve belief that writing is simply thought transferred to the page. But discovering dozens of ways to express a thought requires one to dig deep into a lexical and syntactic repertoire with patience and persistence. This move is much the opposite of techniques of invention such as freewriting and brainstorming, for in this exercise one must slow down and encounter language at a granular level. For a teacher using Erasmian sentence variation as a training exercise, a fair degree of explicit instruction is required to open up the available range of stylistic options.

Inevitably, in this exercise, many sentences will fail to be usable, while others will work in some situations but not others. It's useful to consider *why* a sentence fails in part or in whole. Given how seldom students work at this level, doing so can be groundbreaking. Above all, they experience stylistic options as real choices. There *are* multiple ways to say a thing, each with its rhetorical force. In addition/Besides/Furthermore, students see/discover the value of working with *their* language, finding other ways to say something and finding they can do this repeatedly.

Choosing Words Wisely

Amplification and copia may be means of a lexical progymnasmata, but words are its matter. Efforts to develop *facilitas* with lexis break open the bank of words that a student has available for use and, to push the metaphor, even make additional deposits. For strategies to increase facility with lexis, no better contemporary resource can be found than the anatomy of style Jeanne Fahnestock offers in *Rhetorical Style: The Uses of Language in Persuasion* (2011). The scheme of *Rhetorical Style* mirrors my argument presented here in its style at the level of the word, the sentence, and beyond. Early chapters take up the word before moving onto the sentence, while later chapters address passage construction and interactive features of discourse.

While *Rhetorical Style* is not itself a guide to composing, its principles for analyzing written language direct attention to features any writer or instructor can use to link reading and writing. Each of the first six chapters of *Rhetorical Style* serves as a site for generating a range of exercises in language analysis and stylistic choice. Much of this work is preparatory and sidebar in nature in a writing course, but it seems to me that a certain amount of "word work" in vocabulary awareness is essential to increasing facility with lexis. Let's consider each of these chapters as a starting point for a suite of exercises in lexis.

1. *Translation and linguistic heritage.* Chapter 1 examines words in terms of "language of origin," employing a trifold division of words in English: an Old English core, a Norman-French inheritance, and an injection of learned terms from Latin and Greek. Through close reading of diverse texts, Fahnestock shows how the origins of words contribute to rhetorical effects of "clarity and sincerity" (Old English), "elevation and panache" (French), and "formality and erudition" (Greek and Latin). An immediate impulse upon seeing these analyses yield insights into how word choice operates rhetorically is to look for ways to introduce this "method," aided perhaps only by a dictionary, to students. As an analytical exercise, they can practice locating word origins in the

prose they read as well as write. As a composing exercise, students can "translate" specific words or whole sentences based on word origins, say from core English to Greek and Latin terms, pausing to consider what is gained and lost in translation. For instance, three sentences back, I fretted (Old English) over/debated (Norman French) whether to use "shows" (Old English) or "demonstrates" (Latin), finally opting for the more immediate, shorter word. Of course, a little bit of etymology goes a long way. Students can easily become lost in the minutiae of such exercises. At the same time, for this type of word work to be effective, exercises in etymology can't be a one-off effort. As with *progymnasmata* of old, cyclical use of such strategies pays long-term dividends.

2. *Journaling and word formation*: Chapter 2 of *Rhetorical Style* examines language as living and changing with a focus on how new words are formed and evolve. This compact field guide to morphology, with information on free and bound morphemes, prefixes and suffixes, and clipped and blended words, shows how students and teachers can overlay schema of word formation on the English they read and write every day. In the tradition of a *commonplace book*, students might start a language journal as part of a writing course, collecting scraps of language they encounter, or generate, to place under various headings based on types of word formation. They might consider as well the social uses of new coinages and evolving meanings and discuss choices they made to use or not use particular words and expressions in a piece they have written. But rather than censor themselves, as they might in formal writing, students can thus lay claim to their individual and collective lexis while developing a meta-linguistic awareness.

3. *Bank deposits*: Going further with Fahnestock, students and teachers can explore further aspects of diction, including levels of generality and abstraction in word choice, social and occupational registers, distinctions between written and spoken varieties of English, and the use of slang terms and idioms. As another ongoing exercise, perhaps integrated with the journaling identified above, students could start their own verbal accounting ledger that offers a window into their habitual and emerging choices of words in various contexts of writing, including diction in digital spaces versus more academic voicing. The point to underscore here is that students are estranged in many ways from their own language when they sit down to write. They need to become better acquainted with the vocabulary that is present to them (or accessible, if not necessarily on hand) if they are to compose effectively. These approaches to language in use overlap with the literary stylistics that students have had some exposure to in prior language arts curricula. Here, however, they can go further by exploring, and employing, words rhetorically.

4. *Lexis meets syntax*: The last two chapters on word choice in *Rhetorical Style* visit the tropes (chapter 5) and the schemes (chapter 6) of classical rhetoric to demonstrate their ongoing vitality. Elsewhere I advocate for explicit application of rhetorical figures in composition pedagogy (FitzGerald 2013). Always at issue here is how to balance formal study

of specific lexical features with actual use, whether natural or cultivated. Perhaps, then, the most useful contribution of *Rhetorical Stylistics* to a lexical *progymnasmata* is chapter 6, "Figures of Word Choice," which orients readers—and writers—to lexical effects in sentences and paragraphs. These effects include figures of repetition and variation, two areas where developing writers especially struggle. They may *have* the words in their vocabulary, yet not know how best to use them. To this end, Fahnestock's analysis of figures such as *ploce* (repeated use of a word in a discourse) and *polyptoton* (variant forms of a word, e.g., love/lover/loving) can help students to think not *how do I avoid repetition* (nervously seeking out a possible synonym) but *how can I make strategic use of repetition*. As another exercise, students might experiment to see how long they can use a word or its variations before it gives out on them.

This "hands on" approach to word choice, beyond prescriptive advice on diction, is largely missing in contemporary curricula. Why? No time for what might come across or actually *be* mere busy work? There is always a risk that such exercises, much like skill and drill in grammar and mechanics, will fail to translate into actual practice. It pays to be selective in assigning exercises that focus on lexis or syntax. Here, of course, I am arguing that we should make room for some close work of lexical analysis and experimentation alongside exercises based on imitation at the sentence level or in the construction of paragraphs or practices of sentence elaboration and combining to reclaim the rhetorical resources of words themselves.

CONCLUSION: (RE)CRAFTING COMPOSITION

Recently, the notion of "craft" has arisen as a commonplace. Craft is everywhere. Craft is cool, way cooler than what it replaces. (Side bar: as a final effort in a lexical *progymnasmata*, students might produce short essays examining a single word like "craft" or "cool" for the rhetorical and cultural work it performs.) The field of rhetoric and composition is no exception to an emerging craft aesthetic (Mayers 2005; Rice 2016). I end this essay by suggesting how we might "craft" composition by attending to the material dimensions of words and the labor that adds to their value. I do so as a way to provide a broader frame for this focus on word work. Here, I follow on Danielle Koupf, who in a recent essay, "Proliferating Textual Possibilities: Toward Pedagogies of Critical-Creative Tinkering," looks to "makerspaces" as a way for composition to respond to the creative energies of this moment (2017). For this purpose, Koupf reclaims "tinkering," a term that "has been recovered in a positive light to describe material practices that involve modifying or repurposing heterogeneous parts toward both imaginative and practical ends" (Koupf 2017). Koupf explicitly connects tinkering to pedagogies of style that *make do with* and *make something of* existing parts. She does so in ways that echo my call to attend to words as building blocks of discourse—think "tinker" toys. Indeed, writing is akin to tinkering with words, making something of their assembly into a sum greater than their parts. For students, we might introduce the notion that words are found objects available to be assembled into new creations.

Koupf outlines a course she taught in creative-critical "de/composition" based on work by the poet W. D. Snodgrass. For her course, Koupf's students "decompose" a prior text, and through creative re*work*ing and re*word*ing they see how it was put together: "Just as tinkering with a physical device involves testing how it responds to modifications, tinkering with texts involves testing through rereading and analysis. In noting how the device or text responds to changes, the tinker learns about the device or text itself" (2017). Koupf's students recount what they have learned by tinkering with texts at the "workbench," rather than as finished, polished projects. Attending to words as elements of composition may help students see themselves as makers creatively employing raw materials as so many bits and pieces in an artisan's studio.

Koupf's experiments with *de*composition reveal the creative side of composition, though we know the stakes are high in composing for academic and professional purposes. Words matter. Style betrays. Fearing the wrong word, we may stick to only safe choices. It's fair to say that our active vocabulary is shaped by thoughts of using words incorrectly or of not being the type to use a particular word. Expanding one's vocabulary by tinkering with words requires courage, not unlike trying out a new clothing style. We see this anxiety in quick-fix approaches to vocabulary building to use words to help us fit in to new environments.

A robust genre of phrase books helps writers find the words by simply supplying them. A case in point is *The Academic Phrase Bank* (Morley 2018), primarily addressed to non-native English speakers writing research reports with sections like "Describing Methods" and "Discussing Findings." Another section, "Introducing Work," has headings such as "Establishing the importance of the topic for the discipline" and offers relevant phrases: "X is an increasingly important area of . . ."; "X has been the subject of much systematic investigation . . ."; "Central to the entire discipline of X is the concept of . . . ," etc. In the same genre is *The Only Academic Phrasebook You'll Ever Need: 600 Examples of Academic Language* (Barros 2016) with templates such as "To date, no study has looked specifically at . . ." These guides fill a gap in productive knowledge for writers who, for various reasons, outsource the labor of copia to supplement or substitute for their own. At some level they call to mind a writer's use of the thesaurus to lend variety and distinction to one's prose. But there is also a de-crafting of composition here when writers fail to internalize such phrases. We can empathize with the desire to do quickly what takes years of deepening expertise and a social framework that supports writers through stages of trial and error and rising confidence.

In writing this essay, I repeatedly asked myself, how did I come to write that sentence? How, for example, did I decide above on "empathize" over "understand"? Choose "deepening" to modify "expertise"? When I started that sentence, I did not know that I would pair the phrases "deepening expertise" and "rising confidence." That decision came in the act of writing. It's fair to say the words came to *me* as much as I to *them*. Yet surely that's too simple. It takes much time and practice and a supportive framework to reach the stage where one can attempt/formulate/risk/dare various composing choices, striving for a blend of academic and colloquial voices. You don't see my fits and starts, how I struggled to find/effect a tone that I was happy/satisfied with.

My argument, again, is that we can coach students to a rhetorical style and that this coaching includes attending to *lexis*. I thus want to dispel notions that this return to words is part of any "back to basics" resurrection of current-traditionalism. Quite the opposite, this is a call for us to be committed to discovery/play/experimentation/improvisation. Our students will not find *le mot juste* while waiting for inspiration to strike. They may, however, by assembling and disassembling texts, tinkering with language until the various parts come together. They do so more readily with greater access to the word banks they already possess and by expanding their lexical repertoire by reading, by the uptake of new words, and by writing in response to other texts through acts of imitation, quotation, and forms of language mixing.

A focus on style as *lexis* actually links classical and contemporary understanding of language not with a goal for students to have different or better language but to expand the bank of words at their disposal and use these bank accounts to good effect. Here it is essential to think not in terms of language deficits but of assets, liquidity, and a diversified portfolio—languages of home *and* school *and* work *and* civic engagement. In this respect, approaches to style as *lexis* dovetail with pedagogies of "code meshing" in literacy education (Young and Martinez 2011). For multilingual writers possess multiple vocabularies and need not convert all their linguistic assets into a single currency. As Aristotle observed, "foreign" words lend distinction and interest to prose (1954).

We might further observe that in the multilingual landscape of world Englishes, the lexical domains of many languages, local and global, increasingly come together. And they clash, not unlike in the Early Modern era, during which a recognizable form of English emerged in the wake of an Anglo-Norman fusion. That fusion has resulted in more words, a great profusion of choices, like so many shades of blue (navy, teal, sky, aquamarine, turquoise, midnight, cobalt, cornflower, royal, etc.) with which to paint. A revitalized pedagogy attentive to the resources of *lexis* will not address all the rhetorical and pedagogical challenges associated with style but it may go a long way toward helping students invest in their rich linguistic inheritance and turn a profit.

REFERENCES

Aristotle. 1954. *Rhetoric*. Translated by W. Rhys Roberts. New York: Modern Library.
Bacon, Nora. 2012. *The Well-Crafted Sentence: A Writer's Guide to Style*. Boston: Bedford/St. Martin's.
Bainton, George. 1890. "Mark Twain." In *The Art of Authorship*, 87–88. New York: Appleton.
Barros, Luiz Otávio. *The Only Academic Phrasebook You'll Ever Need: 600 Examples of Academic Language*. Createspace Independent Publishing Platform.
Burke, Kenneth. 1938. "Semantic and Poetic Meaning." *Southern Review* 4: 501.
Butler, Paul. 2008. *Out of Style: Reanimating Stylistic Study in Composition and Rhetoric*. Logan: Utah State University Press.
Carter, Ronald. 1998. *Vocabulary: Applied Linguistic Perspectives*, 2nd ed. London: Routledge.
Christensen, Francis. 1963. "A Generative Rhetoric of the Sentence." *College Composition and Communication* 14 (3): 155–161.
Connors, Robert J. 2000. "The Erasure of the Sentence." *College Composition and Communication* 52 (1): 96–128.
Corbett, Edward P. J. 1971. "The Theory and Practice of Imitation in Classical Rhetoric." *College Composition and Communication* 22 (3): 243–250.
Corbett, Edward P. J., and Robert J. Connors. 1998. *Classical Rhetoric for the Modern Student*, 4th ed. New York: Oxford University Press.
Crowley, Sharon, and Debra Hawhee. 2011. *Ancient Rhetorics for Contemporary Students*, 5th ed. Boston: Pearson.
Daiker, Donald, Andrew Kerek, and Max Morenberg. 1978. "Sentence-Combining and Syntactic Maturity in Freshman English." *College Composition and Communication* 29 (1): 36–41.
Elbow, Peter. 1998. *Writing without Teachers*, 2nd ed. New York: Oxford University Press.
Erasmus, Desiderius. 1963. *On Copia of Words and Ideas (De utraque verborem ac rerum copia)*. Translated by Donald B. King. Milwaukee: Marquette University Press.
Fahnestock, Jeanne. 2011. *Rhetorical Style: The Uses of Language in Persuasion*. Oxford: Oxford University Press.
Fish, Stanley. 2012. *How to Write a Sentence and How to Read One*. New York: Harper.
FitzGerald, William. 2013. "Stylistic Sandcastles: Rhetorical Figures as Composition's Bucket and Spade." In *The Centrality of Style*, edited by Mike Duncan and Star Medzerian Vanguri, 37–56. Anderson, SC: Parlor Press.

Harris, Robert. 2012. *A Handbook of Rhetorical Devices.* Accessed May 8, 2019. http://www.hellesdon.org/documents/Advanced%20Rhetoric.pdf.
Holcomb, Chris, and M. Jimmie Killingsworth. 2010. *Performing Prose: The Study and Practice of Style in Composition.* Carbondale: Southern Illinois University Press.
Kolln, Martha J., and Loretta S. Gray. 2017. *Rhetorical Grammar: Grammatical Choices, Rhetorical Effects*, 8th ed. Boston: Pearson.
Koupf, Danielle. 2017. "Proliferating Textual Possibilities: Toward Pedagogies of Critical-Creative Tinkering." *Composition Forum* 35.
Lanham, Richard. 2003. *Analyzing Prose.* London: A&C Black.
Lanham, Richard A., and James Stodel. 1992. *Revising Prose.* New York: Macmillan.
Leech, Geoffrey, and Mick Short. 2007. *Style in Fiction: A Linguistic Introduction to English Fictional Prose*, 2nd ed. London: Routledge.
Mayers, Tim. 2005. *(Re)Writing Craft: Composition, Creative Writing, and the Future of English Studies.* Pittsburgh: University of Pittsburgh Press.
Micciche, Laura. 2004. "Making a Case for Rhetorical Grammar." *College Composition and Communication* 55 (4): 716–737.
Morley, John. 2018. *The Academic Phrasebank: An Academic Writing Resource for Students and Researchers.* Manchester: University of Manchester.
Myers, Sharon A. 2003. "ReMembering the Sentence." *College Composition and Communication* 54 (4): 610–628.
Ogden, C. K., and I. A. Richards. 1923. *The Meaning of Meaning: A Study of the Influence of Language upon Thought and of the Science of Symbolism.* Orlando: Harcourt, Brace, Jovanovich.
Pinker, Steven. 2014. *The Sense of Style: The Thinking Person's Guide to Writing in the Twenty-First Century.* New York: Viking Press.
Quintilian, and John Selby Watson. 1909. *Quintilian's Institutes of Oratory; Or, Education of an Orator.* London: George Bell and Sons.
Ray, Brian. 2013. "A Progymnasmata for our Time: Adapting Classical Exercises to Teach Translingual Style." *Rhetoric Review* 32 (2): 191–209.
Rice, Jeff. 2016. *Craft Obsession: The Social Rhetorics of Beer.* Carbondale: Southern Illinois University Press.
Richards, I. A. 1943. *How to Read a Page: A Course in Effective Reading, with an Introduction to a Hundred Great Words.* London: Routledge.
Swift, Jonathan. 1907. "A Letter to a Young Clergyman." In *Theories of Style*, edited by Lane Cooper. New York: Macmillan.
Tufte, Virginia. 2006. *Artful Sentences: Syntax as Style.* Cheshire, CT: Graphics Press.
Williams, Joseph M., and Joseph Bizup. 2010. *Style: Lessons in Clarity and Grace.* Boston: Longman.
Young, Vershawn Ashanti, and Aja Y. Martinez, eds. 2011. *Code-Meshing as World English: Pedagogy, Policy, Performance.* Urbana: National Council of Teachers of English.

ABOUT THE AUTHORS

Cydney Alexis is assistant professor of English at Kansas State University. She is coeditor of the forthcoming collection *The Material Culture of Writing*.

Laura L. Aull is associate professor and director of the English Department Writing Program at the University of Michigan. She is author of *First-Year University Writing* and *How Students Write: A Linguistic Analysis*, as well as articles in *Written Communication, Assessing Writing, Journal of English for Academic Purposes, Pedagogy, English Journal*, and other composition and applied linguistics journals.

Anthony Box is in his fourth year of the doctoral program in rhetoric, composition, and pedagogy at the University of Houston.

Paul Butler is associate professor of English at the University of Houston and author of *The Writer's Style, Out of Style*, and *Style in Rhetoric and Composition*.

Jimmy Butts is assistant professor in the English Department at Louisiana State University and the director of the University Writing Program.

Mike Duncan is professor of English at the University of Houston–Downtown. He has written and co-written numerous articles concerning rhetoric and technical communication and coedited the collection *The Centrality of Style*.

William T. FitzGerald is associate professor of English and director of the Writing Program and the Teaching Matters and Assessment Center at Rutgers University–Camden. He is author of *Spiritual Modalities: Prayer as Rhetoric and Performance* and coauthor of *The Craft of Research*.

Melissa A. Goldthwaite is professor of English at Saint Joseph's University. She has authored/coauthored and edited/coedited many articles/book chapters and books, including *The St. Martin's Guide to Teaching Writing, Surveying the Literary Landscapes of Terry Tempest Williams, The Norton Pocket Book of Writing by Students, The Norton Reader, Books That Cook: The Making of a Literary Meal*, and *Food, Feminisms, Rhetorics*.

Eric A. House is an assistant professor at New Mexico State University. His scholarship is interested in the ways in which Black culture remixes definitions and applications of writing and writing administration.

T. R. Johnson is professor of English and Weiss Presidential Fellow at Tulane University in New Orleans. His most recent monograph is *The Other Side of Pedagogy: Lacan's Four Discourses and the Development of the Student Writer*, and he is the editor of the forthcoming collection of essays *New Orleans: The Literary History*.

Almas Khan is assistant director of the Center for Legal English at Georgetown University Law Center. She previously taught in writing programs at the University of Virginia, the University of La Verne College of Law, and the University of Miami School of Law. Khan has published widely in composition studies, critical pedagogy, and law and literature.

ABOUT THE AUTHORS

Zak Lancaster is associate professor of English and Susan & Gene Goodson Faculty Fellow at Wake Forest University. He serves as associate editor of the *Journal of English for Academic Purposes*, and his research on writing in the disciplines has appeared in *College Composition and Communication*, *Written Communication*, *Journal of Writing Research*, *Across the Disciplines*, and other interdisciplinary journals.

Eric Leake is assistant professor of English at Texas State University, where he teaches in the MA in Rhetoric and Composition program. His research interests include empathy, civic literacies, and nonrational rhetorics.

Andrea R. Olinger is associate professor of English at the University of Louisville. Her scholarship articulates a sociocultural approach to the study of writing styles and, drawing on a range of discourse analysis methodologies, explores the role of the body, especially metaphoric gestures, in writers' talk and interaction. Her work has been published in journals such as *Research in the Teaching of English* and *Rhetoric Review*.

Tom Pace is associate professor of English at John Carroll University, where he directs the first-year writing program, writing in the university core curriculum, and the English department's professional writing track. He coedited *Refiguring Prose Style: Possibilities for Writing Pedagogy* and has published essays on style, audience, and information literacy in first-year writing. More recently, he has published on the rhetoric of Generation X in popular culture.

Brian Ray is associate professor at the University of Arkansas, Little Rock. He is author of *Style: An Introduction to History, Theory, Research, and Pedagogy*, one of the Reference Guides to Rhetoric and Composition.

Jarron Slater has appeared in *Rhetoric Review* and the *Journal of Religion and Communication*. He currently teaches at Brigham Young University.

Jon Udelson is assistant professor of English at Shenandoah University. His scholarship focuses on the intersections between creative writing and composition, as well as the disciplinary development of writers and teachers. His work has been published in *Kairos: A Journal of Rhetoric, Technology, and Pedagogy* and the edited collection *Bridging the Multimodal Gap: From Theory to Practice*.

Star Medzerian Vanguri is associate professor of writing in the Department of Media, Communication, and the Arts at Nova Southeastern University. She is editor of *Rhetorics of Names and Naming* and coeditor of *The Centrality of Style*.

INDEX

abbreviations, 114, 118, 125, 126, 129
Abgar, King, 214
Academic Phrase Bank (Morley), 240
Acts of the Apostles: ascension in, 219–23; author of, 213, 223; Luke and, 214, 215–16, 217, 219–23
Adichie, Chimamanda Ngozi, 37, 40–43, 51
aesthetics, 93, 148, 150, 155, 157, 201; poetics and, 151–52, 154; rhetoric and, 149
Aidoo, Ama Aita, 43
Akunyili, Dora, 43
Alexis, Cydney, 3, 8–9, 25, 210n7, 223
Alim, H. Samy, 133, 135, 138
alliteration, 7, 59–60, 61, 156
ALS. *See* Applied Legal Storytelling
Alsup, Allison, 204
Alternate Style, An (Weathers), 120
Amare, Nicole, 66, 67, 71
amplification, 68, 100, 166, 234–35, 236, 237
analysis, 26, 104, 107, 108, 156, 192; comparative, 105; content, 224; discourse, 4, 161; genre, 187; legal, 175, 178; lexical, 239; stance, 99; style, 37, 216, 218; stylistic, 38, 140, 187, 224; stylometric, 213; textual, 25
anaphora, 45, 49
antithesis, 48, 60, 61, 150, 156
Applied Legal Storytelling (ALS), 14, 174–75, 176, 178, 180, 181n17
appreciation, potentialities of, 150, 154, 155
arguments, viii, 8, 9, 12, 13, 45, 52, 63, 69, 70, 73, 76, 79, 96, 100, 104, 107, 134, 141, 142, 151, 153, 154, 156, 189; discovering, 228, 234; generative, 11; lines of, 150, 173; logical, 191; "no conflict," 224; oral, 178; reversible, 216; scientific, 33; stylometric, 217
Argyle, A. W., 215
Aristotle, 115, 228, 229, 242; lexis/syntax and, 233; rhetoric and, 73, 232; style and, 163–64
Armstrong, Stephen, 174
art, 11, 155; communication and, 150; verbal, 228
Association of American Colleges and Universities, 160

Association of Writers and Writing Programs (AWP), 200
Atom Heart Mother (Pink Floyd), vii
attitudes, 10, 57, 109, 101, 110, 151, 153, 154, 156; expression of, 13, 98–99; persistence, 187, 189, 190
audience, 24, 70, 85, 188, 231; academic, 73, 74; epistolary, 38–39; interactions with, 13, 133; of one/of many, 51–52; professional, 67–68; rhetoric and, 74, 164; workplace, 68, 72; writers and, 5, 6, 7, 149, 160
Aull, Laura, 4, 12, 13, 102, 107, 112n2, 118, 187; interactional stance and, 188; voice/identity and, 9
authorship, 224; common, 214, 215–16, 217, 219; determining, 213, 217; forgery and, 223; legitimacy of, 93; style and, 213
autonomy, 17, 59, 200
awareness, 45, 106; genre, 195; metalanguage and, 110; rhetorical, 74; stance, 100, 107, 108–10; stylistic, 194, 195; teaching, 224

Bacon, Francis, 104
Bain, Alexander, 229
Bakhtin, Mikhail, x, xi, xii
balance, 59, 60, 67, 76, 78, 79, 147, 150, 167, 193; grammatical, 48, 73; repetitive, 55
Bartholomae, David, 119
Barton, Ellen, 105, 106, 107, 169
Baur, Ferdinand, 214, 215
Bawarshi, Anis, 187
Bazerman, Charles, 15, 185, 210n4
Beats, Rhymes, and Classroom Life: Hip Hop Pedagogy and the Politics of Identity (Hill), 63
Beaufort, Anne, 70, 79
Beethoven, Ludwig van, 65
behavior, 42, 87, 90, 104
Bergeron, Kat, 3
Berlin, James, viii, xiiin2
Berne, Eric, 118
Between the World and Me (Coates), 7, 37, 44–51
Bewig, Matthew, 181n13

biases, 14, 88, 176
Biber, Conrad, 4
binaries, 16, 45, 56; black/white, 46; false, 227; public/private, 40
Bitzer, Lloyd, 153–54
Bizup, Joseph, 188, 189, 190, 191, 192
Bizzaro, Patrick, 207, 208, 209
Black Lives Matter, 176, 181n10
Boime, Albert, 156
boosters, 13, 100, 166, 167
boundaries: creating/transcending, 14–16; disciplinary, 156, 157, 202, 208; genre, 15; style and, 14–16
Bovon, Francois, 220
Box, Anthony, 14
Bracher, Mark, 65
Bradshaw, Peter, 94
Brammer, Charlotte, 66, 67, 71
Brandt, Deborah, 85, 92, 93
brevity, 8, 25, 35n1, 66, 91, 235, 236
Brown, Elizabeth, 89
Brummett, Barry, 86, 87, 88, 90, 92, 96
Bucholtz, Mary, 4
Buehl, Jonathan, 66, 72, 74
Burke, Kenneth, vii, 12, 128, 155; on collaboration, 153; form and, 148; *hupsos* and, 151; identification and, 60, 61; poetics and, 149; rhetoric and, 148
Bush, George W., 122, 130n9
Butler, Judith, 95, 136
Butler, Paul, ix, 87, 149, 163, 164, 179–80, 204; form and, 148; foundational texts by, 4; genre/style and, 186–87; on lexical/rhetorical choices, 155; style and, 155, 156
Butts, Jimmy, 9, 10

Canagarajah, Suresh, 10–11
Carillo, Ellen, 6
Carr, Nicholas, 128–29
Centrality of Style, The (Duncan and Vanguri), 4, 164, 165
centrifugal/centripetal forces, x, xi, xii
change, 3, 38, 194; rhetorical, 221–22; style and, 4
character strengths, 187, 188, 189, 190
Cher, 121; stupidity and, 126–27
choices: composing, 241; contractive, 168; effective, 111; language, 98, 100, 103, 104, 105, 110, 229; lexical, 155; rhetorical, 155, 156, 161; stance, 110; structural, 208; stylistic, 6, 11, 78, 116, 208, 236–37; word, 237–39, 240
Chomsky, Noam, 114, 165, 167
choppiness, 98, 119
chora, semiotic, 58, 59, 61, 64

chunking, 70, 73, 74, 75, 76, 77, 79
Cicero, xi, 151, 234–35
cipher: energy from, 137–38; evaluations and, 138–39; hip-hop, 133, 134, 138, 143; as linguistic training, 135; setting up, 135–38; style and, 138–42
Cipolla, Carlo Maria, 117
civic life, 62, 241
civility, 13, 161, 162, 173
clarity, viii, 7, 59, 60, 64, 76, 115, 143, 156, 229, 232, 235; achieving, 73; propriety and, 233; rhythm and, 53, 54, 55, 63; style and, 150
"Clarity, Brevity, and Sincerity theory," 235
Clark, Albert, 215
Clark, Gregory, 150
Clark, Herbert H., 188
Clinton, Bill and Hillary, 122
Clooney, George, 121
Coates, Samori, 44–51
Coates, Ta-Nehisi, 7, 37, 44–51
codes, 105, 200; variety/switch/mesh of, 11, 136
Cohen, Joshua, 165, 167
Cohen, Morris, 176
coherence, 63, 156, 188; fake, 14, 190–91, 192
cohesion, 63, 75, 139, 156, 188, 192; achieving, 73, 189, 190
collaboration, 6, 93, 94, 153, 201; cross-disciplinary, 17; exaltation and, 157
collaborative expectancy, 60, 63, 153
College Composition and Communication, 64
commitment: epistemic, 99, 105, 107; institutional, 188, 189
Committee on Style for the US Constitution, 173
common authors: blunders of, 219–20; rhetorical change by, 221–22
commonality, xii, 38, 42, 51, 207
communication, 15–16, 17, 54, 134, 189; art and, 150; audience-based, 73; cross-cultural, 43; idiom of, 203; professional, 76; rhetorical, 67, 69, 76; self-expression and, 149; workplace, 67, 72, 73–74, 80
Communication Across the Curriculum (CXC), 15
Communication Against the Disciplines, 15
Communication in the Disciplines (CID), 15
composition, vii, viii, ix, 99, 100, 135, 139, 140, 187, 201; addressing, 86; civil discourse and, 160–62; college, 230; creative writing and, 185, 199, 202, 203, 206–7, 208, 209; de-crafting,

241; disciplinary nature of, 185, 209; discourse and, 209; forms of, 129; hip-hop-infused, 143; literary studies and, 218; models of, 229; (re)crafting, 239–42; stance studies in, 105–6; static, 141; stupidity and, 128; style and, xii, 5, 8, 12, 103–10, 136, 163–65, 181n7, 228; values and, 162–63, 163–65
composition class, 64, 136, 141, 142, 163, 208; political realities of, 143
composition studies, xii, 6, 9, 11, 54, 120, 166, 210, 230, 231, 233; creative writing and, 15; future of, 16, 64–65; writing and, 209
compositionists, 96, 137, 162, 193, 201, 209
Computers and Composition (Walker), 121
concerns, 162; lower-order, 120; sentence-level, 73–76
connections, 14, 88, 135, 188, 190, 195, 202; building, 192; intersubjective, 60
Connors, Robert, xiiin1, 119, 231
consciousness, 50, 55, 56
consciousness-raising, 110–11
considerations: interpersonal, 10–14, 103; stylistic, 104
consistency, 220; stylistic, 31–32
Contemporary Corpus of American English (COCA), 166
content: debates about, 67–70; form and, 66, 67, 70, 74; style and, 80, 111, 165
contexts, 23, 76, 216; cultural, 89, 161; historical, 89; institutional, 57; rhetorical, 96, 107; social, 57, 161, 186
conventions, 17; disciplinary, 24; generic, 71, 75, 77; genre, 72, 195; pedagogical, 200; static, 210; stylistic, 74, 208
Conzelmann, Hans, 220
copia, 69, 233, 234, 235–37, 241
Corbett, Edward P. J., vii
correctness, 8, 17, 115, 118, 120, 156; common, 119; grammatical, 229
Counseling Psychologist, The, 187, 188, 191, 192, 193
Counter-Statement (Burke), 149–50
Coupland, Nikolas, 10
Cover, Robert, 174
Crawford, John, 44
creativity, 25, 32, 85, 135, 153, 154, 175; culture and, 86
criticism, 102, 138, 143, 151, 165, 178, 222; literary, 148, 229; rhetorical, 231
Critique of Pure Reason (Kant), 116
Crowley, Sharon, viii, 170n3
culture, 14, 51, 160, 239; biases and, 88; creativity and, 86; exemplary, 137; futuristic, 91; identification and, 133; institutional/departmental, 24; modern-day, 92; oral, 61; popular, 85, 86, 87, 88, 96; stereotypes and, 88; style and, 87

D'Angelo, Frank, vii
Dangerous Minds, 85
Dargis, Manohla, 94
Davis, Andre, 178, 179
De Copia (Erasmus), 67, 68, 69, 75, 79
Dear Ijeawele, or A Feminist Manifesto in Fifteen Suggestions (Adichie), 37, 40–43
Deleuze, Gilles, 116
Delgado, Richard, 175
Derrida, Jacques, 116
Detweiler, Eric, 117
Devitt, Amy, 161
dialogue, x, xii, xiii, 6, 54, 219, 222
diction, 11, 13, 14, 156, 178, 179, 213, 229, 230, 231, 232, 233, 238n3, 239; differences in, 216; discourse and, 173; noble, 152
Diekman, Amanda, 89
difference, 43, 51, 134, 138, 203, 216; celebrating, 16; disciplinary, 199; epistemological, 207; field-specific, 110; gender, 99; genre-based, 110, 167; as incorrectness, 206, 208; language, 4, 206, 234; writing across, 8
differentiation, 8, 58–59, 203, 204
digital, 9, 91, 115, 128, 156; elements, 10; visual and, 15
Diogenes Laertes, 115
disciplines, 17, 102, 199, 202, 203, 207, 210n4; academic, 231; writing across, 109
discourse, 5, 7, 133, 134, 135, 136, 166, 177; academic, 107, 156, 162; civil, 13, 17, 160–62, 163, 169; composition and, 160–62, 209; cultural, 38; diction and, 173; framing, 161; interactive features of, 237; investigating, 6; language and, 12; legal, 14, 174; political, 155; public, 13, 128; studies, 12, 161; style and, 203
disidentifications, 6, 39, 44, 51
divides: crossing, 16; framing, 200–202
documents: design of, 72, 77, 78; legal, 174; professional, 67; workplace, 70, 72
Does the Writing Workshop Still Work?, 207
Does Writing Have a Future? (Flusser), 115
Dorf, Michael, 180n4
drafts: peer, 110; struggling with, 73
Dreamers, 46–51
Duffy, John, 160, 162, 164, 169
Duncan, Mike, 16, 57, 164, 165

eavesdropping, 3, 38–39, 40, 44, 47, 48, 51
Economics of Attention, The (Lanham), 194, 205
economy, viii; changes for, 194; information, 194, 205; metaphorical, 203
Ede, Lisa, 39
education, 15, 45; higher, 160; hip-hop-infused, 143; literacy and, 115
effects, stylistic, 98, 100–102, 105, 107, 108, 108 (table), 110, 111
Ehrman, Bart, 220
Einstein, Albert, 114
Elbow, Peter, 54–55, 57, 120, 234
elements: multimodal/visual, 9, 34; style, 7, 73, 75, 76
Elements of Style, The (Strunk and White), 17, 173
Ellington, Duke, 53
embodiment, 181n11; collective, 176; stylistics of, 174, 175–76, 176–80
Emig, Janet, 65
engagement, 49, 100, 103, 106, 133, 177, 231; civic, 62, 160, 241
Enslin, Morton, 221
enthymemes, 153–54
Epistemic Music of Rhetoric, The (Katz), 61
epistemology, 13, 134, 143, 199, 203, 207, 208, 209
Erasmus, 67, 72, 118, 233, 235; brevity and, 236; copia and, 234; copiousness and, 79–80; *facilitas* and, 80; form/content and, 68–70, 74; on variety, 68, 79
error, 10, 117; grammatical, 119; spelling, 126; stupidity as, 118–21; typographical, 119, 120, 121; usage, 119
essays, viii, 10, 11, 16, 26, 37, 59, 60, 66, 87, 239; academic, 166; argumentative, 109, 110, 208; composition, 126, 128; expert, 106
Estrich, Susan, 177–78
ethics, 13, 162; standard of, 160; style and, 163–65
ethos, 13, 16, 52, 56, 73, 74, 90, 117, 214
Eusebius, 214, 215, 223
evaluation, 13, 142, 205; cipher and, 138–39; stylistic, 140
evidentiality, diplomatic, 3, 13, 162, 165–67, 168, 169
exaltation, 12, 149, 153, 157
executive summaries, 71
expectations, 6, 28, 110; academic, 99; collaborative, 63; community, 105; generic, 8; language, 127; stylistic, 7, 71
expression, 9, 101; individual, 156; language, 102, 103; stance, 102, 105, 106, 107, 108, 109, 110, 111; textual, 98

facilitas, 72, 74, 77, 78, 234, 237
Fahnestock, Jeanne, 44, 233, 237, 238, 239
Fairclough, Norman, 103, 104
feedback, 27–28, 31, 137
Fenza, D. W., 200, 201–2
Ferlinghetti, Lawrence, vii
fiction, 156, 200, 202, 203, 204, 207; fan, 217; poetry and, 85; white, 85
Finding Forrester, 86
Fish, Stanley, 120
FitzGerald, William, 16, 105
Fitzmyer, Joseph, 220
Fleury, Anthony, 15, 185
flexibility, 25, 133, 134, 135; stylistic, 235–36; verbal, 234
fluency, 16, 230; lexical, 233; stylistic, 66, 72; syntactic, 231
Flusser, Vilém, 115
Fodrey, Crystal, 105
forgery, 16, 213; convincing, 217–18; early Christian, 214–15, 223; stylometrics and, 218
form, 98, 149–50, 154, 155; content and, 66, 67, 69–70, 74; as covenant, 150; debates about, 68–70; function versus, 111; rhetorical, 127; structure and, 156; stylistic, 128; sublime and, 149; theory of, 148
Foster, Donald, 218
Foucault, Michel, 8
frames, 17, 200–202; analytical, 178; hip-hop-inspired, 142; narrative, 177–78; social, 241
Framework for Success in Postsecondary Writing, 163
Frank, Jerome, 175
Frankfurter, Felix, 173
Freedom Writers, 86
freewriting, 234, 236
French, Norman, 238
Friend, Christy, 162
Fulkerson, Richard, 170n4
"Funeral Elegy, A," Shakespeare and, 128

Garner, Eric, 44
Gee, James Paul, 103–4
gender, 10, 14, 42, 51, 59, 89, 94, 99, 176; conversations about, 37; cultural socialization and, 38; gap, 88; identity and, 96
generalizations, 38, 166, 167, 175, 233
Genius, 139–40
genre, 17, 23, 24, 70, 77, 102, 103, 109, 192, 207, 216, 233; awareness of, 79; conceptualizing, 161; conventions of,

72; instruction in, 71; language and, 161; mastery of, 217; non-academic, 111; as social action, 185, 195; social-turn emphasis on, 161; style and, 71, 186–87; traditional definitions of, 185–86; web-based, 78; workplace, 68, 73, 75, 76, 80; writing, 71, 72, 217
ghostwriting, 61, 85, 92, 93, 94, 223
Gibson, Walker, xi
Goldthwaite, Melissa A., 3, 6–7, 58, 93, 141, 181n5
Gorman, Heather, 216, 217
Gospel of John, 214, 215
Gospel of Luke: Acts and, 214, 215–16, 217, 219–23; ascension in, 219–23; author of, 213, 223; editing habits in, 217
Gospel of Mark, 213, 215, 222; alternate Greek section to, 218; editing habits in, 217
Gospel of Matthew, 215
grammar, xi, 120, 125, 148, 150, 193, 239; abandonment of, 230; check, 66; handbooks, 66; rhetorical, 161; rules about, 17; style and, 104
Grassley, Chuck, 125, 126

Haenchen, Ernst, 220
Hairston, Maxine, viii
Halberstam, Judith, 118
Halliday, M.A.K., 4, 103, 104
Handbook of Rhetorical Devices, A (Harris), 235
Harrington, David, 163
Harris, Robert, 235
Hartley, Clark, 193, 194
Haviland, Susan E., 188
Hawhee, Debra, 62
Hawkins, John C., 217
hedges, 13, 111, 118, 166, 168, 169; boosters and, 167; using, 102, 107
Heidegger, Martin, 116
Henderson, Greig, 150
Her (Jonze), 86, 87, 90–95
Herzog, Werner, 121
Hesse, Doug, 201
Hill, Marc Lamont, 63
Hillbrand, Friedhelm, 129
hip-hop, 133, 136, 137, 138, 142, 143; legacies of, 140; spaces within, 139; translingualism and, 134
history, 49, 68, 155, 207
Hitler (Lewis), 58
Holcomb, Chris, 104
Holmes, Oliver Wendell, Jr., 180n4
Horae Synopticae (Hawkins), 217

Horner, Bruce, 10, 11, 203, 204, 210n5, 210n8
Horning, Alice, 66
House, Eric, 3, 11, 127–28, 206
How I Met Your Mother, 33
hupsos, 151
Hurricane Katrina, style and, 3

identification, 6, 44, 51, 59, 60, 63, 96, 134, 201; authorial, 199; culture and, 133; inviting, 39; potentialities for, 154; theory of, 148
identity, 39, 85, 90, 156, 223; addressing, 86; class and, 96; constructing, 10; expression of, 87, 88; gender and, 96; multiracial, 99; professional-disciplinary, 12, 204; racial, 130n6, 191; social, 103–4; style and, 8–11, 87–89, 88, 95–96; voice and, 9
ideology, 135, 162; language, 5, 25, 33, 206; linguistic, 111; style, 207
idiosyncrasy, 24; style and, 28–39
if-statements, 169
imagination, 86, 201
imitation, 153, 156, 223, 241; early Christian, 214–15
Immigration and Nationality Act, 177
improvisation, 133, 134, 141, 142, 241
In Praise of Folly (Erasmus), 118
independent clauses, 206
indexical meanings, 5, 10, 25, 34
individuality, 88, 135, 186
information, 63, 69, 160, 189, 205; chunking, 70; complex, 75; conveying, 11, 75; processing, 194
imitation, ix, 152, 153, 156, 213, 217, 223, 231, 239, 241; forgery and, 214
Innes, Doreen, 115
inscrutability, 3, 134
Inside Higher Education, 160
Institutes (Quintilian), 234
integration, academic, 187, 188, 189, 190
intensifiers, 165, 166
interpretation, 51, 156, 174, 220
invention, 5, 156, 236; style and, 227; systems of, 234
Invisible Gorilla, The, 33
issue-rule-application-conclusion (IRAC), 175

JAC, 64
Jesus, ascension of, 219–23
Johannson, Scarlett, 94
John the Baptist, 221, 222
Johnson, T. R., 3, 7, 8, 104, 116, 150, 210n6; foundational texts by, 4

Jones, Prince, 49
Jonze, Spike, 86, 93
journaling, 27–28; word formation and, 238
Justin Martyr, 215

Kahn, Almas, 14
Kant, Immanuel, 116
Katz, Stephen, 61
Keith, Damon, 178
keywords, 193–94
Killingsworth, M. Jimmie, 104
King, Stephen, 63, 64
knowledge, 26, 44–51, 52, 137, 179; changing, 17; creating, 199, 201, 204; genre, 70; making, 207; perspective, 169; production of, 202, 241; style, 24, 25; writing, 23, 173, 199, 209
Koupf, Danielle, 239, 240
Kristeva, Julia, 58, 61, 64
Kuhn, Thomas, vii
Kurlinkus, William C., 164

Lancaster, Zak, 4, 12, 102, 106, 107, 118, 165, 166, 186; diplomacy and, 167; interactional stance and, 188; metalanguage and, 187–88; voice/identity and, 9
language, 4, 6, 13, 14, 129, 164, 192, 241; academic, 110–11, 170n4; aesthetic, 90; analyzing, 98–100; attention to, 105; choices and, 98, 100, 103, 104; clear/correct/appropriate, 229; difference in, 203; digital, 128; elements of, 231; epistemic role of, 96; expression of, 191; extemporaneous, 232; genre and, 161; immutability of, 17; ingenuity of, 17; innovation of, 11; legal, 175; manipulating, 194; meaning and, 10; memorable/valuable, 54; metaphorical, 25; multiple, 78; patterned, 169; performance of, 134; poetic, 59; prescriptive, 111; reacting to, 233; rhetorical, 129, 164; simplification of, 114; social action and, 161; struggle with, 227; style and, 25, 28, 31, 34–35, 104, 228; thought and, 228; using, 3, 9, 10, 67, 161; variety of, 69; writing and, 110–11, 191, 232, 234
Language of the Law, The (Mellinkoff), 175
languaging, 133, 204
Lanham, Richard, xi, 4, 55, 56, 57, 90, 95, 148, 186, 194, 205, 235
Leake, Eric, 3, 8–9, 25, 210n7, 223
Lee, Jerry Won, 134, 136
legal system, 179, 180

legal theory, 175–76
Lemon, Don, 127
Leskes, Andrea, 160, 163
Lewis, Wyndham, 57, 58
lexis, 229, 233, 234, 237; rhetorical agency of, 230; style as, 241; syntax and, 228, 238–39
Likimani, Muthoni, 43
linguistics, 14, 25, 103, 128, 161, 162; applied, 99, 100, 105–6, 166; computational, 216; functional, 165
listening: intent, 52; metonymic, 37, 38–39; nature of, 58; rhetorical, 38, 51, 162
literacy, 23, 92, 93, 120, 230; education and, 115; instruction centers, 230; popular culture and, 86
literary studies, 6, 204, 218, 231
literature review, 27; style of, 30 (table)
logics, 51, 73, 138
Longinus, 12, 59, 148, 149, 151, 153, 154, 155
Lordi, Emily J., 47
love letters, ghostwriting, 92
Lunsford, Andrea, 37, 39, 119
Lutosławski, Wincenty, 216

MacDonald, Susan Peck, 4
Maher, Bill, 122
main point, narratives and, 32–33
Malcolm X, 179–80
Malkin, Michelle, 122
manuals, instructional, 217
markers: concede-contrast, 105; generalization, 166, 167; validity, 166
Markus, Hazel, 89
Massumi, Brian, 120
Matsuda, Mari, 176, 177–78, 179
Mayers, Tim, 200
McBride, Renisha, 44
meaning, 156, 203; co-construction of, 16; discursive, 161; language and, 10; making, 103, 104, 111; rhetorically expressed, 142; stylistic, 31
mechanics, 23, 24, 161, 239
media, 48, 139; platforms, 114–15; selfhood and, 89
Mellinkoff, David, 175
memoirs, 37, 44, 45, 46, 48, 51
memorability, 14, 204–5
memoranda, 71, 73, 75, 76
memory, 49, 54, 55, 201; sharing, 50–51
Mertz, Elizabeth, 181n13
metalanguage, 98, 100, 103, 187–88, 190–91, 194; argument for, 104–5; awareness and, 110; developing, 106–8;

formulaic use of, 195; meaningful, 110; sentences and, 107; using, 191, 192–93
metaphor, 6, 25, 38, 49, 69, 134, 137, 201, 205, 236
methodology, 161, 199, 202, 210n1
#MeToo movement, 176, 181n10
Michigan Corpus of Upper-level Student Papers (MICUSP), 110, 111n1, 168, 170n5
Milic, Louis, 67, 186, 193
Miller, Carolyn, 77, 185, 195
Millett, Patricia, 179, 182n18
misspellings, 123, 124, 125, 126, 128
monism: aesthetic, 67, 186; psychological, 67, 186
Mozart, Wolfgang Amadeus, 65
music, xiii, 8, 139, 140, 155
Mussies, Gerhard, 220, 221

narcissists, 28–29, 33, 34
narrative, ix, 8, 32–34, 35, 87, 99, 100, 177–78; arc, 201; ending, 221; main point and, 32–33; rewriting, 223
New Critical paradigms, 229
New Rhetoric, The (Perelman and Olbrechte-Tyteca), 117
New Testament (NT), 16, 213, 214, 216, 217, 220, 223, 224n1
New Writing: The International Journal for the Practice and Theory of Creative Writing (Fenza), 200
New York Times, 26, 122
Newman, Michael, 135
Newsweek, 115
nostalgia, 91, 92–93
nouns, verbs and, 232
Nowacek, Rebecca S., 23–24
Nurius, Paula, 89

Obama, Barack, 122
objectives, 40, 134, 176, 204, 233; communicative, 11; disciplinary-specific, 209
Ochs, Elinor, 4
Odyssey, 208
Ohmann, Richard, 147–48
Olbrechts-Tyteca, Lucie, vii, 117
Olinger, Andrea, 4, 5, 6, 10, 35, 71, 98, 103
On Copia of Words and Ideas (Erasmus), 235–37
On Style (Theophrastus), 115
On the Sublime (Longinus), 148, 149, 151
On Writing (King), 63, 64
Ong, Walter, 61
Only Academic Phrasebook You'll Ever Need: 600 Examples of Academic Language (Barros), 240–41

open-mindedness, 160, 163, 169
openness, 115, 134, 162, 163
ornamentation, 68, 69, 115, 229
other, self and, 59
Out of Style (Butler), 163
outlines, 13, 26, 66, 136, 167, 168, 169

Pace, Tom, 4, 7–8, 90, 103, 148
paradigm, ix, 138, 161, 175, 206, 229, 230, 233; concept of, vii–viii
parallelism, 7, 48, 63
Parsons, Mikeal, 216, 217, 221
pathos, 13, 42, 73
patterns, 161; developmental, 105–6; formal, 150, 155; grammatical, 148; syntactical, 148
Paul, 214, 221, 223
pedagogy, vii, ix, 38, 58, 67, 68, 69, 72, 74, 107, 135, 207, 240, 242; classical, 231; composition, 16, 238–39; critical, 137; developing, 35; feminist, 137; framing, 138; hip-hop, 63, 137; lexical, 228–30; perceptions of, 136; radical, 143; rhetorical, 195, 206; roots of, 137; scholarship and, 228; sentence-based, 231; shared, 210; style, 8, 62, 205, 234; translanguage, 136, 137; writing, 11, 135, 200, 227, 234
Pedagogy, 64
Pennebaker, James, 193
Perelman, Chaïm, vii, 117
performance, 138; musical, 62; oralist, 61; pressure for, 114; verbal, 61
Performing Prose (Holcomb and Killingsworth), 4
Pervo, Richard, 220
philosophy, 155, 156, 167, 214
Phoenix, Joaquin, 86
phrasing, 115, 217
Pink Floyd, vii
Pinker, Steven, 17
Pinnock, Marlene, 44
Pitkin, Walter, 116
plagiarism, 152, 213, 218, 224
Plain English movement, 175
Plato, 62, 115, 128
pluralities, 120, 129, 151
poetics, 148; aesthetics and, 151–52, 154; rhetoric and, 93, 149, 150, 155, 157
Poetics (Aristotle), 232
poetry, 60, 62, 69, 155, 207, 208; fiction and, 85; prose and, 56, 232
politics, 106, 136, 138, 176
Porter, James I., 151
portfolio, 74, 76, 79, 140, 143, 241; assignments, 139; style and, 139

possible selves, 3, 8–9, 89
power: explanatory, 6; institutional, 136; intersubjective, 58; language and, 206
principles: narrative, 221; rhetorical, 103, 162, 164; stylistic, 76
Prior, Paul A., 210n4
production: artistic, 210n8; generic, 210n8; knowledge, 202; literary, 203; theories of, 173
progymnasmata, lexical, 233–39
project management, 70
pronouns, 10, 46, 170n5, 229, 231
propriety, 88, 130n4, 229, 231, 233
prose: diction, 233; poetry and, 56, 232; revising/generating, 230. *See also* writing
Protagoras (Plato), 62
psychoanalysis, 56, 58, 64, 65
psychology, 99, 100, 150, 155, 187, 191
punctuation, viii, 118, 126, 129, 206

qualifiers, modal, 118, 165
Quintilian, 69, 233, 234–35, 236; amplification and, 234; rhetoric and, 87
quotation, 33, 34, 241

race, 46, 59, 176; conversations about, 37; cultural socialization and, 38
racism, 45, 46, 99, 176, 177
Rap Genius, 139
Ratcliffe, Krista, 37, 38, 39, 43, 47
Ray, Brian, 98, 164, 186, 193, 233
reading: epistolary, 39; perceptions/practices of, 96; sponsorship of, 85; writing and, 230
reasoning, 14, 32, 164, 166, 167, 169, 173, 175
Reed, Stanley, 173
reflection, 38, 77, 78, 79, 106, 116, 139, 191
relationships, 94, 95, 163, 164, 165; author-audience, 6, 7, 55, 111; familial, 189; peer, 189; style and, 5–8
remember, 44–51, 205
remix, 141, 142
repetition, 45, 55, 62, 68, 118, 239
representations, 25, 26, 28, 29, 35, 55, 85, 86, 87, 88, 89; style, 31–34, 96
repurposing, 5, 142, 233, 240
research, 13, 70, 99, 100, 143, 169, 190, 207; composition, 103; discipline and, 141; future of, 192; longitudinal, 35; qualitative, 119; style and, 4, 103–10; teaching and, 107
resources, 11; allocation of, 194; inventive, 228; lexical, 231; linguistic, 103; rhetorical, 239; style, 228; verbal, 228

response, 6, 15, 38, 52, 62, 116, 128, 133, 140, 178, 185, 191, 205, 241
revision, 27, 65, 70, 138, 142, 190, 229
Revolution in Poetic Language (Kristeva), 58
rhetoric, ix, 7, 13, 38, 58, 62, 64, 67, 68, 69, 75, 77, 135, 154, 161, 201, 207, 234, 235, 239; aesthetics and, 149; Aristotelian, 216; arts of, 61; audience and, 164; canon of, 149, 155, 157; Ciceronian, 216; classical, vii, 227; communication and, 76; current-traditional, viii, xiiin1, 231; defining, 228; digital, 4, 9, 14; effective, 87; ethics of, 162; feminist, 163; generative, ix, 231; hip-hop, 134; legal, 174; pedagogy and, 195; poetics and, 93, 149, 150, 155, 157; sentence-based, 231–33; style and, viii, 147, 156, 241; theory of, 148; visual, 14, 57; workplace writing and, 73–74
Rhetoric (Aristotle), 229, 232
Rhetoric of Motives, A (Burke), 60, 148, 153
Rhetoric Review, 5, 64
rhetorical figures, 150, 152, 238–39
Rhetorical Listening: Identification, Gender, Whiteness (Ratcliffe), 38
rhetorical style, stupid, 117–18, 121–28
Rhetorical Style: The Uses of Language in Persuasion (Fahnestock), 55, 233, 237, 238
Rhetorical Stylistics, 239
Rhetorical Triangle, 73
rhetors, 5, 44, 67, 96, 224, 230, 234
Rhodes, Keith, 104
rhymes, 134, 135, 140; phantom, 59–60
rhythm, 3, 8, 60, 64, 65, 150, 155; artistry of, 57; clarity and, 53, 54, 55, 63; cultivation of, 56; monotonous, 192; organization and, 56; power of, 58; prose, 216, 233; steady, 56; transposing, 61–62
Rice, Tamir, 44
Rise of Writing, The (Brandt), 92
Roberts, John, 178
Rogers, Joel, 165, 167
Ronell, Avital, 116, 117, 130n4, 162
Roosevelt, Theodore, 53, 54
Rowling, J. K., 123, 124
rubrics, 24, 107
Russell, David R., 161, 185
Ruti, Mari, 57

Samantha (operating system), 93–94, 95
Scalia, Antonin, 180n4
Schiappa, Edward, 122
scholarship, ix, x, 58, 103, 175, 193, 203; composition, viii, 163, 201; narrative, 181n14; pedagogy and, 228
Scholten, J. H., 215

science, 88, 89, 155, 215
self: other and, 59; style/identity and, 87–89
self-expression, communication and, 149
self-mentions, 13, 100, 102, 169
Selzer, Jack, 149
semiotics, 4, 6, 25, 104
sentence fragments, composition and, 208
sentences, 72, 148, 228, 237, 241; concerns about, 73–76; construction of, 191, 192; declarative, 41; flipping around, 190; lexical effects in, 239; metalanguage and, 107; opening of, 109; thesis, 54; varying, 236
Serwer, Adam, 180n4
Shakespeare, William, 218
Shaughnessy, Mina, 119
Short Introduction to the History of Stupidity, A (Pitkin), 116
Simons, Dan, 26
Sirc, Geoffrey, vii
skills, 15, 23, 93, 217, 219, 223, 234, 239; writing, 16, 203
Skinnell, Ryan, 122
slang, 10, 229, 238n3
Slater, Jarron, 3, 11–12, 59, 93
Slightly Stoopid, 129
slogans, role of, 59
Smith, Elliot, 129
Smith, Morton, 218
Snodgrass, W. D., 240
social action, 10, 14, 70, 161, 185, 186, 195
social media, 42, 156
social support, 88, 189, 190
sociolinguistics, 4, 12
Sotto, Eric, 193
space: dialogic, 102, 166; dimensions of, 101 (table); formal/informal, 135; illogical, 126; pedagogical, 138; time and, 137
speech, 155; elite, 229; varying, 236
spell check, 66, 119, 121
spelling, viii, 125, 126
stance, 98–99; academic, 106; attitudinal, 101, 106, 108 (table), 109; consciousness-raising about, 110–11; contrastive, 106; dimensions of, 102–3, 107; epistemic, 100, 101, 102, 105, 106, 108 (table), 109; ethical, 126; examples of, 108 (table); explaining, 100–101; interactional, 101, 102, 105, 106, 108 (table), 109, 188; research on, 103–10; rhetorical, 126; style and, 100–102, 106–8, 111; teaching, 110–11
Standard Edited English, 119, 125
Stanford Study of Writing, 37

Starry Night (van Gogh), 156
Stein, Gertrude, 206, 208
stereotypes, 38, 87, 88, 89, 109
Stiegler, Bernard, 116
Stotsky, Sandra, 170n4
strategies, 17, 73, 169, 236, 237; adaptive, 80; amplification, 234; attenuation, 234; rhetorical, 235; sentence-level, 73; style and, 11–14, 70, 137; stylistic, 7–8, 11–14, 38, 67, 72, 80
structure: form and, 156; generic, 72; sentence, 192, 233; stylistic, 72
struggle, 44–51
Strunk, William, Jr., xi, 17, 164, 173, 206
Students Right to Their Own Language (CCCC), xi
stupid: exploring, 129; playing, 118; term, 129
Stupid Man, 115
stupid style, 9, 114, 116, 118–19; intentional, 123; uses/benefits of, 128–29
stupidity, 9, 10, 129; artificial, 128; characterization of, 115–16, 118–19; as deviant approach, 119; disability and, 120; embracing, 129; as error, 118–21; history of, 115–17; identity politics of, 120; language use and, 126; laws of, 117; patron saints of, 118; presidency and, 125; style and, 114, 116; writing off, 118–21
Stupidity (Ronell), 116
Sturm, Sean, 120
style: academic, 32, 33, 34, 136; acquiring, 68; addressing, 17, 66, 86; civil, 162, 166, 167–69; composition and, 5, 8, 12, 103–10, 136, 163–65, 181n7, 228; concept of, 88, 103, 137, 141; defining, 25, 87, 102, 118, 228; demands of, 147; development of, 3, 34, 104, 121, 138; differentiating, 29 (table); disciplinary, 14, 155, 206–9; discrepancies in, 216; discussion of, 102, 203, 207; emphasis on, 141; epistolary, 38–39; experimental quality of, 4; future of, 8, 80, 129, 147, 148, 157; history of, xi, xii, xiii; impoverished, 228; improvisational, 142; interpersonal, 109; inventive, 5, 227; literary, 204, 215–16; as material practice, 202–5; measuring, 215–16; meta-mastery of, 66; metaphor of, 69; missteps with, 126; narrative, 32–34, 35; nostalgic, 92–93; overlooking, 23–24; perceptions/expectations of, 6; persuasive, 109; portfolio, 139; preferences in, 29–30; proficiency in, 72–80; reclaiming, 228; reflective, 102; research on,

4, 103–10, 201; reversible argument of, 216–18; role of, 68, 96, 199; romantic, 92–93; sciencey, 31–32, 33; similarities in, 213–14; strategies and, 70, 137; stupid, 118–19; teaching, 66, 71, 98, 227; textual, 107; theories of, 67, 100, 148; understanding of, xii, 6, 13–14, 24; universality of, 155; using, 8, 133, 141; writer-audience relationship and, 6; writerly self and, 95–96; writing, 23, 27, 92, 98–99, 148, 173, 174, 175, 227
Style: An Anti-Textbook (Lanham), 56
Style: An Introduction (Ray), 4, 164
Style in Rhetoric and Composition (Butler), 204
Style: Ten Lessons in Clarity and Grace (Williams and Bizup), 54, 63, 188
stylistics, 5, 14, 35, 67–68, 87, 94, 107, 135, 138, 174, 176–80, 194, 210, 217; evolution of, 175–76; literary, 231, 238; teaching, 209
stylometrics, 215–16, 217, 218, 224
subject, style and, 155
sublime, 151–53; formal, 12, 149, 153–56, 157
substance: style and, 51, 90–95, 96, 195; writing with, 227
Swales, John, 166
Swift, Jonathan, 118, 227
synecdoche, 149, 150
syntax, viii, 63, 148, 150, 156, 231, 233; lexis and, 228, 238–39

task, 54, 61, 71, 111, 116, 168, 207, 230
techne, 199, 204, 205, 209, 210
technology, 90, 114, 119, 121, 140, 156; recording, 61; role of, 94
tekne, stupidity and, 119
tension, xiii; seeing/enacting, 28–31; style and, 28–31
Terrell, Timothy P., 174
Tertius, 223
Tertullian, 215, 223
texts, 207; assembling/disassembling, 241; non-academic, 111; style-free, 107
Thaiss, Chris, 24, 25, 28, 163, 169, 202
Theophilus, 223
Theophrastus, 115, 121, 164
theses: argumentative, 208; statements, 208; style of, 30 (table); writing, 26
They Say/I Say, 12
thought, 55; expressing, 236; language and, 228; original, 195; rhetorical, 72
Time and Western Man (Lewis), 57
Tobin, Lad, 87, 88
tourism, 77–78, 79

tradition, xii, 41, 46, 118, 151, 219, 220, 221, 230, 231; current, 241; oral, 141; rhetorical, 87, 103, 134, 163, 228, 232, 234
transdisciplinarity, 12, 149, 157; formal, 154–56
transgender rights, 177, 178–79
translation, linguistic heritage and, 237–38
translingualism, 3, 10, 133, 206, 234; code meshing and, 11; flexibility/resourcefulness and, 134; hip-hop and, 134
trespass, 3, 15, 16, 203
tropes, 12, 38, 68, 156, 236, 238
Trump, Donald, 125, 181n12; misspellings by, 123; rhetoric of, 122; stupidity and, 124, 126; Twitter and, 121, 122, 123, 124
Tufte, Virginia, 147–48
Turner, Stephen Francis, 120
Twain, Mark, 228
Twombly, Theodore, 86

Udelson, Jon, 3, 15–16, 52n1, 85, 133, 181n7
Ulysses, 208
unconscious, 55, 56, 59, 62, 63, 65, 192
usage, viii, 25, 37, 76, 119, 120, 133, 141, 215, 231; differences in, 216; rules about, 17

values, 5, 59, 207; composition and, 163–65; ethical, 162–65; rhetorical, 162–63; style and, 163–65
Van Gogh, Vincent, 156
Vance, John, 4
Vande Kopple, William, 105
Vanguri, Star Medzerian, 107, 164
variety, 14, 68, 69, 136, 221, 239
verbosity, 34–35
verbs: nouns and, 232; strong, 45
vernacular, 10, 103, 120
Vernacular Eloquence: What Speech Can Bring to Writing (Elbow), 54–55, 120
Vitanza, Victor, 120, 121
vocabulary, 160, 217, 238, 240; lack of, 105
voice, 11, 13, 156, 206; clear/appropriate, 24; identity and, 9; imperative/declarative, 70; passive/active, 27, 31, 32, 70, 231
Voting Rights Act, 178

Walker, Janice, 121
Walters, Patricia, 215, 216, 217, 219
Watson, Francis, 217
Weathers, Winston, 119–20
websites, 71; designing/writing for, 76, 77–80

Welch, Nancy, 65
West, Kanye, 127, 128
Where Is Your Body? (Matsuda), 176
White, E. B., xi, 17, 164, 173, 206
Whittaker, James, 121
Why Johnny Can't Write (Sheils), 116
Wilde, Oscar, 114
Williams, Bronwyn, 86, 96
Williams, Joseph, 54, 63, 164, 165, 188, 189, 190, 191, 192
Winterowd, W. Ross, 195
wisdom, 48, 120; institutional-conventional, 203; struggle for, 50
words, 102, 148; cutting off ends of, 18; foreign, 242; formation of, 238; ideas and, 193; inventory of, 228; missing, 118; pool of, 231–33; proper, 227; style and, 240
Wordsworth, William, 208
writers, audiences and, 6, 7, 149, 160
Writer's Style, The (Butler), 155
Writer's Weekly, 85
writing: academic, 24, 98–100, 104, 106–8, 110–11, 122, 128, 160, 162, 165–67, 168, 187, 193, 194; across disciplines, 109; composition and, 185, 202, 203, 206–7, 208, 209; creative, 15, 199, 200, 201, 202, 203, 206–7, 208, 209, 210n1, 210nn3,5,7–8; disciplinary, 14, 110, 185, 192, 207; epistolary, 6, 37–38, 39, 40; ethical, 162, 163; instruction in, vii, viii, 230; language and, 110–11, 191, 232, 234; legal, 174, 176–80, 177, 180; professional, 8, 66, 67, 68, 69, 70–80, 85; programs, 110, 200, 203; as second language, 234; as solitary process, 86; theories of, 209; understanding of, 13–14, 90
Writing Across the Curriculum (WAC), 185
writing class, 23, 86, 111, 174; civil style in, 167–69; as makerspace, 16; professional, 70–72, 74, 76
Writing in the Discipline (WID), 185
Writing in the Real World: Making the Transition from School to Work (Beaufort), 70
Written Communication, 64

Young, Richard, viii, ix, xiiin2
Young, Vershawn Ashanti, 120

Zawacki, Terry Myers, 24, 25, 28, 163, 169, 202
Zenger, Amy, 86, 96
Zirin, Dave, 3

www.ingramcontent.com/pod-product-compliance
Lightning Source LLC
Chambersburg PA
CBHW031101080526
44587CB00011B/768